100 Hikes in the

Inland Northwest

D1124755

By RICH LANDERS
IDA ROWE DOLPHIN
and the Spokane Mountaineers
Maps by Helen Sherman

The Mountaineers/Seattle

This book is dedicated to the memory of Ernest "Pete" Van Gelder, a Spokane Mountaineer who loved, hiked, defended and maintained mountain trails.

THE MOUNTAINEERS: Organized 1906 ". . . to explore, study, preserve and enjoy the natural beauty of the Northwest."

Published by The Mountaineers, 306 Second Avenue West
Seattle, Washington 98119

Published simultaneously in Canada by Douglas & McIntyre Ltd.
1615 Venables Street, Vancouver, British Columbia V5L 2H1

Manufactured in the United States of America

Edited by Jim Jensen
Designed by Marge Mueller; layout by Connie Bollen
Cover: Chimney Rock on the Selkirk Crest in northern Idaho (Photo by Rich Landers)

Library of Congress Cataloging-in-Publication Data

Landers, Rich, 1953-
    100 hikes in the inland Northwest / by Rich Landers, Ida Rowe
Dolphin, and the Spokane Mountaineers.
        p.   cm.
    "Appendix B: Administration/information sources": p.
    Includes index.
    ISBN 0-89886-130-6 (pbk.)
    1. Hiking--Washington (State)--Spokane Region--Guide-books.
2. Hiking--Northwest, Pacific--Guide-books.   3. Spokane Region
(Wash.)--Description and travel--Guide-books.   4. Northwest,
Pacific--Guide-books.   I. Dolphin, Ida Rowe, 1922-   . II. Spokane
Mountaineers (Club) III. Title.   IV. Title: One hundred hikes in
the inland Northwest.
GV199.42.W22S64 1987   87-24635
917.97'37--dc19   CIP

CONTENTS

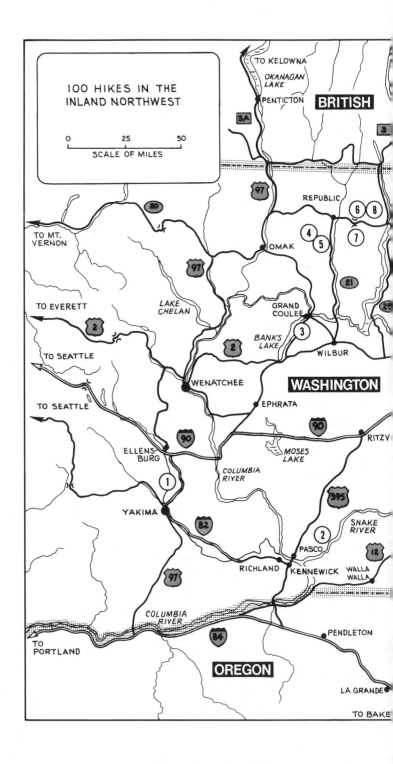

100 HIKES IN THE
INLAND NORTHWEST

SCALE OF MILES
0   25   50

TO KELOWNA

OKANAGAN
LAKE

PENTICTON

BRITISH

3A

3

97

REPUBLIC

6   8

7

4
5

OMAK

TO MT.
VERNON

21

2

LAKE
CHELAN

GRAND
COULEE

25

TO EVERETT

2

BANKS
LAKE

3

WILBUR

2

WENATCHEE

WASHINGTON

TO SEATTLE

EPHRATA

90

TO SEATTLE

90

RITZV

MOSES
LAKE

ELLENS-
BURG

COLUMBIA
RIVER

1

395

YAKIMA

SNAKE
RIVER

82

2

18

PASCO

RICHLAND   KENNEWICK   WALLA
WALLA

97

COLUMBIA
RIVER

PENDLETON

TO
PORTLAND

84

OREGON

LA GRANDE

TO BAKE

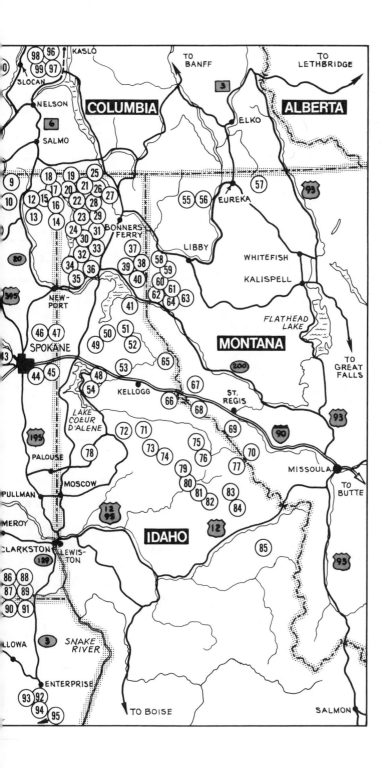

Location	*Hike*	*Page*	*Status*

UMATILLA NATIONAL FOREST

WALLOWA-WHITMAN NATIONAL FOREST

CANADA

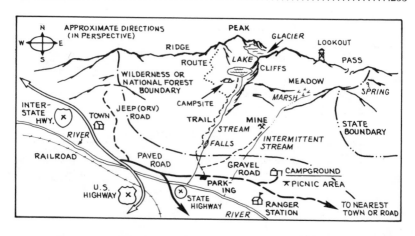

PREFACE

This guidebook originated in 1984 as a project of the Spokane Mountaineers, a club based in Spokane, Washington, for people who are active in the outdoors. Although the Spokane Mountaineers is a separate organization from the publisher of this book, The Mountaineers, which is based in Seattle, the two groups have much in common, including a love for the wild places of the Pacific Northwest.

The by-laws of the Spokane Mountaineers express broad and noble goals: "To encourage a spirit of good fellowship among lovers of outdoor life; to maintain a program of mountaineering trips including mountain climbing, scrambling, hiking, walking, skiing, ski-touring, bicycling, backpacking and snowshoeing throughout the year; to educate aspiring mountaineers in the skills of mountaincraft; to provide capable and experienced leadership for all trips; to endorse the principles of mountain safety as prescribed by the climbing code, and if called upon to provide all possible aid to mountain accident victims; to create greater public awareness of the intrinsic value of our wilderness, forest, primitive, park and monument land, and to seek the preservation of the natural beauty and scenic value of this national heritage; and to preserve by the encouragement of protective legislation, or otherwise, the natural beauty of our great outdoors."

This guidebook was compiled with the assistance of many helpers. Contributors from the Spokane Mountaineers include Mary and Alan Baker, Stan Beck, Chic Burge, Lisa Brooks, Beth Carr, Pat and Gary Cassel, Cris Currie, Sherry Dempsey, Tony Dolphin, Jim Dowell, Virgil Emery, Lynn Erickson, Elizabeth Escher, Gary Gunning, Chris and Mel Hartwig, Dale Hirschfeld, Tom Horne, Don Hutchings, Terri Janek, Loren Johnson, Chuck Kerkering, Julie Kubat, Linda Martin, Don Mattoon, Suzie McDonald, Andie McMaster, Tom McMaster, Mike Merriman, Steve Mitrovich, Dave Moershel, George Neal, Steve Noland, Joe Ohl, Jerry Pavia, Steve and Madge Petrusky, Rod Pharness, Donna Phillips, Sean Ravencraft, Richard Rivers, John Roskelley, Jane Schelly, Sam Schlieder, Susan Scott, Frank and Lou Slak, Nancy Smith, Tom Sowa, Will Venardi, Mary Weathers, Steve Weinberger and Steve Yach.

The authors offer special thanks for assistance from John Carter of the British Columbia Parks Branch; Guy McKee, Luke Konantz, Kelly Liston, Al Garr, Cal Baker and Jim Nash of the Colville National Forest; Cindy French of Priest Lake State Park; Tom Keller and Stewart Wilson of the Clearwater National Forest; Clyde Blake, Pat Hart, Judy Smith, Cort Sims, Jack Dorrell, Bill Cook, Jim Upchurch, Richard Hodge, Mary Ann Hamilton, Jim Myers, and Don Smith of the Idaho Panhandle National Forests; Jon Jeresek, Eric Heyn, William Rockwell, Jeff Adams and John Righter of the Kootenai National Forest; Tom Geouge, Andy Kulla and George Barce of the Lolo National Forest; Jerry Bird and George Weldon of the Nez Perce National Forest; Rich Martin and Steve Bush of the Umatilla National Forest; Robin Gitschlag Rose of the Wallowa-Whitman National Forest; Del Peterson of the Washington Department of Wildlife; Monty Fields of Steamboat Rock State Park; and Gary Yaeger of the U.S. Bureau of Land Management.

INTRODUCTION

"They Ain't Makin' It No More"

The land: As Will Rogers put it, "They ain't makin' it no more." And it's the diversity of this endangered resource that sets the Inland Northwest apart from so many other regions in the country.

The Inland Northwest is the recently expanded version of the "Inland Empire," a term Spokane-area promoters have used for decades to describe the real estate roughly bounded on the west by the foothills of the North Cascades and on the east by the rugged Montana mountains jamming up to form the Continental Divide. The imaginary boundary slips south slightly into Oregon and north a smidgen into Canada.

The Inland Northwest includes the population centers of Libby in Montana, of Nelson in British Columbia, of Enterprise in Oregon, of Coeur d'Alene, Sandpoint, Moscow and Lewiston in Idaho, and of Spokane, Pullman, Walla Walla, and the Tri-Cities area in Washington. It also includes thousands of acres populated only by wildlife and occasional human visitors. This book is designed to introduce you to some of the best hiking opportunities in these wild areas.

Florida has its swamps, California its beaches, Arizona its canyons and deserts. But virtually no place—the only possible exception being the icy, buggy and boggy state of Alaska—could compare with the Inland Northwest for its combination of productive and pristine lands, waters and diversity of wildlife. It's a splendid area to explore on foot.

Roughly half of the Inland Northwest is public land, free of no-trespassing signs and open for hunting, fishing, backpacking and hundreds of other uses. Within the imaginary boundaries are 16 million acres of national forests, 2 million acres of national parks and recreation areas and portions of more than 6 million acres of officially designated or proposed wilderness areas. To put it simply, there's plenty of breathing room in the Inland Northwest and there probably always will be: The region is blessed with just enough glaciers, grizzly bears and rattlesnakes to keep immigration to a trickle.

Threatened Land

It's a false sense of security that leaves many hikers thinking our open spaces will always be inviting. Recent debates over national forest planning have revealed staggering quotas for timber production and road building in the Inland Northwest. Many of the region's traditional trails—even some of the choice ones selected for this book—are threatened to be obliterated by chainsaws or bulldozers in the next 10 years. For perspective, consider that the 1951 USGS Mount Pend Oreille quadrangle showed only about 18 miles of roads. The 1974 Idaho Panhandle National Forests travel plan showed more than 140 miles of roads in that area. And the road systems continue to grow. The 10-year forest plans stretching into the 1990s call for doubling the miles of roads in

Ferns and cedars at Liberty Creek Falls, Liberty Lake County Park. (Rich Landers photo)

many of the forests of this region. The Idaho Panhandle National Forests alone have proposed to double their already burgeoning network of forest roads in the next 10 years from about 6,500 miles to more than 13,000 miles! Combine that with the horrendous timber liquidation launched in the mid 1980s on Burlington Northern timberlands by its subsidiary, Plum Creek Timber Comany, and one can see a gloomy picture for the land.

While islands of protected wilderness are found within the boundaries of the Inland Northwest, it is sobering to realize that most of our favorite retreats have little or no official protection from development. The wide-open spaces might always be here, but what good will they be if the trees become stumps and the trails become roads and the trout streams become silt-choked funnels for erosion?

11

At the time this guide was published, Idaho's congressional delegation still had not agreed on wilderness legislation that would protect the state's last remaining roadless areas, such as the Mallard-Larkins region above the North Fork of the Clearwater River. It's been a long battle. About 46,000 acres of Long Canyon and the Selkirk Crest were recommended for wilderness designation by conservation groups and Idaho Governor John Evans in 1985, while the Forest Service was recommending only 22,875 acres. Thanks to conservationists in northern Idaho, it appears as though there will be some sort of lasting protection for Long Canyon and the Selkirk Crest. But nothing is certain.

Montana, too, was still working on wilderness legislation in 1987. Conservationists were working hard to win protection for the state's remaining pristine areas, resorting in some cases to the restrictive wilderness designation only because they cannot trust forest managers to preserve the recreational qualities of our wild lands under the open rules of multiple use. Fish Lakes Canyon, Hike 56, is just one of many examples of beautiful trails that have been degraded by roads. In this case, a 5½ mile trail leads into a pretty canyon with fine trout fishing. But in 1986, a logging road was built to within ¼ mile of the first fishable lake. It's an old story. Soon people will be tramping a shortcut from the logging road to the lakes. The trout will quickly disappear and soon thereafter the scenic trail will become neglected both by hikers and trail crews. An area that once made a fine weekend outing will become a ¼-mile nature walk.

For information on what conservationists are doing to save the last pristine areas in the Inland Northwest, write Inland Empire Public Lands Council, P.O. Box 2174, Spokane, WA 99210.

Disappearing Trails

In the 70-year history of the Spokane Mountaineers, club members have tramped along many of the 15,000 miles of trails in the region. It's largely from that experience that this book is written. Because the Spokane Mountaineers is a group of all types of people, so too is this book a collection of trails for everyone from iron-thighed backpackers to parents who want to tote their babes on short excursions. Volunteers from the Spokane Mountaineers have provided much of the information. Additional information has been provided by the Spokane County Parks Department, U.S. Bureau of Land Management and the U.S. Forest Service, the agency which is as much a friend as foe of the people who prize the country's trail systems.

But as vast as the the public land is in the Inland Northwest, hiking opportunities are drying up like desert mud puddles. Hundreds of miles of trails in this region are being destroyed or neglected. It's a national trend. In 1944, the Forest Service was maintaining about 150,000 miles of trails and 107,000 miles of roads. By 1983, trails had decreased 34 percent to about 98,800 miles while roads had increased more than 200 percent to about 321,000 miles. Even this mileage for trails is inflated. Many of these so-called trails actually are roads. (For example, see Bottleneck Lake, Hike 31.) Many trails have been abandoned since aircraft have replaced lookouts and fire crews in fighting forest fires.

Many others have simply been gobbled up by roads and clearcuts.

In the three years of research for this book, several trail candidates had to be dropped after being singled out for timber sales. The Monumental Divide near North Baldy in Washington's Pend Oreille County has been intercepted by sprawling clearcuts. Several prime trails in the Kettle Range near Republic, Washington, have been neglected because of proposed timber sales. Notable among them is the Thirteenmile Trail, which winds through the area's last virgin stand of Ponderosa pines. (The Kettle Range spurred controversy when it was curiously left out of the Washington Wilderness Act passed by Congress in 1984. Lawsuits filed by the Sierra Club and other conservation groups so far have stalled actual cutting in several prime natural areas.) Several hikes in the book, including Graham Mountain, Hike 53, are scheduled to be gone in the next few years.

Part of the problem is that the Forest Service is steadily becoming tied to the pickup truck. It used to be that forest rangers knew every mile of trails in their districts. Now it's common to meet Forest Service personnel who have never been off the forest roads. Trails aren't a major consideration in the Forest Service's "services" anymore. Timber production and road building eat up most of the budgets. Consider that in fiscal year 1984, the Idaho Panhandle National Forests' Bonners Ferry District had a budget of $1.8 million. Of that only $24,000 was allotted for recreation purposes and only another $17,000 was designated for trail work.

This explains why hundreds of miles of trails that look inviting on a map turn out to be disappointing, if not totally eliminated by neglect. This book can't do anything about the trend other than to alert its readers and hope they protest with constructive comments and letters to the proper politicians and agencies.

Keep in mind that within the Forest Service are many dedicated workers who love the land and believe in trails. For instance, the Bonners Ferry Ranger District, singled out in the example above, employs one of the most dedicated trail maintenance coordinators in the agency. Despite a meager budget, Pat Hart has used hard-working crews and recruited volunteers to construct excellent trails in the Northern Selkirks. The problem is, there aren't enough Pat Harts in Washington, D.C.

Trails Need Friends

Therein lies another purpose of this book. People have blasted guidebooks as evil works that spoil the wilderness by encouraging crowds to get out and trample the flowers. Indeed, a guidebook does invite more people into fragile areas. The authors encourage readers to study the section "Heading Out on Foot" and learn the techniques for treading lightly on these places. We beg you to pack out your garbage and even to sack up some that's been left behind by less considerate people. We pray that you'll camp away from the fragile shores of lakes and streams and keep their waters pure by keeping soap and latrines far away. And we hope you'll avoid campfires when possible and never cut or scar a living tree.

But we also hope that by buying and using this guide you'll become a friend of Inland Northwest hiking trails. Once you see the peaks, meadows and lakes along these routes, you can't help but become an advocate who will help protect them against the interests that see no good in wildlands because they selfishly can see no profit.

So read on, hike on and be a good friend to the trails.

How to Use This Guidebook

This book does not seek to tell everything about the trails and areas it describes. A hiker who doesn't want to put any effort into exploring a trail and its surrounding area needs a guide, not a guidebook.

This book purposely leaves out some detail for two major reasons. First, we don't want to ruin all of the surprises. We want to encourage hikers to be looking and discovering with every step down an unfamiliar trail. Second, since people and nature never quit changing the land, detailed information has a way of being out of date before it's out in print. New roads, clearcuts and other man-made alterations are constantly being made and nature never stops its doodling with wind, fire, flood, drought and other modes of change.

For each hike we offer a summary of the following information:

Distance of hike: usually a round-trip distance, although there can be variations according to the possibilities described in the text.

Approximate hiking time: figures allow ample time for the steady walker to take a few breaks and snap a few photos; "overnight" identifies hikes suitable for camping.

High point and elevation gain: helps peg the difficulty of a hike and offers clues to how snow and weather might affect hiking conditions; gain is computed by subtracting elevation of lowest point from highest elevation.

Difficulty: a subjective evaluation to give hikers a quick reference to skills required. Generally, the term "easy" means well-defined trails with little elevation gain; "moderate" means rougher trails and more elevation gain; "difficult" means trails could be difficult to find in some areas and terrain can be steep and rough. The text will elaborate on difficulties.

Hiking season: months the trails typically are free of snow and suitable for walking.

United States Geological Survey (USGS) maps: the name of the USGS topographical map or maps covering the hike.

Information: who to contact for up-to-date trail information and additional maps. (See addresses and telephone numbers in Appendix B.)

The narrative for each hike will discuss directions to trailhead and give a brief description of the hike, including information on landmarks, history, some possible difficulties one might encounter and the availability of bonus activities such as berry picking and fishing.

Making Way with Maps

The maps in this book—indeed, the book itself—are not designed to replace the need for topographical maps. The maps recommended for each hike are as essential as the boots on a hiker's feet.

Also, it's essential, especially when driving forest roads and hiking backcountry trails, to carry additional references, such as appropriate Forest Service road and trail maps.

USGS topographical quadrangle maps cost about $2.50 each, which includes the helpful attention of the map experts in the map distribution room if the maps are purchased in person at the Spokane USGS office, Room 678, U.S. Courthouse, W920 Riverside. If maps cannot be picked up, they can be ordered from the regional distribution center by writing USGS, Box 25286, Denver Federal Center, Denver, CO 80225. A mailing fee of $1 is charged for orders under $10. No mailing fee is required for index maps or for orders over $10.

Most of the hikes in this book are scattered through nine national forests. All of these maps can be purchased for $1 from the Forest Service Information Center, Main Floor, U.S. Courthouse, W920 Riverside, Spokane, WA 99201. Or they can be ordered directly from the supervisor's office in each forest (see Appendix B). In some cases, special wilderness maps also have been published. (The Kootenai National Forest has produced a Cabinet Wilderness map; the Wallowa-Whitman National Forest has produced an Eagle Cap Wilderness map; the Umatilla National Forest has produced a Wenaha-Tucannon Wilderness map; British Columbia Parks has produced maps for Kokanee Glacier and Valhalla provincial parks.) These maps are useful. Often they designate heavily used trails. But it's a good idea to have the overall forest map, too, as an aid in navigating forest roads to the trailhead. From the United States, topo maps of Canada can be difficult to obtain. Northwest Map Service, W713 Spokane Falls Blvd., Spokane, WA 99201, telephone (509) 455-6981, carries a complete supply of topos, including those for Canada.

When writing for the latest forest maps, note that the Idaho Panhandle National Forests headquarters in Coeur d'Alene, Idaho, is headquarters for the Kaniksu, Coeur d'Alene and St. Joe national forests. However, each of these forests still has a separate map.

Following Forest Roads

Beware that many of the forests are still in the process of renumbering their roads with a seven-digit system that could take years to transfer to maps and signs. When the project is complete, there will be logic to the numbering system. But until then, new road signs often will not agree with numbers on old maps and old road signs won't correlate with new maps. Hang in there.

Desert lupine studded with raindrops. (Rich Landers photo)

Heading Out on Foot

We all crave the outdoors in one way or another, but for too many people the experience is like getting a massage from a gorilla. The fun is overruled by the misery. Granted, humans weren't designed as well as the mule for carrying a load. Ancient paintings show the Egyptians carried loads on their heads—and they rarely grew more than 5½ feet tall. The Chinese irrigated their rice paddies by painfully hauling water in buckets tied to the ends of a stick draped across their shoulder blades. However, much of the burden has been removed for modern hikers. Sophisticated modern packs distribute weight neatly to shoulders and hips; miles of marked trails have been groomed and four-color maps take much of the mystery out of route finding.

All a modern pilgrim needs to explore the wilds on foot is:
- A pack load of equipment (more or less depending on the length of the visit) and some idea of how to use it,
- A realistic evaluation of physical limitations, and
- And a moderate level of fitness.

Getting Tuned

As the sunset hours of long mountain walks have approached, the fittest hikers have gasped the Tired Walker's Prayer: "If you pick 'em up, O Lord, I'll put 'em down." After a hearty hike, anyone has the right to be tired. There's satisfaction in hard work. But a difference exists between being pooped out and being knotted in a ball of cramps and blisters. Some sort of pre-trip fitness program should be included in the preparation for a backpacking trip. Many of the dayhikes covered in this book are perfect training walks for the longer backpacks.

Be Realistic

Backpackers should either prepare their bodies for the trip or modify the trip to the limitations of their bodies. Also, they should make sure the same considerations have been made for others in the party. Especially during the heat of the summer, it's often important to get up early so most of the mileage can be logged during the coolest part of the day. This also allows some grace time, should unexpected discoveries or emergencies occur along the trail. In the words of Ben Franklin, "He that riseth late must trot all day."

A person's body works much harder than normal on a backpack. While some people actually lose weight on an extended trip, it's not wise to go backpacking with the intention of dieting. Hikers have good reason to eat heartily and drink far more water than they think they need. Hikers always should carry water in their packs, even if they're sure a spring is just ahead. Being sure isn't always a guarantee. To keep body thermostats working in the comfort range, hikers add or peel off layers of clothes during the day. It's important to avoid any rush that might tempt hikers to neglect first aid to the inevitable hot spots on their feet. These are buds ready to bloom into juicy blisters if tape or moleskin isn't applied immediately. Besides, it's good to stop occasionally for a snack, a photograph or a moment of nature observation. As Gandhi said, "There's more to life than increasing its speed."

Gearing up

Because backpacking dealers carry so much ultra-light equipment these days, few backpackers get away without packs that weigh a ton. They think they have to buy it all. John Muir carried less for a 1,000-mile hike than most of us pack along for a stroll in Riverside State Park. All he said he did to prepare for an expedition was to "throw some tea and bread in an old sack and jump over the back fence." While in the wilderness he said he lived on "essences and crumbs" (he ate mostly bread, dried to prevent molding) and his pack was as "unsubstantial as a squirrel's tail."

Most hikers aren't happy traveling quite so sparsely. But most aren't game to imitate Sherpas of the Himalaya, who are capable of going all day carrying 60-pound loads. On multi-day solo hikes, a pack doesn't need to be more than about 35 pounds. With friends along it can be made considerably lighter by sharing the weight of common items.

Equipment is both boon and bane to many backpackers. One of the advantages, however, is that lightweight equipment such as tents, sleeping pads and stoves eliminate the need to cut firewood for cooking or tree bows for insulation and lean-tos. It has never been easier to travel through the wilderness without leaving a trace of your visit. A list of recommended gear is published in Appendix A, but a few items require elaboration.

THE TEN ESSENTIALS

First, never go anywhere in the backcountry—not even on the short dayhikes covered in this book—without the Ten Essentials:
   1. Map
   2. Compass
   3. Flashlight
   4. Knife
   5. Matches in waterproof container
   6. Fire starter
   7. Extra clothing
   8. Extra food and water
   9. First aid kit
   10. Sun protection (includes sunglasses and sunscreen)

OTHER GEAR

The old standby, wool clothing, still is handy to have along in the mountains, although modern polypropylene, pile and breathable waterproof fabrics have revolutionized the way hikers dress. Wool, polypropylene and pile—unlike cotton—offer warmth even when wet.

For short hikes on established trails, there's no need to spend $100 on hiking boots. Rugged running or walking shoes are cheaper, more comfortable and more functional in or out of the mountains. But for the hiker who plans a lot of backpacking and scrambling on and off trails, it's wise to consider the rugged but lightweight boots many manufacturers are making. Just be sure to break them in before tackling a substantial hike.

Always carry some sort of rain gear. One hiker might prefer a parka and bibs made of a breathable waterproof fabric. Another hiker might prefer a coated nylon poncho and chaps.

Down bags are terribly expensive, but they're still the lightest way to a warm night's sleep. Fiberfill products are good investments, though. They are a few ounces heavier than down and add a few inches of bulk to the pack, but they cost as much as 40 percent less. Moreover, a bag made of a fiberfill, such as Polarguard, will dry faster and retain warmth better when wet.

Most good tents are made of breathable waterproof fabric or of uncoated nylon with waterproof floors and separate waterproof rain flies. Some hikers still use a tarp to make a lean-to, but many hikers prefer the all-element protection (that includes protection from mosquitoes) of a tent.

Packs are a huge topic in themselves. Some people swear by frame packs, some insist on soft packs with no frames. Look them over. Talk to dealers, read the catalogs and buy one. Just be sure it fits.

Organizing a Pack

Organizing a backpack is as personal as the way one arranges underwear in a chest of drawers. Nevertheless, a backpacker is smart to take a logical approach to the task. Keep frequently used items, such as maps, trail snacks, drinking cup, insect repellent and sunglasses, handy in the outside pockets of the pack. Organize gear in plastic bags or stuff sacks so it's easy to find and protected from rain. After all, if something furry licks your feet in the middle of the night, you don't want to be fumbling for your flashlight.

Dinners and breakfasts go in one bag buried in the pack. Lunches are packed in another bag near the top of the pack for easy access on the trail. Some items, such as powdered drinks, are ideal for stuffing in pots, helping to take advantage of every square inch of space in the pack. Large items, such as tents and camp shoes, can be strapped to the outside of the pack. A rain cover for the pack will keep everything dry. (See Appendix A for equipment list.)

Wilderness Etiquette

Somewhere between 30 and 50 million Americans every year leave the cities—where people are employed to dispose of our garbage and sewage—to tramp through the wilderness where there is no one to pick up after them. The result in some areas has been devastating. The cumulative effects of all this nature loving has destroyed vegetation, eroded trails, polluted streams and degraded some areas with human waste.

For those who don't want the backcountry to go the way of the cities, here are some tips on wilderness etiquette.

Camp in places already trampled by other campers rather than packing down another area of vegetation. Avoid camping on fragile shores of lakes and streams. Consider tenting on higher knolls and ridges, which usually have fewer bugs. In the age of tents, tarps and foam pads, a hiker should cut green trees and boughs for shelter only in an emergency.

Never use soap near a lake or stream. Many backpackers find they don't need soap at all; using sand for pots and simply rinsing off their bodies works fine for the duration of a hike, even if it lasts several days. Hikers who must use even biodegradable soap should lather up and rinse using a pot of water hauled well away from the lake or stream.

Dig personal latrines AT LEAST 100 feet from any trail, campsite or water source. A personal latrine can be dug with a stick or boot heel. It only needs to be about 6 inches deep. Cover the waste with dirt and replace the duff to hide the digging. It's also wise to carry a butane lighter to burn toilet paper before burying the waste. Few things are worse than walking into a lovely campsite surrounded by piles of wilting tissue. Scrape away the duff and burn the paper on bare dirt. Then be sure the ashes are cool before scraping them into the latrine for a proper burial.

When confronted with equestrians, give them the right of way. Walk toward the horses to make sure they see you, then step off the trail and let them pass. A few friendly words not only is a neighborly way to greet the rider, but also alerts following horses to a hiker's presence so they don't spook.

Keep groups small to minimize impact to camping areas.

Leave pets at home. One hiker might think his dog is cute, but when it poops in the trail, barks at night, jumps on other people and their equipment, chases deer and squirrels or ruins the fishing by taking a swim in a wilderness lake, one should be able to understand why others won't share the sentiments.

And, of course, never bury trash. Critters will soon dig it up. Pack out all garbage.

Camping With and Without Campfires

In most cases, wilderness travelers should avoid campfires unless there's a designated fire pit. Sure, fires are romantic, but so are candles. Consider these good reasons for NOT building a campfire:

1. The smoke gets in your eyes and fouls your hair and clothes.

2. Sparks burn holes in expensive coats, tents and raingear.

3. Light from the fire blots out the surroundings, including many of the stars. This leaves one in a little compartment even while visiting a vast wilderness.

4. Noise from the fire blares over sounds of owls, crickets and coyotes.

5. Fire chars rocks and earth, leaving unsightly scars for other wilderness lovers to see.

6. Gathering fuel for fires has left many campsites bare of wood, and trees bare of branches as high as a camper can reach.

7. Campfires increase the potential for forest fires.

8. Fires are messier than stoves for cooking. A stove is ready instantly; a fire must burn down to coals before it's ready.

9. Fires take more time than stoves to extinguish. If there's no water, one must let a fire burn out completely and stir with dirt. If one uses water to douse the fire, putting it out before its time, unsightly chunks of charred wood and a messy camp will be left behind.

Hikers who insist on building fires should avoid making a fire ring with rocks. Simply scrape away the duff down to bare dirt and build a SMALL fire. Let it burn out to ashes so they can be extinguished, cooled, scooped and scattered away from the campsite. Then replace the duff to hide the scorched ground.

Fishing the Backcountry

Most of the trails described in this book lead to, along or near a lake or stream that holds fish. That's the nature of the Inland Northwest. Fish are common in the backcountry; so are anglers.

Hikers should be aware, however, that the supply of fish is not endless. Native backcountry fisheries, such as that of the west-slope cutthroat trout found in many northern Idaho streams, have evolved in relatively sterile mountain waters by eating virtually every food item they see. Thus, they are fairly easy to catch and are prone to being fished out.

Many streams have special regulations limiting the catch. Hikers should heed these state regulations, for their own good and that of the fisheries. There's nothing wrong, when regulations permit, with taking a fish or two for a meal. But don't be a pig—even when the daily limit of fish is high. Native trout streams can't take heavy harvest; neither can mountain lakes. Rainbow and cutthroat trout do not spawn naturally in most high mountain lakes. They must be stocked, a few hundred at a time, usually on a rotation of every three years or so. Sometimes this is done by aircraft from funds derived from the sales of required state fishing licenses. But often, as in the case of lakes nestled below mountain peaks, the fish must be carried in on the back of a biologist or a horse.

Limit your catch; don't catch your limit. Practice catch-and-release techniques. Pinch down the barbs on flies and lures so fish can be released easily with little or no handling. Let them swim away and please another mountain angler some day.

Safety Considerations

The Ten Essentials recommended earlier are advised because backcountry hiking entails unavoidable risk. Every hiker must assume this risk. The listing of a trail in this book does not guarantee it will be safe. Trails vary greatly in difficulty. Hikers vary greatly in their skill and physical conditioning. On some hikes, routes may have changed or conditions may have deteriorated since the descriptions were written. Also, trail conditions can change even from day to day and hour to hour, owing to weather and other factors. A trail that is safe when dry might be dangerous during adverse weather. A trail easily negotiated by a well-conditioned, agile, properly equipped hiker may be a nightmare for an out-of-shape novice.

Hikers can minimize risks on the trail by being knowledgeable, prepared and alert. This book is not designed to fully prepare a hiker for exploring the backcountry. Many good general backpacking books are available. Also, backpacking courses are offered through clubs or schools in many communities.

It's important for all hikers to recognize their own limitations. Look ahead. If adverse conditions are stacking up against your skill and conditioning, abandon the trip. Resort to an easier trail. It's better to bag a questionable outing than to be the subject of a mountain rescue.

Remember, there are no telephones or quick means for assistance in the backcountry. The wilderness is a free and exciting place to visit, but it's not a place to be without good ol' common sense.

Water in the Wilderness

Many hikers conjure up images of dipping a cup into a cold mountain stream for a long draw of sweet, clear water. Many other hikers are haunted by memories of diarrhea and severe intestinal disorders caused by drinking so-called "pure" mountain water.

No one can unconditionally guarantee that a backcountry water source is safe for human consumption, not even from free-flowing streams in our most pristine wilderness areas. No reference to water sources in this book is a guarantee the water is safe to drink. Each individual must accept the responsibility to determine whether to play it safe or take a risk when drinking mountain water.

Playing it safe means either carrying water from home or treating water obtained in the backcountry to prevent contracting microorganisms that can cause illness. For example, giardiasis is an intestinal disorder caused by a microscopic organism, Giardia lamblia. This parasite is found all over the world and even in some treated municipal water systems in the Inland Northwest. Giardia are carried in the feces of some animals and even humans. Cysts of Giardia can contaminate surface water supplies even though they can look clear, feel cold, smell clean and taste pure. One hiker might drink from a Giardia-infested stream and show no symptoms while another could suffer diarrhea, loss of appetite, abdominal cramps, gas and bloating.

With proper diagnosis, the disease is curable with medication prescribed by a physician. But at best, giardiasis is an inconvenience; at worst, a backcountry hiker suffering from diarrhea could become dehydrated to the point of immobility.

Prevention is the key. First, help avoid the spread of Giardia by burying human waste far from water sources and leaving pets at home. Second, treat all water before drinking or even brushing teeth.

The National Park Service recommends boiling water a minimum of one minute to destroy Giardia at altitudes below about 4,000 feet and five minutes at higher altitudes. Other experts recommend boiling for 10 minutes at any altitude. Boiling is perhaps the surest method of fighting against the myriad organisms that can go bumph in your tummy.

If boiling is impossible, many experts say iodine treatments can be effective. The National Park Service, however, points out that while iodine and less-effective chlorine compounds work well against most waterborne bacteria and viruses, they are not as effective as heat in killing Giardia. Also, be sure to carefully follow directions in treating water with chemicals.

The jury is still out on filtration devices. Experts disagree on whether certain filters are effective in screening both Giardia and inhibiting bacterial growth within the filters themselves. Filters can be nice in areas such as the Wenaha-Tucannon Wilderness, where water sources are scarce and occasionally turbid. But smart hikers should consider additional treatment as well.

Hiking in Bear Country

An old joke explains the two sure ways to tell a grizzly from a black bear. When you see a bear, it is said, climb a tree. If the critter climbs up after you, it's a black bear; if it rips the tree out of the ground and shakes you out, it's a grizzly.

However, since several of the hikes suggested in this book lead into grizzly country, hikers should take a little more serious approach to the subject.

All bears deserve respect. However, grizzlies are notorious for their infrequent but highly publicized attacks on humans. Grizzly populations in several areas covered by this book are small, with the exception of Kokanee Glacier Provincial Park, which has been known to close trails because of bear activity. It's a good idea to check with park or forest rangers to get reports on bear activity before hiking or camping in grizzly country. Avoid areas with recent sightings. Always cook and keep food hung away from camp. Avoid opening a can of tuna, for instance, and draining the juice near a campsite—yours or anyone else's. In fact, tuna is a bad food choice for grizzly country. Stick with dried, oil-free foods that are less seductive to an animal's olfactory senses. Also, hikers should avoid wiping peanut-buttery knives on their pants. The clothes worn while cooking and eating should be left in a pack outside the tent and preferably hung in a tree with the food.

Several years ago, rangers at Glacier National Park were asking hiking anglers to pack out fish entrails in plastic bags. The idea was to avoid littering the shorelines with bear bait. Logically, backpackers weren't particularly fond of tramping through bear country on warm summer days with bags of fish guts; few complied with the request. The park subsequently went back to the standard policy of asking anglers to puncture the air sacks on the entrails and throw them back into the middle of the streams or lakes away from the shores. Probably the preferred method for disposing of fish viscera is to build a hot fire away from tent sites and burn it. Better yet, backcountry travelers could catch and release their fish to totally avoid the problem.

Experts warn against wearing perfumes, deodorants, hair sprays or cosmetics that might have some flowery appeal to bears. Some evidence also suggests that women should avoid bear country during their menstrual periods.

Bear experts agree there's no foolproof way to avoid an encounter with a grizzly short of staying out of bear country altogether. All one can do is minimize the already minimal risks. Don't hike alone in bear country; stay together with a group. If a grizzly is spotted in the distance, abandon the trip or give the animal a very wide berth.

Surprise is a common element in many bear attacks, especially in encounters with sows that have cubs. Bear bells don't have official endorsement from the Forest Service or Park Service, but hikers won't hear any bear experts saying they "shouldn't" be worn.

Some backpackers carry the small but piercingly loud air horns made for bicyclists in the hope that a loud blast might scare away a bear that wanders into camp. There is evidence this will work. But, again, no guarantees. Carrie Hunt, a University of Montana graduate student who had been studying bears for eight years in the mid 1980s, researched the effectiveness of potential bear repellents. At the time this book was published, she said she had not been able to try the alternatives on enough bears to make any solid recommendations.

Hunt, like thousands of other wilderness travelers, does not hesitate to venture into bear country armed only with her wits. In one encounter with a sow, Hunt thought she had enough time to climb a nearby tree. However, even after making a side trip to usher away the cubs, the bear was staring up from the base of the tree before Hunt was out of reach. "I just froze," Hunt said. "I didn't even look at her. I felt she was waiting for me to do something. Finally a friend yelled from some distance and the bear ran away."

Hunt emphasizes that every bear encounter is a different situation. "You have to rely on your gut feeling to what the situation is," she said. "Never run unless you're positive you can get 15 feet up a tree before the bear gets to you. At full charge, a grizzly can hit 30 mph, or 44 feet per second." By comparison, an Olympic sprinter can only manage 33 feet per second.

In the rare event that a bear charges, Hunt recommends playing dead by rolling into a fetal position to protect one's face and vital areas. She notes that in most cases a bear attack is a one-swat affair. A study by Steve Herrero of the University of Calgary indicates that playing dead is statistically the best way to survive an attack by a grizzly that is being defensive of cubs or territory.

After reading the experts' advice, keep in mind that it is not intended to scare hikers away from bear country. Use this information to go prepared into our wildlands. Grizzlies are extremely wary and elusive. To even see a silvertip is a rare prize indeed.

Rattlesnakes

Perhaps more misconceptions have been spread about rattlesnakes than about any other creature in the west. No, they aren't slimy; they don't hypnotize potential prey; they don't have to coil to strike; and they don't go slithering each day hunting for a human to kill. But they are a potential hazard in some of the areas covered by this book, such as the Columbia Basin of eastern Washington, portions of the Kettle Range and the Wenaha-Tucannon Wilderness.

Nationally, about 12 people die each year from poisonous snake bites, according to The Medical Letter on Drugs and Therapeutics. To put that in perspective, about 30 people die each year from bee or wasp stings. Furthermore, nearly half of the snakebite victims are people who keep, collect, handle or attempt to kill the snakes. An even smaller fraction of these victims are struck by western rattlesnakes, the only poisonous snakes found in the region covered by this book. Generally, rattlers only bite those who are careless, foolish, ignorant or just plain unlucky.

Western rattlesnakes get their name from the rattles at the end of their tails. The snakes use the rattles to warn intruders that they are getting too close. Invariably, rattlers would rather retreat than hold their ground or make an advance on anything larger than a ground squirrel.

In the extremely rare instance where a hiker surprises a rattler, the snake might strike. Humans rarely die from rattlesnake bites. About 20 percent of these bites are "dry"; that is, no venom is injected. The other 80 percent of the time, the victim is most likely to suffer symptoms such as pain, swelling and nausea. Sometimes permanent damage after a snakebite is due not to the snake's venom but to overreactions in application of first aid.

Treatment of snakebites continues to be controversial. Some physicians still recommend using ice packs, or administering the cut-and-suck method described in most field manuals or in over-the-counter snakebite kits. However, other experts say making an incision is unnecessary and risks damage to nerves; they say cold treatments increase tissue damage. Generally, experts agree that victims of serious poisonous snakebites should receive antivenin. Since it is impractical for hikers to carry antivenin, which must be kept cool, one must know only one generally accepted first aid treatment for snakebite: Apply a broad, firm, constrictive bandage immediately over the bitten area and bandaging as much of the limb as possible. DO NOT CUT OFF CIRCULATION. Immobilize the limb and seek medical attention as soon as possible.

Backcountry in the Inland Northwest

A library could be filled with books about the wealth of natural beauty, history and wildlife in the Inland Northwest. Terrain ranges from desert dunes to glaciered peaks; wildlife ranges from the common

Wood ducks. (Rich Landers photo)

white-tailed deer to the rare and endangered mountain caribou, which is found nowhere else in the United States. Along with this natural diversity is a spectrum of human intervention. Some of it is destroying our natural areas; some of it is responsible for its preservation. Following is but a sampling of what backcountry hikers will experience in some of the special areas covered by this book.

Juniper Dunes Wilderness

The Juniper Dunes Wilderness, situated about 15 miles northeast of Pasco, Washington, is one of the areas given protection under the 1984 Washington Wilderness Act. But that is about the only similarity it shares with other wilderness in the state. Juniper Dunes is managed by the U.S. Bureau of Land Management (BLM), not the Forest Service. It is desert country rather than alpine. And most people wouldn't even consider it pretty. The vegetation that has taken hold on the ever-changing dunes is fragile and there's no reasonable way to make camping easy or comfortable.

The 7,140-acre wilderness is the last remnant of an ecosystem that once spread over 250,000 acres down to the Snake and Columbia rivers before agriculture gobbled it up. It was set aside primarily as a natural sanctuary. The ecosystem includes some of the largest sand dunes and the six largest remaining natural groves of western junipers in the state. The dunes, formed by the nearly incessant southwesterly winds, are up to 130 feet high and ¼ mile wide. The juniper groves are up to 150 years old and represent the northernmost limits of the species.

One of the major complications in managing the wilderness, BLM officials say, is that much of the surrounding area has been a popular off-road-vehicle (ORV) playground for years. While hiking into the wilderness where all vehicles are prohibited, one still can see where the knobby-tire tracks of a few renegades have left deep scars in the unstable hillsides. ORV clubs in the Tri-Cities area have helped to educate riders that the wilderness is off-limits to vehicles. A fence built along the western boundary of the wilderness in the mid 1980s also helps. BLM is trying to acquire additional land near the wilderness to set aside for ORV use.

No fires are allowed and no drinking water is available in the Juniper Dunes. But what a privilege it is to have this gem set aside for the mule deer, coyotes, kangaroo rats, Swainson's hawks—and the few people who will come here to study and soul search in a sanctuary of the past.

Kettle Range

Although Congress deleted the 80,000-acre Kettle Range from the 1984 Washington Wilderness Act, the Kettle Crest itself has not been riddled with roads. Conservationists are still fighting many timber sales threatening to encroach on this scenic area, which is blessed with rolling mountains and flowered meadows in the area's only roadless mountain terrain.

The north and south sections of the Kettle Crest Trail combine for about 42 miles of ridge trail crossed by only one road, State Highway 20 at Sherman Pass. This is some of the best scenery in Ferry County, but certainly not all of it. Another 14 trails in the Kettle Range account for 80 miles, 61 of which are proposed by conservationists for inclusion in a hiking area. This classification would be less restrictive than a wilderness area but still protect the trails and scenic beauty. So far the Forest Service has turned its back on these plans. Meanwhile, many trails have been neglected for years, including the classic route through the virgin stand of Ponderosa pines in the Thirteenmile drainage.

Wenaha-Tucannon Wilderness

Established in 1978, the Wenaha-Tucannon Wilderness is composed of 177,412 acres, of which 110,995 are in Washington, the remainder in Oregon. Though its northerly trailheads are only 150 miles from Spokane, this area of the Blue Mountains is seldom visited by hikers. Unless one is in the wilderness in late October and early November during the elk hunting season, it is common to cover miles of trails without seeing another human.

The area consists of horizontal basalt flows thousands of feet thick that have been deeply and steeply eroded by streams. Trails either follow the broad rolling ridgetops near 6,000 feet or parallel the streams 2,000 to 3,000 feet below. Scenic vistas are common on all ridge trails and along the Wenaha River. Camping areas are determined by water availability. Most high-elevation springs identified on the maps remain flowing even during dry summers, though some may require a steep descent from the trail (Sheephead and Table Camp Springs near Trail No. 6144) or they may be only a murky trickle (Rettkowski, Twin and Clover Springs near Tril No. 6144). With summer temperatures into the 90s and water sources sometimes over 5 miles apart, the hiker is advised to carry more than the usual quart bottle of water.

The area is relatively dry and is sparsely forested on south-facing slopes. The western half receives more precipitation and thus is more heavily forested. Trails are generally snow-free by late June, although the higher elevations in the western sections often have snow into July.

Aside from the rugged basalt canyons, the characteristic that makes this area unique for Inland Northwest hikers is the large number of Rocky Mountain elk. It is common to see over a dozen per day along the trails.

The dry climate makes mosquitoes rare, but horseflies can be bothersome. Don't confuse them with the unusually large numbers of hummingbirds that choose these mountains for their breeding grounds. (Hikers wearing colorful clothing or bandannas often will get "buzzed" by hummingbirds here.) Rattlesnakes are common at lower elevations.

The flora is the same as one would expect to find anywhere else in eastern Washington, although the Mountain Mahogany is found nowhere else in the state. Grand firs seem to outnumber the Douglas firs, and yew trees grow in profusion along the streams. Beautiful Ponderosa pine-grass parklands cover the higher slopes above the Wenaha

River in the southeast corner's Smooth Ridge/Moore Flat area.

Campgrounds near trailheads are small and primitive. Reaching any trailhead will involve a 10- to 30-mile drive over dusty dirt roads, either south from the Pomeroy, Washington, area or from Dayton, Washington. Oregon approaches are all off of Forest Road No. 62. These roads are generally poorly marked, and in Washington only, their southern most portions are included on the Wenaha-Tucannon Wilderness map. State highway maps are useless here. The visitor is advised to obtain the USGS 1:100,000 meter scale topo map of Clarkston for information on approach roads.

Salmo-Priest Wilderness

The country of northeastern Washington and northern Idaho called the Salmo-Priest was a hunting ground of the Kalispel Indians before it was invaded by white men surveying the border between the United States and Canada in 1861. The area's history was heavily influenced by Father Peter DeSmet and other Jesuit missionaries, the namesakes for Priest Lake.

In 1908 the international border between the U.S and Canada was surveyed and in 1927 the boundary swath, maintained as a linear clearcut today, was cut through the dense forest. By 1925, a trail had been built from Salmo Mountain and along the South Salmo River, and the Shedroof Mountain lookout had been constructed. Between 1924-29 the west side of the wilderness was swept by fires from which much of the area has never recovered. From the '30s into the '50s, the Forest Service used cabins and lookouts at Ace High Camp near Helmer Mountain and at Crowell Point, Thunder Mountain, Shedroof Mountain, Round Top, Little Snowy Top and Pass Creek Pass. Salmo Cabin, which is along Salmo Loop, Hike 18, was staffed until 1951. It has been vandalized, but it still stands and occasionally is used as a shelter by soggy hikers. Lookout towers still exist in one form or another on Salmo, Sullivan, Little Snowy Top and Round Top mountains.

A road was built to the head of Deemer Creek in 1938. In 1963 it was extended to the Salmo Mountain lookout and in 1968 it was reconstructed in preparation for timber sales in the area. In 1968, Spokane firefighter, Ray Kresek, began to drum up support to save the Salmo area. In 1970, the Forest Service backed off its plans to build roads and harvest the Salmo's timber, and, in 1971, recommended about 21,000 acres for wilderness study in the first Roadless Area Review and Evaluation (RARE I). Finally, after years of work by conservationists, 41,335 acres of the area were included in the 1984 Washington Wilderness Act for official wilderness designation. Thousands of adjoining acres in Idaho's Upper Priest Lake area are proposed as an addition to this wilderness, but Idaho wilderness bills had failed to receive Congressional approval at the time this book was published.

Hikers should be aware that Colville National Forest officials adopted a policy in 1987 prohibiting new mileage and trail number signs from being posted inside the wilderness. Eventually, signs will indicate destinations only; trail numbers will be posted only at trailheads.

The wilderness and proposed additions offer a variety of trails from the cedars along the Upper Priest River to the treeless Crowell Ridge that leads to Gypsy Peak. The Upper Priest area is known as being the highest precipitation zone in Washington east of the Cascades, so be prepared for wet weather. Elevations range from the Upper Priest River at 2,900 feet to Snowy Top Mountain, one of the highest points in the region at 7,548 feet. A few miles away is 7,309-foot Gypsy Peak, the highest point in eastern Washington. The area is rich with dense forests of western hemlock and some of the largest cedar in eastern Washington and northern Idaho—some up to 10 feet in diameter. Mycologists around the world know the Priest Lake area for its abundance and variety of mushrooms, more than 1,000 documented species.

But it's a wilderness backed into a corner. From the summit of Snowy Top, one can see a road or a powerline or a clearcut in every direction. The Upper Priest drainage is a protected spawning area for bull trout and west slope cutthroats. Big game species, too, are making a last stand against development.

Mountain caribou, found in the United States only in northeastern Washington and northern Idaho, were federally protected as an endangered species in 1983. The grizzly bear and bald eagle are other threatened and endangered species found here. This is the only remaining area in Washington and Idaho where the grizzlies are known to live on a regular basis. While many other species of wildlife abound in this region—including deer, black bears, elk, mountain goats, bighorn sheep, lynx, wolverines and Washington's healthiest population of cougars— it's the existence of these endangered species that distinguishes this wilderness from any other area in the country.

American Selkirk Mountains

East of the Priest River drainage, the Selkirk Mountains of Idaho are a hiker's heaven. From the mile-long scramble to Hunt Lake to the 35-mile Long Canyon Loop, hikers of all abilities can find suitable scenic routes punctuated with trout-filled lakes and gleaming granite peaks.

With the notable exception of Long Canyon, virtually every major drainage in the Selkirks has been pegged for timber sales and roads. This generally means good road access to some trailheads near the Selkirk Crest, but it also means that roads have gobbled up miles of good trails. Many of the trails in this region were originally constructed by the Civilian Conservation Corps between 1933 and 1942. Since then, many of them have not been significantly improved.

The Selkirks, actually a 250-mile-long mountain range running from Sandpoint, Idaho, well into British Columbia, are on their last legs against human intrusion. Some of the Selkirk Crest has been recommended for wilderness designation and some for roadless classification, but roads and clearcuts already have scarred virtually everything below. Still, the area has some breathtaking scenery.

The Selkirk Mountains region averages about 75 lightning fires a year and another 20 caused by man. In 1967, the 16,400-acre Trapper

Peak fire and the 55,960-acre Sundance fire devastated large areas of the Selkirks covered by this book. The Sundance blaze was dramatic and intense. In a single afternoon it advanced 28 miles through the Roman Nose Peak and Pack River areas. Then it suddenly pooped out. Silvery snags on ridges and hillsides remain as monuments to the burn.

Coeur d'Alene and Pend Oreille

A broad swath of mountains roughly from Sandpoint, Idaho, south to St. Maries and from Spokane, Washington east to the Idaho-Montana border is dominated by two large lakes that are remarkably like those found high in the mountains.

Lake Coeur d'Alene extends 23 miles south from the city of Coeur d'Alene. It covers 77 square miles and has 109 miles of shoreline. Major tributaries are the St. Joe and Coeur d'Alene rivers, both of which are the sources for hikes in this book. Just to the north is Lake Pend Oreille, which dips down to the mind-boggling depth of 1,150 feet, so deep that it was established as a Navy submarine testing base during World War II. The lake is 43 miles long, 6 ½ miles wide and has 111 miles of shoreline.

Coeur d'Alene (pronounced "core-da-LANE") is of French origin meaning "heart of the awl" or "sharp-hearted." It's not clear whether the term was most commonly used by European fur traders describing the shrewd Indians confronted in this region or by the Indians as they referred to the greedy traders. Pend Oreille (pronounced "pon-der-AY") is another French name meaning "Indians who wear earrings."

Mineral exploration played a major part in the history of this region. Mining began in 1881 when gold was discovered in what was later to be called the Silver Valley. The area later was acclaimed to be the richest silver, lead, zinc and antimony mining area in the United States and was once ranked with the 20 richest known mineralized areas in the world. Now that many of the minerals have been taken and market prices have made it uneconomical to mine, much of the land is left permanently scarred; some of its waterways are permanently polluted with heavy metals.

The great forest fire of August, 1910, raised further havoc with the region. When it was over, 78 firefighters and 7 civilians were dead. The Idaho towns of Wallace, Kellogg, Osborne, Burke and Murray were ravaged. The Montana towns of Taft, DeBorgia, Saltese, Haugan and Tuscor were consumed. And a 3-million-acre path 260 miles long and 200 miles wide from the Salmon River north to Canada was charred. Most of the destruction occurred in just two days.

Several of the hikes selected for this book seek out the most pristine and scenic areas remaining in this region. While one might use the word "spectacular" to describe the peaks of the Cabinet and Eagle Cap wilderness areas, one would be inclined to describe the Coeur d'Alene and Pend Oreille areas as "picturesque." Most of the mountains are rounded and the valleys are timbered. The highest summit in the area is Stevens Peak, elev. 6,826 feet (see Stevens Lakes, Hike 66), and there are no glaciers or sky-scraping pinnacles.

Wildlife management has played a major role in reviving this country. For instance, the healthy elk herds in the Coeur d'Alene area developed almost entirely from four plants totaling 237 head made between 1925 and 1939. And trout streams are beginning to get some respect after years of abuse from logging and mining.

St. Joe/Mallard-Larkins

The 32,331-acre Mallard-Larkins Pioneer Area and the regions surrounding the nearby St. Joe River drainage, are an Eden-like refuge for fisheries, big game and backcountry explorers. The Mallard-Larkins averages more than 60 inches of annual precipitation, compared to only 25 inches in the western reaches of the St. Joe National Forest. Within this national forest alone are 560 miles of fishable streams and 17 fishable high mountain lakes. The trail systems are relatively good, servicing both hikers, horsepackers and large numbers of hunters who flock to the area each fall to hunt the excellent populations of elk.

As in most of the forests in this part of the country, the trail systems were largely designed for servicing lookouts and fighting forest fires. The cabin on Mallard Peak is a monument to this era. The structure was built in 1929 from materials that included 3,750 pounds of cement mix packed in on the backs of men and livestock over 43 miles of trails. The cabin was decommissioned in 1957. Now that roads have punched into the area, the hike to the peak (see Mallard-Fawn Lakes, Hike 74) is an easy day's walk. The cabin was refurbished by Spokane lookout buff Ray Kresek in 1981.

Use in the St. Joe is concentrated along the St. Joe River, the upper reaches of which are part of the Wild and Scenic River System. Use in the Mallard-Larkins centers around 12 alpine lakes that are beginning to show the wear and tear. The name Mallard-Larkins is derived from two prominent peaks in the area. The origin of the name Mallard is not clear, but Larkin is the name of a former homesteader in the North Fork of the Clearwater River. The homestead is now inundated by Dworshak Reservoir.

Clearwater National Forest

Hikes 81-84 in the Clearwater National Forest cover territory explored by Lewis and Clark in their famous expedition of 1805-06. The trailhead for Hike 84 to Lost Lakes is situated on the historic Lolo Trail west of the Lochsa River drainage and Lolo Pass. The expedition nearly starved as it followed this Indian trail through the Clearwater country. Today, however, the area is rich with elk and deer; indeed, it is one of Idaho's most prolific producers of elk and west slope cutthroat trout.

The Forest Service has published a descriptive brochure on the expedition's travels in this area. It's called "Following Lewis and Clark across the Clearwater National Forest."

Cabinet Mountains Wilderness

The Cabinet Mountains, which slice narrowly through the Big Sky of northwestern Montana near Libby, are soaked in some areas by up to 100 inches of annual precipitation. The steep terrain is scenic and wet with cascading waterfalls. Cedar forests thrive to a timberline of about 7,000 feet. Mosquitoes seem to thrive everywhere.

Within the range is the 94,272-acre Cabinet Mountains Wilderness, established in 1964. The high point is 8,712-foot Snowshoe Peak (see Leigh Lake, Hike 61). Only three small glaciers still hang in the jagged peaks. This wilderness, along with the smaller Ten Lakes Scenic Area to the north near Eureka (see Ten Lakes, Hike 57), are the only scenic areas in this region that haven't been laced with logging roads.

The wilderness is home for a small population of grizzly bears, thousands of trout, plenty of elk, some mountain goats, bighorn sheep, black bears and a variety of other creatures.

Selway-Bitterroot Wilderness

The 1.3-million-acre Selway Bitterroot Wilderness, encompassing the Selway River, a part of the national Wild and Scenic River System, was officially secured by the 1964 Wilderness Act. It is named after the Selway River, which drains its core, and the Bitterroot Range, which bounds it on the east. It ranges from 1,800 feet on the Selway to 10,000 feet along the Bitterroot Divide. It is blessed with 1,000 miles of trails. Although some of them are in less-than-pristine condition, the wilderness trail system is excellent.

Since the Selway-Bitterroot is on the outer limits of the region this book covers, the authors have included only one hike within its boundaries (see Cove Lakes, Hike 85). This hike penetrates the popular Selway Crags, a dramatic line of glacier-carved peaks 8,000 feet high at the northwest edge of the wilderness. While a good trail system covers this region, the Forest Service, to its credit, also is managing a large portion of the Crags as a pristine area with no trails. Life is fragile here, where plants must survive in the thinnest of soils, endure long winters and cram a growing season into a short two or three months.

Hikers should look beyond the Crags to other tempting areas for exploration in the Selway. The hiking season begins in early June on lowland trails, such as the trail along the Selway River, long before high country trails are open. Most of the wilderness is densely forested with Douglas fir, spruce and lodgepole pine. It is host to a large population of elk, good numbers of moose, some black bears and many other creatures. Virtually all of the lakes and streams hold trout. The wilderness is accessible from U.S. Highway 93 in the Bitterroot Valley south of Missoula and from the Selway River area off U.S. Highway 12 along Idaho's Lochsa River.

Eagle Cap Wilderness

The Eagle Cap Wilderness is a ruggedly captivating collection of glacier-cut valleys, shimmering peaks and waterfalls and more than 50 mountain lakes in the Wallowa Mountains of northeastern Oregon. The centerpiece in the 220,416-acre preserve is 9,595-foot Eagle Cap Peak, although it isn't the highest mountain within the wilderness boundaries. Sacajawea Peak and the Matterhorn, adjacent to each other on a

Mule deer in camp, Eagle Cap Wilderness. (Rich Landers photo)

long ridge above Hurricane Creek north of Eagle Cap, are both about 9,800 feet.

The wilderness, situated just west from the rim of Hells Canyon of the Snake River, was established in 1940. It has four main access areas. The most heavily used is the paved highway to Wallowa Lake, south of Enterprise, Oregon, and just 1 mile from the wilderness boundary. Other main routes are the Hurricane Creek Road, Imnaha River Road and Lostine River Road. All the roads have developed campgrounds. They lead to five main trails into the heart of the wilderness, the major portion of which usually is free of snow by early July. Beginning in mid September, the area is infiltrated by hunters. Fishermen will find more than 37 miles of streams and 23 lakes stocked with rainbow trout, brook trout, bull trout, cutthroats and golden trout.

Oregon's original mountain goat herd was transplanted into the wilderness in 1944. Since then, the herd has increased slowly. They are most often seen at Ice Lake, the Matterhorn, Sacajawea Peak and Chief Joseph Mountain. (The area is rich with history of Chief Joseph, leader of the Nez Perce.) A bighorn sheep herd introduced to the Lostine area was decimated by a rare viral disease during the winter of 1986-87.

Timberline in the Wallowas varies from about 8,500 to 9,000 feet, from which the autumn hiker can look down on a patchwork of golds and greens among the trees struggling for existence in a world of crumbling granite, limestone and marble. There's a price to pay for country this beautiful. For instance, at a trail junction along Hurricane Creek a Forest Service sign pointing up the seemingly vertical slopes of the canyon says "Echo Lake 3 miles." One can see where a hiker tried to scratch the 3 into an 8. Somebody else tried to make the 8 into an 18. The sign had other comments about the last 3 miles to Echo Lake, such as "Pure hell!" and "With Jesus, 4 hours."

The popular Lake Basin area of the wilderness is heavily used, particularly in August (see Lake Basin, Hike 95). It's not an area for solitude. Most trails are liberally splattered with horse manure, and hikers abound. To help counter human impact, wilderness rangers have been enforcing regulations that prohibit camping within 200 feet of a lake. The fine is $40.

Kokanee Glacier/Valhalla Provincial Parks

Of all the hiking areas covered in this book, none is more spectacular than these two provincial wilderness parks preserved in southeastern British Columbia near Nelson.

Kokanee Glacier Provincial Park is a 63,232-acre wilderness in the Slocan Range of the Canadian Selkirks. Established in 1922, it is one of the oldest of the splendid parks in British Columbia's provincial park system. It is named after the glacier that clings to the easterly slopes of 9,154-foot Kokanee Peak in the center of the park. The park has more than 30 lakes. It is rugged country with a short summer hiking season. Most of the park lies at elevations above 6,000 feet, with half of it above 6,900 feet. The park is speckled with signs of early mining, and grizzly bears still roam within its boundaries.

Valhalla Provincial Park was designated in 1983 as a 122,560-acre preserve in the West Kootenays to protect an extraordinarily scenic mountain area from encroaching logging and mining. The park extends from the shorelines of the fjord-like Slocan Lake at 1,750 feet to high alpine meadows and rugged spires reaching elevations of more than 8,200 feet. The park has a healthy population of grizzlies along with black bears, deer, mountain goats, some moose and a variety of smaller creatures, including unfearing white-tailed ptarmigan, which turn white in winter. Many of the trails in the park are still primitive; some are accessible across Slocan Lake via water taxis. Contact the British Columbia Parks Division for a brochure and more information. (See Appendix B.)

1 YAKIMA RIM SKYLINE TRAIL

One way 18 miles
Hiking time 2 days
High point 3,630 feet
Elevation gain 1,930 feet
Moderate

Hikable March through October
USGS Yakima
Information: Washington
   Department of Wildlife, Region
   3 Office in Yakima

This is a desert trail that can be forbiddingly hot during summer, but delightful in spring and fall. During spring, a hiker would be better off leaving Desert Solitare home and bringing a field guide to western wildflowers. In summer and fall, leave all the books home and bring water. The hike winds through the L.T. Murray Wildlife Area managed by the Washington Department of Wildlife.

The 18-mile Skyline trail, completed in 1977, follows the wasteland ridges above the Yakima River between Yakima and Ellensburg. The south trailhead is accessible via Interstate 82 and Selah. The north trailhead is accessible from Ellensburg only by crossing through Umtanum Creek, which may or may not be a good idea in anything but a four-wheel-drive.

To reach the south trailhead from I-90 at Ellensburg, head south toward Yakima on I-82. Drive 28 miles and take the Yakima Firing Center exit (also the first exit to Selah). Turn right at the first stop sign, drive ¼ mile and turn left on Harrison Road. Follow Harrison 2 miles and turn right on Wenas Road. Drive 2¾ miles to where the paved road bends left. Continue straight onto the gravel of Gibson Road. Turn right after ¼ mile on Buffalo Road and right again in ½ mile onto an unmarked dirt road. The road proceeds 2 rough miles to a parking area

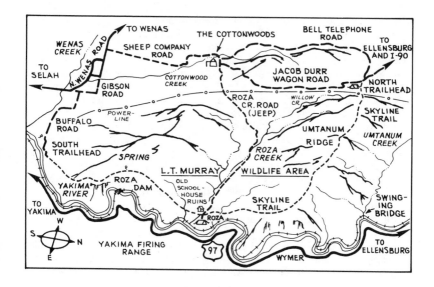

Yakima Rim Trail near Umtanum Ridge. (Rich Landers photo)

with chemical toilets (but no water). The nearby trailhead is signed L.T. Murray Wildlife Area. Vehicles with reasonable clearance can be shuttled to the north trailhead (a parking lot with a huge wood L.T. Murray sign) via Sheep Company Road and Durr Road.

From the south trailhead near Selah, the trail heads steeply up a rimrock ridge overlooking the Yakima River Canyon. To the west, if the sky is clear, a spectacular view of Mt. Adams and Mt. Rainier can be seen. Twin Springs, about 4 miles from the trailhead, supplies the only water for man and beast on the way to Roza Creek. A pipe provides water for people; a trough supplies water for horses and wildlife.

Hikers gain more than 1,500 feet, one false summit after another, before heading down to a campsite at Roza Creek, the trail's midway point. The stone foundation of an old schoolhouse provides the shelter for cooking. Weeds and sagebrush provide the windbreak for tents. A rough road leads to this Roza Creek campsite, enabling hikers to shuttle a car here for a dayhike option. There is a reasonably reliable water source less than 2 miles up Roza Creek from the campsite.

Be alert for red-tails and other hawks. The state Wildlife Department has identified this area as having one of the densest nesting raptor populations in Washington. The area also sports coveys of Hungarian partridge. And be warned that an occasional rattlesnake could be seen.

From Roza Creek, the trail climbs 2,200 feet in 2 miles, but in fairness to the trail, this is where the fun often begins in spring. The Skyline Trail is not a wilderness experience. From the ridges you can see I-90, Canyon Road, Roza Dam, Ellensburg or Yakima, an abandoned microwave station and, on this north section of the trail, occasional off-road vehicles. But hikers who visit this area at the right time in April are in for a spectacular desert display of blooming buttercups, yellow bells, lupine and violets, plus bitterroots, balsamroot, wild onions and cactus.

The trail becomes an old wagon road as it leaves the Yakima rim and bends west along the rim of Umtanum Creek. With good binoculars, hikers occasionally can spot a band of bighorn sheep in the basalt hills below. No optics are required to see the Stuart Range of the Cascades to the northwest. The trail continues along Umtanum Ridge to the north trailhead. From the Umtanum campsite near the north end of Durr Road, a trail leads a couple of miles along the creek to Umtanum Falls. The other follows the creek east 5 miles down to the Yakima River and Umtanum Creek fishing access where there is a suspension bridge over the river and another campsite.

COLUMBIA RIVER
Juniper Dunes Wilderness

2 JUNIPER DUNES

Round trip 4½ miles
Hiking time 3 hours
High point 920 feet
Elevation gain 70 feet
Easy

Hikable March through October
USGS Rye Grass Coulee, Levy
** SW, Levy SE and Levy NE**
Information: Bureau of Land
** Management, Spokane Office**

This wilderness is not likely to be a destination for masses of nature lovers. It has no towering peaks, trout-stuffed streams or gin-clear lakes. Rather it is a small, parched gem of unheralded nature naked to the dry winds that have shaped its character.

The Juniper Dunes Wilderness includes six groves of the largest concentration of western juniper trees in the state. But this is desert coun-

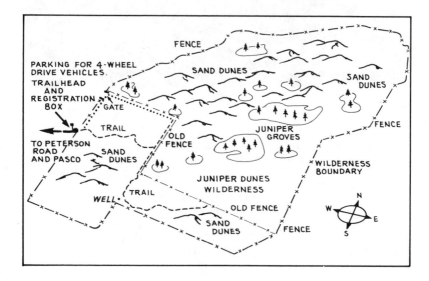

Juniper Dunes Wilderness. (Rich Landers photo)

try. No fires are allowed and no drinking water is available. Perhaps most people would prefer to see it as a dayhike, especially in early morning and late evening when wildlife is active. But by hauling in water for a small, clean camp, one can comfortably enjoy the peacefulness of this 7,140-acre sanctuary.

From the first U.S. Highway 395 interchange coming into Pasco, Washington, from the north, take the Highway 395 exit to Walla Walla. Drive 2 miles and turn left onto the Pasco-Kahlotus Highway. Drive 5¾ miles to a crop-spraying facility and airstrip and turn left on an unsigned gravel road listed on maps as Peterson Road. (If the paved road begins to make a sweeping right turn, you've gone about 200 feet past the turnoff.) Drive 4⅛ miles on Peterson Road and turn right on a dirt road. Go about 100 feet to a parking area hidden in the sage. Do not proceed farther unless equipped with an off-road vehicle or four-wheel-drive; it is easy to get stuck in loose sand, especially when it is dry. From the parking area follow the road past the big dunes used by off-road vehicle enthusiasts; bear right on the first prominent spur road. It's 3½ miles from the parking area to the wilderness boundary. Vehicles must be parked at the boundary.

The area is ripe for wandering, with no designated trails. But the area is somewhat featureless to the untrained eye, and one could become disoriented. For a good introduction to the area, hike along the road that crosses the wilderness boundary. Walk about 1½ miles to an old fence line. Turn north and walk along the old fence line for a mile toward some juniper groves. From here, one can retrace his steps with no danger of getting lost. Or one can continue, following the old fence as it heads west to the new fence on the wilderness boundary. Follow this fence south to complete the loop back to the trailhead.

To reach the most scenic portions of the area, one must hike cross-country about 3 miles northeast toward the densest concentration of junipers and the fringe of the large 130-foot dunes that bank up against the northern boundaries of the wilderness.

One also can enter the wilderness from the north on Rpyzinski Road, which ends just before the boundary. However, this access is on private land and cars cannot be left overnight. It would be wise to stop at the farm house near the end of the road to ask permission to park a vehicle for the day.

COLUMBIA RIVER
Steamboat Rock State Park

3 STEAMBOAT ROCK

Round trip 5 miles
Hiking time 3–4 hours
High point 2,220 feet
Elevation gain 1,000 feet
Moderate
Hikable April through October

USGS Barker Canyon, Electric
City, Steamboat Rock SE,
Steamboat Rock SW
Information: Steamboat Rock
State Park

Steamboat Rock is a spectacular basalt butte jutting up from Banks Lake in central Washington. For generations it was used as a landmark by Indians, then by settlers and today by pilots. Hikers can explore nearly 640 acres on top of the butte, from which one can contrast close views of the desert with the glaciered spectacle of the North Cascades in the distance. April and May are the best months to explore this Columbia Basin scabrock country. Comfortable temperatures plus a remarkable variety of wildflowers, blooming cactus and nesting waterfowl

Heading up to Steamboat Rock. (Monty Fields photo)

around Banks Lake provide pleasures hikers won't find in alpine country. Be warned, however, that it's not surprising to occasionally see a rattlesnake in this area.

From Coulee City, Washington, drive north on State Highway 155 about 14 miles to Steamboat Rock State Park, which is just south of Electric City and 13 miles south of Grand Coulee Dam. There's no mistaking Steamboat Rock, which rises 1,000 feet above Banks Lake. The park includes two excellent campgrounds and a day-use parking area just north of the second campground.

The trail to the top of Steamboat Rock begins across the road to the west of the second campground. The route leads up toward the east rim, gaining most of the 1,000 feet in elevation in the first steep pitch. The trail is much more gentle as it leads from the east rim to the west rim. Then it heads north up a short pitch to the top of the butte. Hikers can walk around the perimeter of the relatively flat top of Steamboat Rock and return on the same trail.

Drinking water is available only at the campground. Banks Lake is open year-round for fishing. It is particularly well known for its largemouth and smallmouth bass and walleyes, along with perch, crappie and kokanee. Water sports such as skiing also are popular.

Interesting places to visit in the area include the Dry Falls interpretive center and Sun Lakes State Park just south of Coulee City on State Highway 17. The exhibits at Dry Falls tell the story of the geological phenomena that created the fascinating landscapes in this region. The

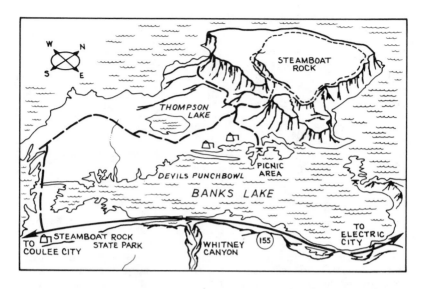

center also houses an exhibit explaining the Blue Lake Rhino Cast discovered above Blue Lake.

Lake Lenore caves are situated about 10 miles south of Dry Falls. A short hike from the parking area, well marked on Highway 17, leads to shelters used by prehistoric man.

KETTLE RIVER
Unprotected

4   SWAN LAKE

Round trip 1½ miles
Hiking time ½ hour
High point 3,650 feet
Elevation gain negligible
Easy

Hikable June through September
USGS Aeneas
Information: Colville National
   Forest, Republic Ranger
   District

This trail is an example of a feature that's all too often forgotten by campground planners. It's an easy hike, not so much an adventure as an antedote for the guilt of too many hot dogs and s'mores. But its brevity and simplicity might be just what it takes to lure parents with little ones—or little ones with their parents—away from the roads to an outing on foot.

From Republic, Washington, drive south on State Highway 21 about 6½ miles and turn west on Scatter Creek Road No. 53. Drive 7 miles to Swan Lake campground.

Swan Lake Trail No. 14 is a 1½-mile loop that begins at the north end

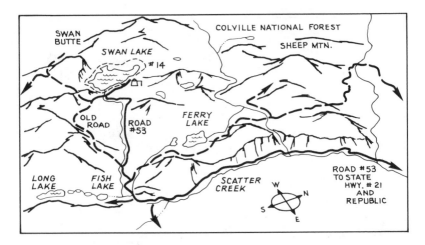

of the campground near the community kitchen and ends nearby at the junction with the access road to the campground. If the trail has been maintained, one simply has to get on the trail and walk. The lake is in view virtually the whole way as the trail makes its way around the shores. Watch for huckleberries and thimbleberries in July and August. Chipmunks and squirrels are familiar sights on the trail; waterfowl usually can be found on the lake.

The campground is well developed, complete with a volleyball area and a large, covered kitchen built by the Civilian Conservation Corps in 1933. This is the only structure of its type in the Colville National Forest.

Swan Lake. (Rich Landers photo)

Cattails and lily pads on Fish Lake. (Rich Landers photo)

KETTLE RIVER
Unprotected

5 FISH LAKE-LONG LAKE LOOP

Round trip 1½ miles
Hiking time 1 hour
High point 3,300 feet
Elevation gain negligible
Easy

Hikable May through October
USGS Aeneas, Bald Knob
Information: Colville National
    Forest, Republic Ranger
    District

    This is an easy dayhike, particularly appealing to fishermen, parents with kids and campers looking for a way to burn off marshmallows. Both lakes are accessible by road, but Long Lake is the most peaceful of the lakes in the area. No motors are allowed on the lake and anglers are re-

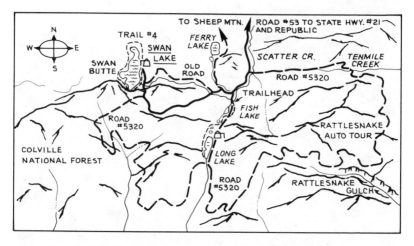

stricted to fly fishing. Fish Lake is stocked with rainbow trout and Long Lake is stocked with cutthroats. The lakes are alive with ducks and other birds that delight children.

Drive south from Republic, Washington, on State Highway 21 for 8½ miles and turn west on Scatter Creek Road No. 53. Follow this paved road about 6 miles and turn left at the sign to the Long Lake campground. (Follow the road farther for turnoffs to Ferry Lake and Swan Lake, both of which have campgrounds and fishing. See Hike 4 for a daytrip around Swan Lake.) Drive ¼ mile to the trailhead at the north end of Fish Lake, which by late summer is reduced to a small swampy pond.

From the well-marked trailhead, hike about ½ mile to Long Lake campground. Find the trailhead in the middle of the campground for another trail that circumnavigates Long Lake. The trail has little elevation gain, but there are a few sections of rough talus, especially on the east side of Long Lake.

KETTLE RANGE
Semi-primitive

6̄ KETTLE CREST NORTH

One way 29 miles
Hiking time 3–5 days
High point 7,135 feet
Elevation gain 1,130 feet
Moderately difficult

Hikable June through September
USGS Sherman Peak, Copper
Butte, Mt. Leona
Information: Colville National
Forest, Republic Ranger
District.

The Kettle Crest Trail is one of the premier hikes in the Colville National Forest. It runs across the tops of rolling mountains and through flowered meadows in the area's only roadless mountain terrain.

Although Congress snubbed Kettle Range for official wilderness designation in 1984, the crest itself has not been riddled with roads. Conservationists are still fighting timber sales threatening to encroach on this
scenic area. Sections of the trail south of Boulder/Deer Creek Summit
were rerouted in the mid 1980s and did not appear on USGS maps in
1986.

Water is sparingly available along this trail. Springs developed with
stock troughs are identified on the accompanying map. Other sources
are identified in the text. The Forest Service recommends that all water
found on the crest be treated for human consumption.

The best way to explore this well-maintained 29-mile trail is to ar-
range for a car shuttle from one trailhead to the other or to organize two
hiking groups, one beginning from the south and one from the north.
When the two groups rendezvous on the trail, they can exchange car
keys.

Wapaloosie Mountain on the Kettle Crest. (Rich Landers photo)

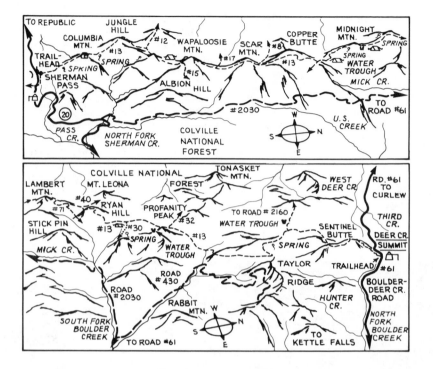

To reach the south trailhead from Kettle Falls, Washington, drive west across the Columbia River to the junction with State Highway 20. Turn left onto Highway 20 and drive about 23 miles to Sherman Pass. Turn right into the trailhead parking area, which is well marked at the summit. A picnic area and pit toilets are available at the trailhead.

To reach the north trailhead from Kettle Falls, follow Highway 395 across the Columbia River; stay on Highway 395 heading north 16⅛ miles and turn west onto Boulder/Deer Creek Road No. 61. This road is paved for ¾ mile before becoming a good gravel road that's scheduled for more improvements. Follow this road 12 miles to the pass and look for the sign boards and trailhead to the left. Deer Creek Summit campground, with picnic tables and campsites but no toilet, is on the right. (For hikers planning to do their own car shuttle, it is faster to go west from Sherman Pass or Deer Creek Summit and use State Highway 21 between Curlew and Republic than it is to use highways 395 and 20 to the east.)

Heading from Sherman Pass north, Kettle Crest Trail No. 13 begins at elev. 5,581 feet. Switchbacks soon lead up a moderate slope and two springs (from PVC pipe along the side of the trail) are passed within the first mile. The trail begins to open into grassy alpine meadows as it winds along the west side of Columbia Mountain. The trail junction to Columbia Mountain is about 2 miles from the Sherman Pass trailhead. The hike southeast to the top of Columbia Mountain, site of an old cabin-style lookout, gains 662 feet in 1 mile. This is a pleasant side trip or a nice dayhike in itself. The lookout cabin is the oldest lookout still existing in this region. It's a unique construction for forest lookouts, built between 1914 and 1916.

In this stretch of the hike, as on many parts of the first 10 miles, there are numerous open meadows covered with the reds, yellows, blues and whites of summer wildflowers. Indian paintbrush and lupine abound. Occasionally a browsing deer can be spotted.

After passing the Columbia Mountain trail junction, Trail No. 13 swings slightly east then northwest along the side of Jungle Hill, elev. 6,544 feet. At about 4 miles, a PVC pipe provides spring water at the side of the trail before the saddle of Jungle Hill. This is a pretty wooded area of gently rolling hills. After passing Jungle Hill, the trail heads east then begins a switchback descent to the north—down and then back up the ridge. At about 5¾ miles, there is a trail junction with the spur heading west toward a stream. It is not necessary to take the trail spur west to get water. Continue up the hill on Trail No. 13, where water is available at either of two switchbacks by cutting left (west) on obvious mini-trails 30-40 feet off the main trail.

The first good campsite is at 6¾ miles, about halfway between Jungle Hill and Wapaloosie Mountain. The site is an old outfitter's camp, nestled in a grove of trees about 100 yards past a spring. The site offers a pleasant view of a valley to the southeast.

Heading toward Wapaloosie Mountain, the trail continues to climb gently through flower-filled meadows. It reaches the crest, where one can enjoy the scenery on both sides of the ridge. The trail passes to the west of 7,018-foot Wapaloosie Mountain back out to the ridge, then to the west of 7,046-foot Scar Mountain. The trail descends about a ½ mile then gradually climbs for about a mile to the top of 7,140-foot Copper Butte. Being the tallest mountain in the area, views from the many open areas on Copper Butte are superb. The trail down (north) from Copper Butte descends about 1 mile with many switchbacks through dense trees.

There's a spring just off the east side of the trail about 1¼ miles north of Copper Butte and just south of 6,660-foot Midnight Mountain. From Midnight Mountain, it's another ⅔ mile to a trail junction just west of 6,525-foot Lambert Mountain. Bear left (northwest). A spring can be found ⅓ mile past the junction. The trail leads ½ mile, then heads north and then northeast, passing the junction of a ½-mile trail to Mount Leona.

A campsite with water exists at the old Ryan Cabin site shown on Forest Service maps, but it can be tricky to find. Ryan Cabin Trail No. 30, which is no longer maintained, leads east from the crest trail north of Ryan Hill ¼ mile to the site of the decaying cabin.

From the intersection of Trail No. 13 and old Trail No. 30, it is 9-plus miles to the Boulder/Deer Creek Summit. The stretch has no good camping areas and few water sources. In a pinch, water is available from a stock trough along a feeder trail heading down to Forest Road No. 2160 northwest of Profanity Peak. From Ryan Hill, the trail winds through mostly wooded areas and skirts small open meadows. Rare Turk's cap lilies can be seen periodically in the woods. One also passes boulder fields, rock cliffs and scree areas en route to the trailhead.

7 KETTLE CREST SOUTH

One way 13 miles
Hiking time 7 hours or overnight
High point 6,923 feet
Elevation gain 1,523 feet
Moderately difficult

Hikable mid June through
    September
USGS Sherman Peak
Information: Colville National
    Forest, Kettle Falls Ranger
    District

This southern section of the 42-mile Kettle Crest Trail heads south from Sherman Pass on State Highway 20. Wildlife is abundant, including deer, coyotes, grouse, black bears and song birds with relatively good numbers of the elusive lynx. Listen for the shrill whistle of the varied thrush in the timber and the squeaks of pikas in the talus slopes. The Washington Wildlife Department manages this region as a trophy mule deer area, which means it has a high percentage of mature bucks with antlers four-points or better on each side. Deer seem to use the trail as much as or more than hikers.

Good views are available intermittently for the entire length of the trail with a particularly pleasing vista from the southern ridge of White Mountain, site of a demolished lookout. Long before the Forest Service arrived, young Indians of what now are the Colville Confederated Tribes made a pilgrimage to the top of White Mountain as a rite of adulthood.

Columbia Mountain Lookout, with Sherman Peak and Kettle Crest in the distance. (Rich Landers photo)

Here they built rock cairns to commemorate the visions of their ceremonial retreat. Today, one can still see some of the cairns from the summit (a few, however, were stacked by bored Forest Service lookouts) and the area is still occasionally used by tribal members. Please respect the area and leave the cairns intact.

From Kettle Falls, Washington, head west on State Highway 20 for 26¼ miles to Sherman Pass, elev. 5,587-feet. From the parking area, there are two trailheads, one of which is for the section of the Kettle Crest trail that heads north from the pass. For this hike, take the trail that heads south, walk about 200 yards down to the east and follow the signs across the highway where the trail continues south along the Kettle Crest.

Hikers who want to shuttle a car to the end of this hike should drive 14 miles west from Kettle Falls on Highway 20 and turn left (south) on Forest Road No. 2020 (South Fork Sherman Road). Drive 6½ miles and turn left onto Forest Road No. 2014 (Barnaby Creek Road). Drive 4¼ miles and turn right on Forest Road No. 250 and go 4½ miles to the well-marked trailhead. (The Forest Service has plans to re-route the trail and move the trail slightly by 1990.)

From Sherman Pass heading south, Kettle Crest Trail No. 13 switch-backs gently uphill, winding around the east side of Sherman Peak. The trail then roller-coasters along the shoulders of Snow Peak, Bald Moun-

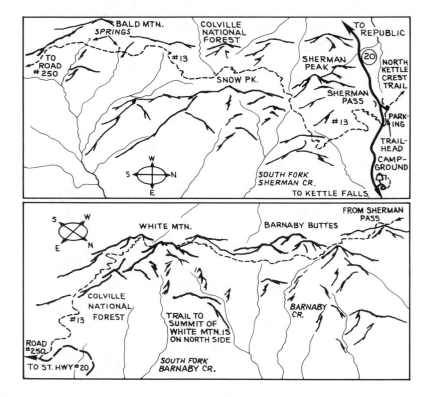

tain, Barnaby Buttes and White Mountain. It crosses several talus slopes, but the hiking is generally easy with only a few steep grades and a long switchbacking downhill near the southern trailhead. Camping spots are available along the way, but dependable water sources are scarce. Unless one hikes in early June, when snow patches still can be found, carry all necessary water.

KETTLE RANGE
Unprotected

8 HOODOO CANYON

Round trip 6 miles
Hiking time 3–5 hours or
** overnight**
High point 3,720 feet
Elevation gain 880 feet
Moderately difficult

Hikable May through October
USGS Jackknife
Information: Colville National
** Forest, Kettle Falls Ranger**
** District**

This is a short dayhike or overnighter through a lightly used and surprisingly lush area of the Colville National Forest. Hoodoo Canyon, which is near a popular developed campground, is a scenic feature of nature tucked away for hikers to explore.

From Kettle Falls, Washington, drive west on State Highway 20 across the Columbia River and turn right onto State Highway 395 toward Canada. Drive north about 6 miles and turn west onto Forest Road No. 460. Go about 6 miles and turn left onto Forest Road No. 9565. Drive

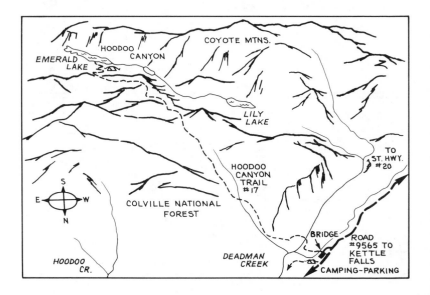

Hoodoo Canyon, with Emerald Lake in the distance. (Rich Landers photo)

another 3 miles to the trailhead and parking area on the south side of the road.

From the parking area, the trailhead begins at the edge of the timber about 100 feet upstream from the well-used fire ring. Don't be lured astray by game trails. Hoodoo Canyon Trail No. 17 descends quickly to a wide footbridge over Deadman Creek. The route is well maintained as it climbs through a stand of timber with abundant wildflowers. After about 2 miles, the trail breaks out of the timber with a view of Lily Lake, 500 feet below. Hoodoo Canyon is narrow with numerous rock outcroppings. The trail skirts the edge of the canyon, then descends steeply with sharp switchbacks on an unmaintained trail the last ¼ mile to Emerald Lake at 3,200 feet. Although the lake is about 10-15 feet deep in early spring, it dwindles to a small pond by late summer. There is room enough for several campsites. The trail ends here, but the canyon and stream run another ¾ mile southeast into larger Trout Lake, which has an improved Forest Service campground. The Forest Service has plans to build a trail connecting the Hoodoo Canyon area with Trout Lake before 1990.

PEND OREILLE RIVER
Unprotected

9 ABERCROMBIE MOUNTAIN

Round trip 2¾ miles
Hiking time 2 hours
High point 7,308 feet
Elevation gain 2,408 feet
Moderately difficult

Hikable late June through
September
USGS Abercrombie Mountain
Information: Colville National
Forest, Colville Ranger District

Abercrombie Mountain and its neighbor, Sherlock Peak, are the two prominent high points between the Columbia River on the west and the Pend Oreille River on the east. Hikers who reach their summits (also see Sherlock Peak, Hike 10) enjoy panoramic views of both drainages.

From Colville, Washington, head east on Third Avenue, where a sign points to "Ione, Newport—Highway 20." At the edge of town, turn left (north) at the airport and go 1½ miles to a Y, staying to the right toward

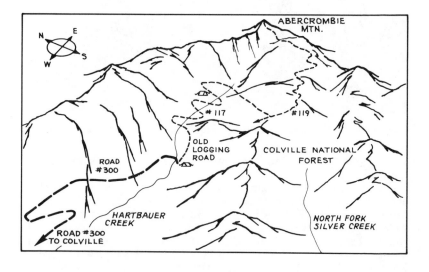

Abercrombie Mountain from Pend Oreille River. (Rich Landers photo)

Northport. Follow Northport Road 24 miles to another Y, staying to the right toward Deep Lake. Continue 7½ miles past Deep Lake to Leadpoint and turn right onto Silver Creek Road No. 4720. At an unmarked Y 1½ miles up this road, stay to the left. At the next intersection, turn left onto Road No. 7078, where a sign says "Abercrombie Mt. 12 miles," and drive 4½ miles. Turn onto Road No. 300, a less developed road that may be muddy in spots, and drive 8 miles up to the trailhead at the end of the road. A good camping area has been established here; water is available a few hundred feet back down the road.

The trail begins as an old logging road for about 1 mile. In the first ½ mile, it passes one campsite and several places where water is available. Beyond the first ½ mile, there is no reliable water source. At 1 mile, the trail dead-ends ends at Trail No. 119. Head left (east) on Trail No. 119, where a sign says it is 1¾ miles to Abercrombie. The trail is mostly gradual with switchbacks through dry, open country. At the ridgetop there is a large rock cairn, the first of several that mark the rest of the way along a faint trail north to the summit. The last ½ mile is fairly steep, but not overly difficult. A USGS survey marker has been installed at the summit, and the burned remains of a lookout tower still can be found. The peak offers exceptional views of the Columbia River Valley, the Salmo-Priest Wilderness, Canadian peaks and, on a clear day, the North Cascades.

Hikers could extend this into a longer backpacking trip, leaving from the campsite on Silver Creek at the end of Road No. 070, shown on Colville National Forest maps. From here, hikers could go up either South Fork of Silver Creek Trail No. 123 or Sherlock Peak Trail No. 139 to the ridgetop. From there they could bushwhack northerly to the Abercrombie Trail No. 119 and return to their vehicle on Silver Creek. There is no defined trail on the ridge and no water, save for possible snowbanks in early July. But it is open and easy going.

PEND OREILLE RIVER
Unprotected

10 SHERLOCK PEAK

Round trip 2½ miles
Hiking time 1½ hours
High point 6,365 feet
Elevation gain 905 feet
Moderately difficult

Hikable late June through
  September
USGS Deep Lake
Information: Colville National
  Forest, Colville Ranger District

This is a short but steep hike to a scenic viewpoint on top of Sherlock Peak overlooking both the Columbia and Pend Oreille River drainages. Summit baggers could extend this hike to include a cross-country walk along a mostly open ridge to Abercrombie Mountain (see Hike 9).

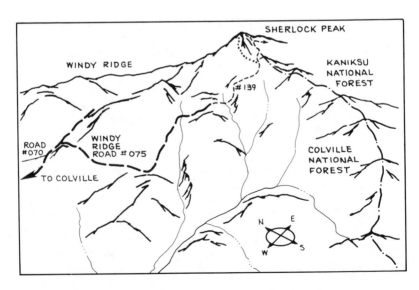

On the ridge south of Sherlock Peak, Abercrombie Mountain in the background. (Rich Landers photo)

From U.S. Highway 395 in Colville, Washington, head east on Third Avenue, where a sign points to "Ione, Newport—Highway 20." Drive 1 mile and turn left (north) at the airport onto Aladdin Road. Drive 2 miles and bear right at a Y toward Northport. Continue 23 miles and bear right at a Y toward Deep Lake. Drive 7 miles and turn right onto Silver Creek Road. Drive ½ mile and bear left at a Y (there's an undeveloped campsite here by a stream) and continue on County Road 4720 about 1 mile and cross a cattle guard onto national forest land. Drive almost ½ mile and bear right onto Forest Road 070. Drive about ½ mile to a Y and bear right onto Forest Road No. 075 (Windy Ridge). Drive about 4½ miles up to a small campsite where rough roads branch to the left and right. Cars without high clearance should park here. It's 1¾ miles from here to the trailhead at the end of the road that takes off to the left.

The trail is steep, but it's only 1¼ miles to the ridge. Hike about ½ mile to an open area, where there is a cold spring, the only water available along the trail. At the top of the ridge the trail splits. Bear left, going across and down the other side of the ridge and to the south. The trail is faint, but from here it makes no difference. Sherlock Peak lies to the north (left), an easy ½-mile cross-country hike away. From the top, one can enjoy views of the Columbia River Valley, the Salmo-Priest Wilderness, many peaks in Canada and, on a clear day, the North Cascades. Using a topo map, one can easily plot a cross-country hike through the sparsely timbered saddle 4 miles north to Abercrombie Peak.

11 SPRINGBOARD TRAIL

Round trip 2½ miles
Hiking time 1–2 hours
High point 3,600 feet
Elevation gain 420 feet
Easy

Hikable late May through
**   October**
USGS Lake Gillette
Information: Colville National
**   Forest, Colville Ranger District**

This is a pleasant dayhike designed for campers and picnickers visiting the chain of lakes along the Little Pend Oreille River. The trail is easy, with only a few switchbacks, and leads to a soothing view of lakes Sherry, Gillete and Thomas. The Forest Service provides brochures at the trailhead to explain features and history along the route. An example of a tidbit one would pick up explains the name of the trail: "Springboards, as they were called, were once leaned against large trees so loggers could cut above the swollen base, or 'churn butt.'"

From Colville, Washington, drive east on State Highway 20 about 24 miles and turn east following the signs toward the Lake Gillette Recreation Area. Follow this road about 1 mile to Gillette campground. The trailhead is at the far end off the road that loops through the campground. No parking is available at the trailhead. Hikers who aren't camping at the campground should park along the road just outside the campground entrance.

The sign at the trailhead says Springboard Trail/Rufus Trail No. 148. Rufus Trail is open to motorcycles and is an old dirt road. But hikers share this route for only a few minutes before coming to another sign.

Daisies along Springboard Trail. (Rich Landers photo)

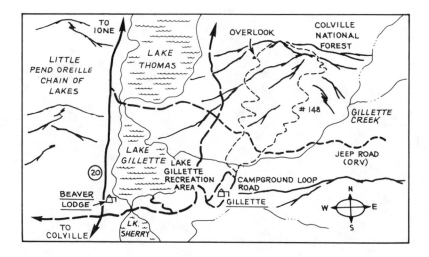

The Rufus Trail (and motorcycles) go straight ahead. The Springboard Trail (and hikers) head to the left. From here the trail crosses a meadow and creek with a wooden bridge before reaching a fork. Stay to the left to follow the self-guided interpretive trail described in the brochures usually available at the trailhead. Seven points of interest along the trail are explained in the brochure, including white pines and the natural results of a 1931 forest fire. The trail passes through many open areas and meadows. It's about 1 mile to the end of the trail and a view from 3,600 feet of lakes Sherry, Gillette and Thomas.

The trail then loops back on a less traveled but still identifiable route, returning to the fork described at the beginning of the hike. At two points in the hike, the trail crosses the Rufus Trail, but signs once again make it clear that motor bikes should not use the Springboard Trail.

SULLIVAN LAKE
Unprotected

SULLIVAN LAKE

One way 4 miles	Hikable May through October
Hiking time 2 hours	USGS Metaline Falls
High point 2,920 feet	Information: Colville National
Elevation gain 320 feet	Forest, Sullivan Lake Ranger
Easy	District

This is an easy hike beginning from one of the most popular developed campgrounds in the region. The trail winds from cool, shaded creek crossings to open scree slopes along the east shore of Sullivan Lake. While the campground is large, the lake is as unspoiled as a mountain lake served by paved roads can be.

From Metaline Falls, Washington, continue north on State Highway

Sullivan Lake and Hall Mountain. (Rich Landers photo)

31 as it climbs 2 miles to the signed junction to Sullivan Lake. Turn right and follow this county road 4 miles to Sullivan Lake campground. Turn left onto Forest Road No. 22 and drive ¼ mile, then turn right into the campground and look for the trailhead for Trail No. 504. (A ½-mile nature trail also begins nearby.)

The trail starts with an easy climb to a viewpoint overlooking the north end of Sullivan Lake, then works down and gently rolls its way south along the east shore through timber, open rock slides and dense

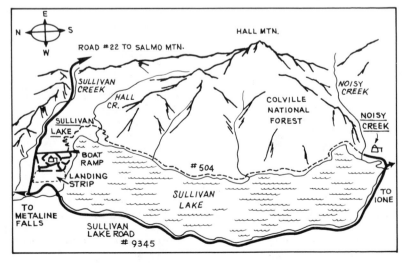

alders. The trail is well maintained for 4 miles to its southern trailhead at Noisy Creek campground. Hikers could have a car shuttled to this campground via the paved road on the west side of the lake if they're not up to the 4-mile hike back to the starting point.

SULLIVAN LAKE
Unprotected

13   HALL MOUNTAIN

Round trip 5 miles
Hiking time 3 hours
High point 6,323 feet
Elevation gain 1,070 feet
Moderate

Hikable late June through
    October
USGS Metaline Falls, Pass Creek
Information: Colville National
    Forest, Sullivan Lake Ranger
    District

Hall Mountain looms unobtrusively over the clear waters of Sullivan Lake. The mountain is the home for one of Washington's most famous herds of bighorn sheep. The sheep are so prolific, the Washington Wildlife Department traps a few of the animals every few years for relocation to other parts of the state.

From Metaline Falls, Washington, continue north on State Highway 31 as it climbs 2 miles to the signed junction to Sullivan Lake. Turn right and follow this paved county road 4 miles to Sullivan Lake campground area. Continue past the campground area on Forest Road No. 22 for 3 miles and turn right on Johns Creek Road No. 500. Drive 7½ rugged miles to the trailhead at the end of the road.

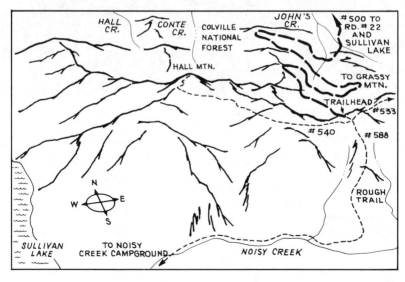

Bighorn sheep on Hall Mountain. (Rich Landers photo)

About ⅔ mile up the trail, there are two closely spaced junctions. Trail No. 533 is a pleasant ridge route east to Grassy Top Mountain (see Hike 14). Trail No. 588 is a steep, washed-out trail plunging down to Noisy Creek campground. To reach Hall Mountain, head west on Trail No. 540. With most of the elevation gained on the access road, Trail No. 540 gains only 800 feet in the 2½ miles to the summit. The trail is rocky in places but easy to follow. No water is available. Carry binoculars and hike early in the morning or late in the afternoon for the best opportunities to spot bighorn sheep.

14 GRASSY TOP MOUNTAIN

Round trip 7½ miles
Hiking time 4–5 hours or
  overnight
High point 6,375 feet
Elevation gain 1,000 feet
Moderate

Hikable late June through
  September
USGS Pass Creek
Information: Colville National
  Forest, Sullivan Lake Ranger
  District

This is an excellent ridge-running walk for good views of the Idaho Selkirks, the Priest Lake area and portions of Salmo-Priest Wilderness.

From Metaline Falls, Washington, drive north on State Highway 31 about 2 miles past the Pend Oreille River bridge and turn right toward Sullivan Lake on County Road No. 9345. Drive southeast 4 miles to Sullivan Lake Ranger Station and campground. Turn left (east) on Forest Road No. 22 along Sullivan Creek for 5 miles to the junction with Forest Road No. 2220. Turn right (south) on Road No. 22 across Sullivan Creek, climbing for 7 miles almost to Pass Creek Pass, where the trailhead is situated at elev. 5,400 feet. Parking is limited to only a few vehicles along the road. (Note: Nearby to the north is the trailhead for Shedroof Divide Trail No. 512.)

Grassy Top Trail No. 503 descends sharply to cross the head of Pass Creek before climbing a well-kept path through heavy timber and below a towering granite ledge. A mile later the trail levels off through a thinning forest and acres of beargrass. Watch for an opening to the east of the trail: a good lunch spot/campsite overlooking the North Fork of Granite Creek. Priest Lake and the Selkirk Crest can be seen in the distance. The trail continues gently on, wandering in and out of the timber

On the route to Grassy Top Mountain. (Rich Landers photo)

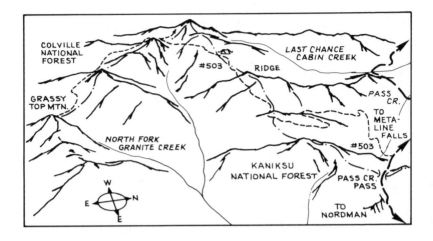

along a ridge before connecting with Trail No. 533, which heads west to Hall Mountain. About 3 miles from the trailhead there's a choice of either following the trail the last ½ mile to Grassy Top, elev. 6,253 feet, or climbing a steep, unmarked trail up an open slope to a grand viewpoint at 6,375 feet.

SULLIVAN LAKE
Salmo-Priest Wilderness

15 CROWELL RIDGE

Round trip 16 miles
Hiking time 2 days
High point 6,790 feet
Elevation gain 520 feet
Moderate

Hikable July through mid
**   October**
USGS Gypsy Peak
Information: Colville National
**   Forest, Sullivan Lake Ranger**
**   District**

This is a scenic, mostly treeless ridge hike in the Salmo-Priest Wilderness that involves about 1 mile of off-trail navigation through slopes of beargrass and talus to reach Gypsy Peak and Watch Lake. A shorter route to Gypsy Peak begins at Bear Meadow, but it is no match in scenery for the Crowell Ridge hike described here. Roads could be the limiting factor for some hikers. The road to Bear Meadow is impassable to passenger cars; the road to the Sullivan Mountain trailhead is very poor with deep drainage ditches that could bump the bottoms of cars with low clearance.

From Metaline Falls, Washington, drive north on Highway 31 about 2 miles past the Pend Oreille River bridge and turn right toward Sullivan

Lake. At the Sullivan Lake Ranger District administration buildings, turn north at a sign for Sullivan Creek Highline and Crowell Ridge. Follow Forest Road No. 2212 about 3 miles and turn left on Forest Road No. 245 toward Sullivan Mountain Lookout. Drive this rough road to the trailhead, which leaves the north side of the road on a switchback just below the lookout.

Crowell Ridge Trail No. 515 weaves through open timber before breaking out of the trees for most of its distance. About 7 miles from the trailhead, the trail heads decidedly downhill to the northeast toward Bear Meadow. Using a topo map, leave the trail before it descends and follow the ridge north toward Watch Lake. Hikers should contour to the east of the first knob after leaving the trail, then contour to the west side of the ridge for about 1 mile over the talus until they come to the bowl above Watch Lake. Descend to the saddle south of Gypsy Peak and then down to the lake. Carry plenty of water; no reliable source is available until the end of the hike at Watch Lake. This is a fragile camping area, definitely not suitable for groups of more than about six. The area around the lake can be boggy in July or after heavy rains.

Watch Lake and Gypsy Peak, Salmo-Priest Wilderness. (Rich Landers photo)

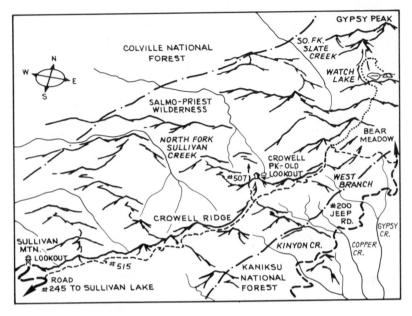

This is a popular elk, bear and mule deer hunting area in the fall. Also keep an eye out for bighorn sheep that frequent Crowell Ridge during spring and summer.

SALMO RIVER
Salmo-Priest Wilderness

16 SHEDROOF LOOP

Round trip 21 miles
Hiking time 2 days minimum
High point 6,520 feet
Elevation gain 3,600 feet
Difficult
Hikable July through mid
October

USGS Salmo Mountain, Helmer
Mountain, Continental
Mountain
Information: Kaniksu National
Forest, Priest Lake Ranger
District; Colville National
Forest, Sullivan Lake Ranger
District.

Hikers can combine trails in the Salmo-Priest Wilderness of Washington and proposed wilderness additions in Idaho to make a rugged loop. Problem is, two of the trails connecting the Shedroof Divide have been poorly maintained in recent years. Check with the Priest Lake Ranger District for the conditions of Trail Nos. 311 and 312 before attempting this loop. Also, water can be difficult to find on the divide during some years.

From Priest River, Idaho, drive north on State Highway 57. A few miles past Nordman, the road turns to gravel and becomes Forest Road No. 302. Continue about 5 miles past Granite Falls campground and turn left onto Road No. 662 toward Hughes Meadows. (Note that the Kaniksu forest map identifies this as Road No. 1662. This is a mistake.) Drive 2 miles and bear left at the junction with the Hughes Ridge lookout road. From here it's about a mile to the Hughes Meadows ranger cabin (generally unstaffed) and the trailhead near the creek. Because of new grizzly management plans, the Forest Service says the trailhead could be moved to a less conspicuous spot on the road just before the ranger station. Officials say this trailhead will be signed and easy to find.

From the trailhead, hike a ways and bear left onto Trail No. 311. The trail leads up Jackson Creek, with plenty of water at lower elevations, but becoming dry near the Shedroof Divide. It is about 7½ miles from the trailhead to Shedroof Divide Trail No. 512. Turn right and head north on Trail No. 512, passing an undependable spring along the slopes of Thunder Mountain. This is the best part of the trip, hiking the high divide between Upper Priest River and the Salmo drainage, with peaks in every direction. It's about 6 miles from here to the junction with Hughes Fork Trail No. 312, with a few possible campsites along the way. Also, there's an unmaintained trail that leads to the summit of Thunder Mountain. Another possible campsite can be found about ¼ mile past the junction with Trail No. 312. To complete the loop, head down Trail No.

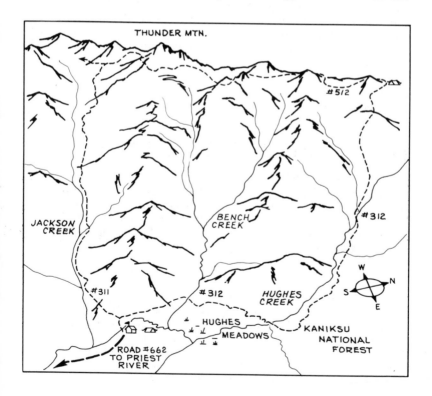

Forest Service buildings at Hughes Meadows, with Shedroof Divide in the distance. (Tony Dolphin photo)

312. This trail has been poorly maintained in recent years. But when maintained, it is a reasonably good route down the Hughes Creek drainage 7½ miles, skirting the west side of Hughes Meadows and back to the trailhead. Beware that some unmaintained fire-control trails cross through this area.

SALMO RIVER
Salmo-Priest Wilderness

17 SHEDROOF DIVIDE

One way 18 miles
Hiking time 2 days minimum
High point 6,450 feet
Elevation gain 1,050 feet
Moderately difficult
Hikable July through mid
   October

USGS Salmo Mountain, Helmer
   Mountain
Information: Colville National
   Forest, Sullivan Lake Ranger
   District

This is an up-and-down ridge hike along the Shedroof Divide in the Salmo-Priest Wilderness bordering the west side of the Upper Priest River drainage. It skirts around four small peaks and through open meadows with many pleasant views, although clearcuts have crept right up to the wilderness boundary in many places. Water is scarce, particularly from late July through September. The hike is most enjoyable with a car shuttled to each trailhead and hiked one way.

Shedroof Divide, Salmo-Priest Wilderness. (Rich Landers photo)

To reach the north trailhead (also used for Salmo Loop, Hike 18) drive east on Forest Road No. 22 from Sullivan Lake about 6 miles to the junction with Pass Creek Pass Road. Continue on the same road toward Salmo Mountain, but note that the road number has now changed to No. 2220. Continue past the junction of Forest Road No. 270 about 1½ miles (past one trailhead) to the end of the road and the trailhead for Trail No. 535.

To reach the south trailhead, drive east from Sullivan Lake on Road No. 22 about 6 miles. Here one has to turn right to continue on Road No. 22 toward Pass Creek Pass. Follow this well-maintained road to the pass; the trail begins about ¼ mile farther east. (The Forest Service says it may be re-routing this road before 1990.)

From Pass Creek Pass, begin climbing immediately on Trail No. 512 around Round Top Mountain before beginning the ups and downs that lead around Mankato, Helmer, Thunder and finally Shedroof mountains. Only about three good campsites can be found near the trail. At Shedroof Mountain, head west on Trail No. 535, passing a good campsite which has a seasonal trickle of water, about 4 miles to the trailhead. No dependable water sources can be found along the trail, although early season hikers should find some sources on the south flank of Helmer Mountain, 1 mile north of Helmer Mountain, on the north side of Thunder Mountain and northwest of Shedroof Mountain on Trail No. 535. Trail Nos. 511 and 526 are good bail-out routes to Forest Road No. 2220 at Gypsy Meadows.

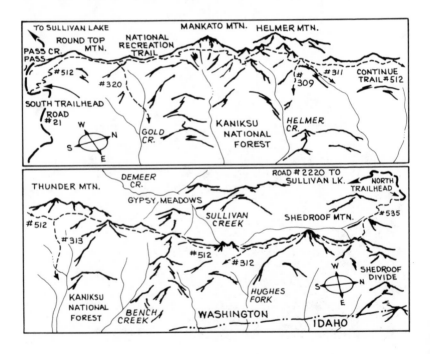

Little Snowy Top Lookout, Salmo-Priest Wilderness. (Rich Landers photo)

SALMO RIVER
Salmo-Priest Wilderness

SALMO LOOP

Round trip 18 miles
Hiking time 2 days minimum
High point 6,400 feet
Elevation gain 2,250 feet
Moderately difficult
Hikable July through mid
October

USGS Salmo Mountain,
   Continental Mountain.
Information: Colville National
   Forest, Sullivan Lake Ranger
   District

This loop exposes the Salmo-Priest for what it is: a lush nugget of wilderness that narrowly escaped development encroaching from every direction. The trail plunges down to the Salmo River and leads back up to airy peaks and ridges on the Washington-Idaho border. This is some of the wildest country left in Washington, among the state's last sanctuaries for grizzly bears, mountain caribou and lynx.

From Metaline Falls, Washington, drive north on State Highway 31

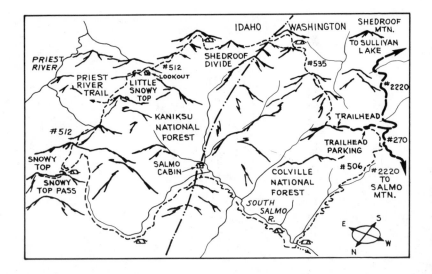

about 2 miles past the Pend Oreille River bridge and turn right toward Sullivan Lake. From Sullivan Lake, drive east on Forest Road No. 22 about 6 miles to the junction with Pass Creek Pass Road. Continue on the same road toward Salmo Mountain, but note that the road number has now changed to No. 2220. Drive past the junction of Road No. 270 about ½ mile to the trailhead. Parking is available here. A car can be shuttled to the other trailhead, which is at the end of the road another mile farther.

The route begins on Trail No. 506 at 5,910 feet and immediately plunges downhill 3½ miles to the South Salmo River at 4,150 feet. It's an enjoyable walk, since the trail switchbacks downhill pleasantly through old growth cedars and hemlocks, moss-carpeted logs and lacey ferns. But be warned that this north-facing slope can still be burdened with snow well into July. Good camping areas can be found on both sides of the river, which holds small cutthroat trout. (Some people stay overnight here and head out the same way the next day.)

To continue the loop, cross the river and bear right at the junction with the unmaintained trail that heads left toward the Canadian border. From the junction it's 2⅓ miles to the Salmo Cabin, which is an easy ¼-mile walk down and to the right from the main trail. In the past, this trail was signed, but the Forest Service says it plans to remove the signs. The cabin is situated by a stream and a good camping area. The cabin was built in the 1930s and used as a backcountry station until 1951. Today, unless hikers take the initiative to refurbish it, the cabin has been reduced to a dirty, deteriorating mess that could be used as shelter only in a pinch. Hikers planning to do the loop in two days should push on at least another 3½ miles to a decent campsite just below Snowy Top Pass. Water is abundant to this point. From here it's another ¾ mile uphill to a better but dry campsite right at the pass on the shoulder of 7,572-foot Snowy Top Mountain. (Summit baggers should allow two hours to scramble to the summit and back from the pass). Water is not available at the pass and is scarce on Shedroof Divide, especially in August and September.

From the pass, continue south on the Shedroof Divide Trail No. 512 to the junction with the Little Snowy Top Trail, which leads 1 mile to the lookout above. This is an excellent side trip, although plenty of good views of the Idaho Selkirks to the east and Gypsy Peak to the west are yet to come on the main Shedroof Divide trail. A few hundred yards past the Little Snowy Top junction is the junction to the Priest River trail, which switchbacks steeply 4½ miles east to the river bottom. This is not recommended for people who value their knees. Continue hiking 6 miles passing infrequent water sources from Snowy Top Pass to Shedroof Mountain. Leave the Shedroof Divide and head northwest on Trail No. 535 about 4 miles to the trailhead. If a car was not shuttled to this trailhead, it's a 1-mile walk to the Trail No. 506 parking area.

UPPER PRIEST RIVER
Proposed wilderness

 # 19 UPPER PRIEST RIVER

Round trip 17 miles
Hiking time 2 days
High point 3,600 feet
Elevation gain 840 feet
Easy

Hikable mid June through mid
October
USGS Continental Mountain
Information: Kaniksu National
Forest, Priest Lake Ranger
District

This is a dark, dank trail through a virgin red cedar forest. It is an easy walk with the musical rumble of the Upper Priest never far away. The river is part of the federal Wild and Scenic River System and reaches into an area proposed as an addition to the Salmo-Priest Wilderness.

From Priest River, Idaho, drive north on State Highway 57 about 37 miles to Nordman. Continue another 14 miles on Forest Road No. 302 (Granite Creek) to Granite Falls campground. Now drive 1½ miles and bear right at the road junction onto Forest Road No. 1013. Drive about 11 miles and look for the trailhead sign and parking area on the left side of the road. (Drivers who start up a sharp switchback have gone about ½ mile too far.)

The trail is constantly ambushed by springs and streams, and often visited by deer and the occasional moose and grizzly bear. Good campsites can be found at Rock Creek, Diamond Creek and Malcom Creek. Camping also is available at Upper Priest Falls (also called American Falls), but these sites are dirty and overused generally by less than ethical hikers who occasionally come in on the short 2-mile route from Forest Road No. 637. These hikers save time getting to Upper Priest Falls, but they miss one of the best lowland hiking trails in Idaho.

Upper Priest River. (Chuck Kerkering photo)

The last ¾ mile of trail to the 40-foot tumbling falls is not maintained, but it's fairly easy for attentive hikers to follow. Cutthroat and bull trout inhabit the Upper Priest, but beware that the Idaho Fish and Game Department has enforced a fishing closure on the river for many years.

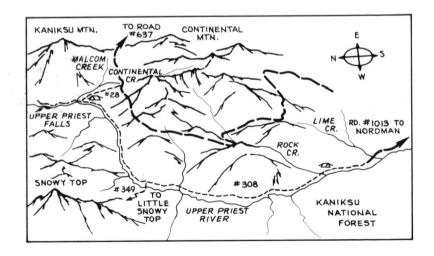

20 UPPER PRIEST LAKE-NAVIGATION TRAIL

Round trip 12 miles
Hiking time 6–7 hours or
  overnight
High point 2,640 feet
Elevation gain 200 feet
Moderate

Hikable late May through mid
  October
USGS Priest Lake NE, Upper
  Priest Lake
Information: Kaniksu National
  Forest, Priest Lake Ranger
  District

From Priest River, Idaho, drive north on State Highway 57 to Nordman. At the fork at Nordman, turn right toward Reeder Bay and continue north along the west shore of the lake to Beaver Creek campground. Follow the signs to the trailhead parking area. Here there are toilet facilities along with the start of a ¼-mile canoe portage trail that heads down to the thoroughfare between Priest and Upper Priest Lakes.

(To reach the north trailhead, bear left at Nordman onto Forest Road No. 302. Drive to the end of the pavement and continue past campsites at Stagger Inn and Granite Falls to the trailhead for Hatchery Trail No. 300, 20 miles from Nordman. From the trailhead, it's 4 miles to Navigation campground, but the route is not as scenic as the walk in from the south trailhead.)

From the Beaver Creek trailhead, Trail No. 291 heads into a cedar forest. After about 1½ miles, it skirts Armstrong Meadows where there is a beaver pond. It then ducks back into the woods. Although it has a few uphills and downhills, the elevation gain in this portion of the hike is negligible.

Upper Priest Lake from Plowboy Campground. (Sam Schlieder photo)

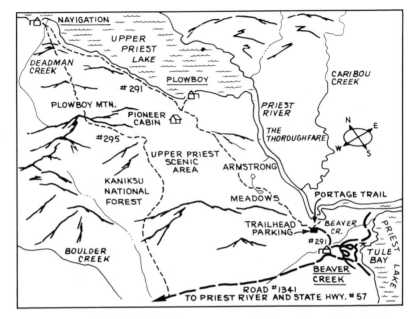

About ¼ mile before Plowboy campground, there is a pioneer cabin from earlier days when settlers lived around the lake. Continue on to Plowboy, which is situated on the shore of Upper Priest Lake. The campground has several picnic tables, fire pits and pit toilets, used by both hikers and boaters. Other scattered campsites can be found in the area.

It's a total of 3 miles to Plowboy, the half-way point to Navigation which is reached by continuing northwest on the trail along the undulating shore of Upper Priest. Navigation has pit toilets and numerous campsites. Picnic tables in this area were destroyed by unusually high winds in a 1976 summer thunder storm that blew down hundreds of trees. The area was closed for several years before it could be cleared.

To explore the northerly trail to the Hatchery trailhead, cross Deadman Creek and follow the trail on the north bank. There is also a trail (4 miles round trip) from Navigation campground to the top of Plowboy where the remnant of an old lookout tower exists. About fifty feet east of the lookout is an open area with an excellent view of the Selkirks. This Plowboy trail continues down the other side of the mountain with many switchbacks, coming out at Plowboy Mountain Trail No. 295 trailhead, located about 2½ miles west of Beaver Creek campground.

Fly fishing for native cutthroat trout can be good at Upper Priest Lake, but check Idaho Fish and Game Department fishing regulations for special closures and size restrictions. The inlet streams to Upper Priest Lake, including Upper Priest River, are closed to fishing.

Side trips in this area include the Lakeshore Trail, which begins near Beaver Creek campground at Tule Bay and heads south, hugging the lakeshore for 6 miles. The trail offers a good view of Chimney Rock across the lake on the Selkirk Crest (see Hike 34). There are two other access points to the Lakeshore Trail along the road to Tule Bay.

21 UPPER PRIEST LAKE-TRAPPER CREEK

Round trip 10 miles
Hiking time 6–8 hours or
  overnight
High point 2,634 feet
Elevation gain 200 feet
Moderate
Hikable May through October

USGS Upper Priest Lake
Information: Idaho State
  Department of Lands in
  Cavanaugh Bay and Kaniksu
  National Forest, Priest Lake
  Ranger District

Priest Lake visitors can get away from the crowds at the main lake with this hike to a secluded area at the north end of Upper Priest Lake. Vehicles are not allowed in this area and no water skiing is allowed on Upper Priest, making it more the playground of hikers, anglers and canoeists. It once was the playground of mountain caribou and grizzly bears, both of which are now endangered but still clinging to existence in this region.

From Priest River, Idaho, drive north on State Highway 57 to Nordman. At Nordman, bear left at the Y onto Forest Road No. 302. The pavement ends after 4 miles. Continue on Road No. 302 past campgrounds at Stagger Inn and Granite Falls (the Roosevelt grove of ancient cedars, shown near Granite Falls on the Kaniksu National Forest map, is worth a stop for pictures). Less than 2 miles past the campgrounds, the road forks three ways. Take the middle fork, staying on Road No. 1013 as it winds through the forest. Stay on the main road, passing the turnoffs to Hughes Meadows and several other spur roads for about 3 miles and turn right onto Forest Road No. 655. The trailhead for Trapper Creek Trail No. 302 is ½ mile east on this road, about 22 miles from Nordman.

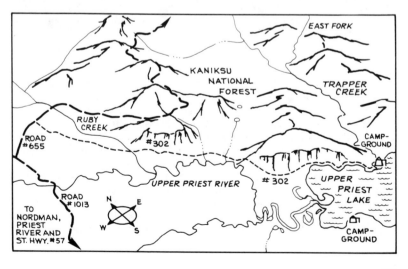

Trapper Creek Trail to Upper Priest Lake. (Chuck Kerkering photo)

The trail leads gently through a cedar forest, breaks into some openings and back into the woods. It's a peaceful hike with some ups, downs and stream crossings. During spring runoff, a staff is useful. The trail emerges at the northeast shore of Upper Priest Lake, 4 miles from the trailhead. A short distance before arriving at the lake, there is a dilapidated cabin, reminiscent of the early history of the area which was busy with miners and trappers. From the lakeshore one can see Navigation campground across the lake to the west and Plowboy Mountain which dominates the west shore. (Plowboy campground is not visible from here.) The trail continues eastward, skirting the shore for 1 mile to Trapper Creek campground, a wooded area with good campsites. Water is available from Trapper Creek, which is just east of the campground.

22 WEST FORK LAKE

Round trip 12 miles
Hiking time 8 hours or overnight
High point 5,800 feet
Elevation gain 720 feet
Moderate
Hikable mid June through
September

USGS Smith Peak, Shorty Peak,
Caribou Creek, Grass Mountain
Information: Kaniksu National
Forest, Bonners Ferry Ranger
District

The trail leads to West Fork cabin, which is open to public use with a wood stove and room for about six adults. The trail also leads to Hidden and West Fork Lakes, two of the largest mountain lakes in the Idaho Selkirs. Both are stocked with cutthroat trout. West Fork Lake is situated in a remote area where one can climb up to views of country in which grizzly bears and woodland caribou have found their last remaining refuge in this region.

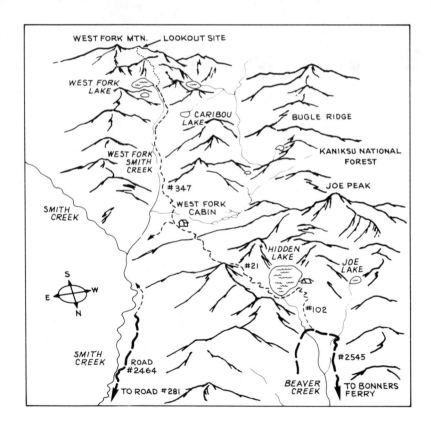

West Fork Lake, Idaho Selkirks. (Jerry Pavia photo)

From Bonners Ferry, Idaho, drive north 15 miles on U.S. Highway 95 to the junction with Highway 1. Bear left on Highway 1, drive about 1 mile to the Copeland Bridge Road and turn left. Cross the Kootenai River and turn right at the junction with the Westside Road. Drive about 10 miles and make a sharp left turn on the well-maintained Forest Road No. 281 (Smith Creek Road). After about 8 miles, the road makes a sharp turn to the right. At this turn, bear left on Forest Road No. 655/2545 (Cow Creek/Beaver Creek Road). Drive about a mile and bear left onto Road No. 2545. From here it is about 3 miles to the unmarked but obvious trailhead just after a left turn in the road.

Begin on well-used Trail No. 102, which begins by switchbacking steeply through an old burn. After ½ mile it begins to level off for the next ½ mile to Hidden Lake. Plenty of campsites are available.

Continue up and around the northeast side of the lake overlooking the water to a trail junction and bear south on Trail No. 21. Hike down from the saddle about 2 miles through brushy areas and big cedars to West Fork cabin, which is well used and open on a first-come first-served basis. Continue south about ⅓ mile and bear right at the junction onto Trail No. 347 toward West Fork Lake and mountain. Cross a branch of West Fork Smith Creek, down through more old cedars and ferns and through some rocky and boggy areas about 2½ miles to a junction on a small saddle. The main trail heads down to the lake ¼ mile below. The other fork of the trail leads up an unmaintained route to the old lookout site on West Fork Mountain for views of West Fork Lake, Smith Peak and Lions Head.

SELKIRK CREST
Unprotected

23 LOOKOUT MOUNTAIN

Round trip 5 miles
Hiking time 3–4 hours or
overnight
High point 6,727 feet
Elevation gain 1,527 feet
Moderate

Hikable June through September
USGS Caribou Creek
Information: Idaho State
Department of Lands at
Cavanaugh Bay

The north face of Lookout Mountain is a nearly vertical 200-foot cliff forming a broad U shape often admired by hikers and canoeists looking up from Upper Priest Lake. From the summit of Lookout Mountain looking south, one sees a magnificent view of Priest Lake and Upper Priest Lake. The Forest Service designated the peak as a fire observation point in 1921 and erected the first lookout house on the summit in 1929. Unstaffed for 30 years, a new tower was built by the Idaho Department of Lands in 1977. In 1983, Spokane lookout buff Ray Kresek and others be-

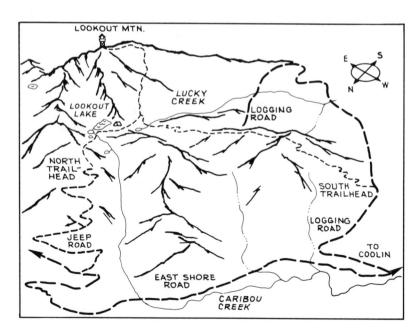

Ridge near Lookout Mountain, Idaho Selkirks. (Stan Bech photo)

gan a project to restore the lookout to its original design, a project that could put it on the National Register of Historic Places.

From Priest River, Idaho, drive north on Highway 57 about 21½ miles and turn right toward Coolin. Drive 5⅓ miles to Coolin and turn right on East Shore Road toward Cavanaugh Bay. Continue 10½ miles (going from pavement to gravel at Cavanaugh Bay) to Indian Creek campground and store; then drive past Lionhead campground. About ¼ mile past Milepost No. 21, a logging road branches off to the right, leading 2 miles up to the south trailhead. (Hikers can extend the hike described below by leaving a vehicle at this trailhead and taking another vehicle to begin the hike at the north trailhead.) To reach the north trailhead, continue on the main gravel road for another 2¼ miles to the next road that angles off to the right. Drive 2¼ miles past two switchbacks and turn right onto a road marked on the 1969 USGS map as a jeep trail. If driven slowly and cautiously, an ordinary car can make it up the 3½ miles to the north trailhead.

The route begins at 5,200 feet and heads ¾ mile uphill to Lookout Lake at 5,564 feet. The lake is the only year-round reliable source of water on the trail. Three small campsites are situated along the trail on the west side of the lake. The lakeshore itself is marshy, with a boulder field along the south end. Overnighters often camp here and dayhike to the summit.

From the lake, follow the trail about ½ mile to a junction. From here it is about 1¼ miles to the summit of Lookout Mountain. The last ¼ mile to the summit is on a steep road. At the top, hikers will find a wooden lookout shelter along with a modern lookout tower. Also, there's an out-house nearby in a clump of trees.

Those who want to extend the hike 3½ miles to the south trailhead can return to the trail junction and continue southwest down the trail. Logging operations interrupt the trail about 1¾ miles down. By stumbling through the debris on the north side of the ridge, hikers should be able to pick up the trail again in a few hundred yards. If not, a logging road, albeit longer and less scenic, curves around to the south trailhead at 3,480 feet.

SELKIRK CREST
Proposed wilderness

24   TWO MOUTH LAKES

Round trip 6 miles
Hiking time 4 hours or overnight
High point 5,880 feet
Elevation gain 1,720 feet
Moderate

Hikable late June through
  September
USGS The Wigwams
Information: Kaniksu National
  Forest, Bonners Ferry Ranger
  District

Once there were two good routes to this scenic area near the Selkirk Crest. However, the Idaho Department of Lands has not maintained the route on its land coming from the Priest Lake side (west) of the crest for years. As of 1987, the department had no future plans to do so. The remaining route, approaching from the east on Forest Service land, is better maintained, although it is inaccurately shown on Kaniksu National Forest maps as recently as 1985.

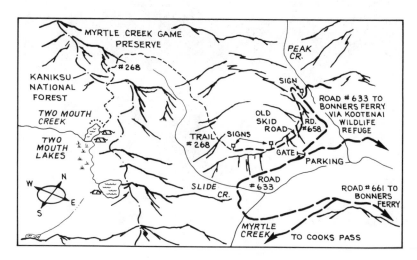

The area is wild and stunning. It has been officially classified as grizzly habitat.

At Bonners Ferry, Idaho, take the City Center exit off U.S. Highway 95. Head west on Riverside Street along the Kootenai River, following signs to the Kootenai National Wildlife Refuge. Bear right when the paved road forks and turns into a gravel road. Drive 1½ miles to the refuge headquarters and turn left on Myrtle Creek Road No. 633, which is well maintained. Drive about 10 miles up the main road.

Begin hiking on Road No. 658, which is barricaded at Road No. 633. Hike about ½ mile and look for a sign marking a skid road heading uphill to the left. Follow this skid road, which eventually becomes Trail No. 268 in the Slide Creek basin. (Slide Creek can gobble up about 100 feet of the trail early in the year, making it difficult to negotiate.) The trail winds around the basin and climbs a pass before dropping down to the lakes from the north. This trail is reasonably easy to follow if maintained to keep the alders cut back. Before dropping down to the lakes, consider hiking the open ridges for spectacular views. Lower Two Mouth Lake is beautiful and interestingly shaped, sitting right on the Selkirk Crest. Only two campsites exist since the surrounding area is marshy. One or two campsites also are available near the outlet of Upper Two Mouth Lake. The Forest Service asks hikers to minimize use of the marshy areas between the two lakes because of their fragile nature.

The route from the Priest Lake area once led through Idaho State Lands property up Two Mouth Creek. But it is badly overgrown, clogged with blowdowns and almost impossible to follow.

Main Two Mouth Lake, Idaho Selkirks. (Cris Currie photo)

25   LONG CANYON LOOP

Round trip 35 miles
Hiking time 4–5 days
High point 7,200 feet
Elevation gain 5,360 feet
Moderately difficult
Hikable July through September

USGS Smith Peak, Pyramid Peak,
  Shorty Peak, Smith Falls
Information: Kaniksu National
  Forest, Bonners Ferry Ranger
  District

This is a classic backpacking trip, leading up beneath ancient cedars and hemlocks through one of the last unlogged drainages of the American Selkirks. Then it climbs up to a lake-studded ridge and plunges back to the Kootenai River Valley. Long Canyon is flanked by two of the three highest mountains in northern Idaho, Smith Peak at 7,653 feet and Parker Peak at 7,670 feet. (The highest is Fisher Ridge—not to be confused with lower Fisher Peak—at 7,682 feet.) Within the canyon are four lakes, reached only by difficult bushwhacking from the main trail through dungeons of devils club. Long Canyon Creek holds some small rainbow and brook trout. The main Long Canyon trail, called Canyon Creek Trail No. 16, has been rebuilt and maintained since the early '80s by several Bonners Ferry-based volunteer groups, including hikers and horsepackers. (Note: Because of extensive reconstruction since 1980, trails marked on Forest Service and USGS topo maps are inaccurate in many places.)

From Bonners Ferry, drive north 15 miles on U.S. Highway 95 to the junction with Highway 1. Bear left on State Highway 1 and turn west at the Copeland turnoff. From here it's 10 miles—crossing the Kootenai River and heading north at the Westside Road junction—to Canyon Creek Trail No. 16. The trailhead is on the west side of the road; parking is on the southeast side of the creek. The hiking loop ends at the trailhead for Parker Ridge Trail No. 221, which is on the Westside Road 3

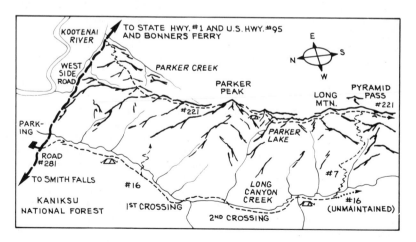

Tributary of Long Canyon Creek, Idaho Selkirks. (Jerry Pavia photo)

miles southeast of the Trail No. 16 trailhead. A shuttle car can be left here.

From the trailhead, walk uphill to a road, turn left, then head up again to the right on an old road that's beginning to look like a trail again. Shift into low gear; the trail is fairly steep and occasionally brushy for the first 2 miles before becoming a gentle combination of ups and downs. Look at the bright side: this steep ridge of slate thwarted the roads that would have led to the logging of this pristine canyon years ago. (The Forest Service has plans to reroute this lower section of trail by 1992.) Carry water; it's 3 dry miles before the trail comes close to the creek at the first available campsite. From there the trail is dry for another 3 miles to the next camping area and the first creek crossing, which can be difficult in high water during June. Water is abundant along the trail from this point on to Pyramid Pass. Other good campsites are at 8 miles and 11 miles, where there's a very large campsite along the unnamed creek that flows out of Smith Lake.

At about 12 miles, Trail No. 16 crosses Long Canyon Creek again before coming to the junction with Trail No. 7, which switchbacks up about 4 miles toward Pyramid Pass. (Trail No. 16 beyond this junction is no longer maintained because of forest management decisions protecting grizzly habitat.) About ½ mile below Pyramid Pass, turn left onto Trail

No. 221. The ridge above Long Canyon is graced with several lakes, usually stocked with rainbow or cutthroat trout. The lakes offer good campsites, although in some cases, such as Parker Lake, the best campsites
are on the ridges above the lakes. It is important to stock up with water
at the lakes for the rest of the trip. The trail from the junction of Trail
No. 221 to Long Mountain is steep, rugged, poorly maintained—and dry.
Beyond Long Mountain Lake, stay on the ridge until the trail reappears.
This is generally a delightful open hike, but the trail constantly fades
away. After passing Parker Lake (about 9 miles from the end of the
trail), the only dependable water is at a spring near a small trail sign 5
miles from the Westside Road trailhead. The last mile of the trail has
been partially reconstructed, but it's still brushy and partially obliterated by skid roads. The Forest Service has plans to improve it.

SELKIRK CREST
Proposed roadless

26 TROUT-BIG FISHER LAKES

Round trip 10 miles
Hiking time 9 hours or overnight
High point 7,400 feet
Elevation gain 3,000 feet
Moderately easy

Hikable July through September
USGS Pyramid Peak
Information: Kaniksu National
    Forest, Bonners Ferry Ranger
    District

Many hikers consider this one of the premier overnight trips in
Idaho's Selkirk Mountains. The lakes are high and uncrowded and the
trails lead to open ridges with excellent views.

At Bonners Ferry, Idaho, take the City Center exit off U.S. Highway
95. Head west on Riverside Street along the Kootenai River, following
signs to the Kootenai National Wildlife Refuge. Bear right when the
paved road forks and turns into a gravel road. About 14 miles from Bonners Ferry, turn left on Forest Road No. 634 (Trout Creek Road). Follow
the Trout Creek Road west for 9½ miles to the well-marked trailhead.
The road is rough gravel and rock, best suited for pickup trucks or small
cars with good clearance. Allow about 50 minutes to drive the last 9½
miles.

Trail No. 13 heads uphill about ½ mile to a junction. (Pyramid-Ball
Lakes, Hike 28 describes the trail to the left.) Bear right on Trail No. 13
following the signs toward Pyramid Pass. At the next intersection, follow the signs to Trout Lake. Most of the trail is wooded with occasional
open sections in the 2½ total miles to Trout Lake. Virtually no water is
available along the trail. The trail levels out and then drops 300 feet to
the lake, where campsites are available for about three tents at each
end. The lake is stocked with cutthroat trout. A scramble to the 7,500-
foot ridge above offers good views.

The hike to Big Fisher Lake covers another 3 miles and takes about
2½ hours. The trail has been rerouted up to the ridge and there are more
switchbacks than are shown on the topo map. The trail is well marked,

Trout Lake, Idaho Selkirks. (Loren Johnson photo)

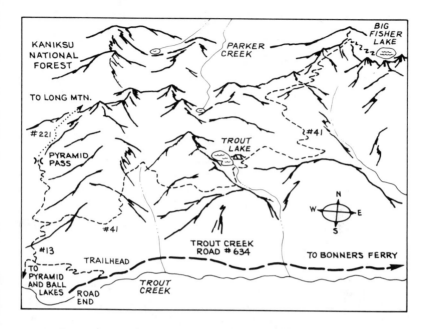

but there is no water along the trail. After climbing the ridge, a steep, rocky section of trail drops almost 700 feet into a granite cirque where the lake is situated in the shadow of Fisher Peak. Here there are plenty of campsites, also trout.

SELKIRK CREST
Proposed roadless

27   FISHER PEAK

Round trip 13 miles
Hiking time 7-8 hours
High point 7,580 feet
Elevation gain 3,170 feet
Moderately difficult

Hikable July through September
USGS Pyramid Peak
Information: Kaniksu National
  Forest, Bonners Ferry Ranger
  District

Here's a hard and healthy dayhike into one of the Selkirk Mountain's last truly wild and unroaded areas. This is officially recognized as habitat for grizzly bears and endangered woodland caribou. From the peak, one can look into Long Canyon, a wilderness candidate and one of only two major unroaded drainages left in northern Idaho.

From Bonners Ferry, Idaho, drive north on U.S. Highway 95 for 15 miles and turn left onto State Highway 1 at the Copeland junction. Drive 1 mile, then turn left on a gravel road marked with a National Forest sportsmen's access sign. Drive to a T, which is West Side Road No.

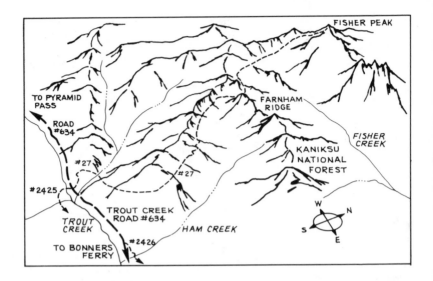

417 and turn left. Drive 14¾ miles and turn right onto Road No. 634 (Trout Creek Road). Trailhead No. 27 to Fisher Peak is on the north side of the road 5½ miles up from the turnoff. Trout Creek Road is not suitable for vehicles with low clearance, although many standard short-wheel-base compact cars will make it.

The trail begins at elev. 4,413 feet, and heads steadily uphill. The grade is not unreasonably steep, but it is relentless and becomes faint in

Boletus mushrooms on Fisher Peak, Idaho Selkirks. (Tony Dolphin photo)

some places. Blazes help define the trail in these sections. About ½ mile up, the trail crosses a stream that could be difficult to cross during runoff. This is the only reliable water source on the hike. From there the trail proceeds up to Farnham Ridge, where the views are better and the trail becomes more gentle until the last ¼ mile to the rewarding vista waiting atop Fisher Peak.

SELKIRK CREST
Proposed wilderness

28 PYRAMID-BALL LAKES

Round trip 5 miles
Hiking time 4 hours or overnight
High point 6,710 feet
Elevation gain 1,310 feet
Moderately easy

Hikable mid July through
**   September**
USGS Pyramid Peak
Information: Kaniksu National
**   Forest, Bonners Ferry Ranger**
**   District**

This is a short, reasonably easy hike for dayhikers and overnighters alike. The lakes are sunk into rocky cliffs near the crest of the Selkirk Mountains in settings one normally would have to hike much longer dis-

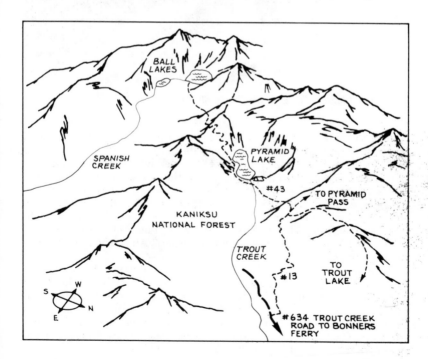

Ball Lake, Idaho Selkirks. (Jerry Pavia photo)

tances to enjoy in this region. It takes only an hour to reach Pyramid Lake; it's less than an hour farther to Ball Lake.

At Bonners Ferry, Idaho, take the City Center exit off U.S. Highway 95. Head west on Riverside Street along the Kootenai River, following signs to the Kootenai National Wildlife Refuge. Bear right when the paved road forks and turn left on Forest Road No. 634 (Trout Creek Road). Follow the Trout Creek Road west for 9½ miles to the well-marked trailhead. The road is rough gravel and rock, best suited for pickup trucks or small cars with good clearance. Allow about 50 minutes to drive the last 9½ miles.

Trail No. 13 heads uphill about ½ mile to a junction. Turn left onto Trail No. 43 toward Pyramid Lake. (See Trout-Big Fisher, Hike 26 for the trail heading to the right.) From here the trail winds gently uphill about ½ mile to Pyramid Lake. The shallow lake is in a cirque of rock cliffs and stocked with cutthroat trout. Campsites are available for about six tents. The trail continues around the east shore of Pyramid Lake and up another mile, mostly switchbacks, to Ball Lakes.

29   MYRTLE LAKE

Round trip 10 miles
Hiking time 6 hours or overnight
High point 7,090 feet
Elevation gain 1,850 feet
Moderately difficult
Hikable mid June through
  September

USGS Roman Nose, The
  Wigwams, Smith Peak
Information: Kaniksu National
  Forest, Bonners Ferry Ranger
  District

This tiny gem of a lake is surrounded by timber. It's not as scenic or popular as some of the other Selkirk Mountain lakes that seem to hang from steep granite cliffs. But therein lies the attraction to many hikers.

At Bonners Ferry, Idaho, take the City Center exit off U.S. Highway 95. Head west on Riverside Street along the Kootenai River, following signs to the Kootenai National Wildlife Refuge. Bear right when the paved road forks and turns into a gravel road. Drive 1½ miles to the refuge headquarters and turn left on Forest Road No. 633 (Myrtle Creek), which is well maintained. Drive about 9½ miles and, shortly after crossing the bridge over Jim Creek, turn right on Forest Road No. 2406 (Jim Creek). Neither the topo maps nor the 1985 Kaniksu National Forest map show the upper reaches of this road accurately. It has been extended to gobble up about ¾ mile of trail. Pass several spur roads and

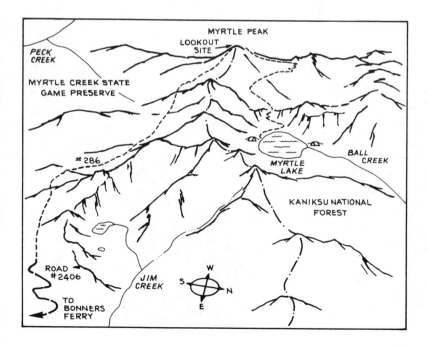

switchback up to the end of the road to the new trailhead.

It begins as an old skid road through the brush, but within a few hundred yards Trail No. 286 becomes a scenic footpath. It heads relentlessly uphill on a southeast exposure that can be hot on sunny summer days. After about 1 mile, the trail winds through slabs of rock. The tread is often difficult to find, but hikers have maintained a good system of rock cairns. As it nears the top of the Selkirk Crest, the trail offers views of Kent and Harrison lakes. The trail leads to a scenic grassy pass just under the old Myrtle Peak lookout platform. As late as mid July, the trail from this point and down a ridge to a saddle above the west side of the lake can be covered with snow. Generally, there should be no problem glissading or kicking steps over this short stretch. Approaching the saddle keep a sharp eye out for the trail, which plunges sharply over the steep ridge to the right toward the lake. Finally the trail winds through an open forest to the lake, which has two small campsites at the north end and two at the south end. The shoreline is very brushy and boggy, but fishing can be good for cutthroat trout.

Myrtle Lake, Idaho Selkirks. (Rich Landers photo)

30   HARRISON LAKE

Round trip 6 miles
Hiking time 4 hours or overnight
High point 6,182 feet
Elevation gain 1,080 feet
Moderate

Hikable mid June through
  September
USGS The Wigwams, Roman Nose
Information: Kaniksu National
  Forest, Bonners Ferry Ranger
  District

One of the most beautiful alpine lakes in the Selkirk Mountains, Harrison Lake, is accessible by two trails, both of which will be described here. However, this book features the north route, which has been reconstructed and maintained by volunteers with cooperation from the Forest Service. It's a little longer, but it's the best trail for hiking.

North Route

At Bonners Ferry, Idaho, take the City Center exit off U.S. Highway 95. Head west on Riverside Street along the Kootenai River, following signs to the Kootenai National Wildlife Refuge. Bear right when the paved road forks (left fork is gravel). Drive 1½ miles from the fork to the refuge headquarters and turn left just beyond the headquarters on Forest Road No. 633 (Myrtle Creek Road) which is well maintained. Drive about 14 miles and turn right on Forest Road No. 2409 (Upper Myrtle Creek Road). The poorly maintained road is marked with a sign. Drive 1½ miles to the trailhead at the end of the road.

Trail No. 6 is an old skid road for about ¾ mile. After the third creek crossing (negotiated by hopping rocks), the road is wet for a short stretch. To keep feet dry, a hiker can walk on the railroad ties laid along

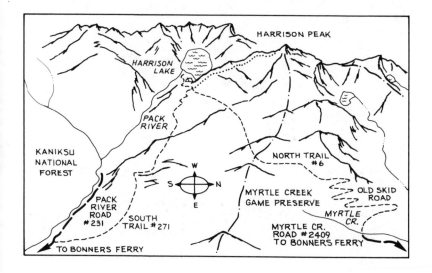

the edge of the road in the worst sections. Soon the trail leaves the road bed, heading up the hill to the left. Watch for this intersection. It could be easy to miss as the road continues and the trail is narrow and not well traveled. Rocks have been placed across the road at the trail junction.

The first third of the trail is narrow and brushy. It leads gently uphill with a few short, steep sections. It then widens out and switchbacks up the hill. At the top of the ridge, the trail narrows again and wanders

Harrison Lake and Harrison Peak, Idaho Selkirks. (Will Venard photo)

along almost level. It crosses a few rock slabs where it is marked with cairns, and drops down into the Pack River drainage (great view here) to the junction with Trail No. 271 coming from the south. Pay attention here. Coming back, it is easy to miss this trail junction and head out Trail No. 271. (Just before the trail crosses the rock slabs is a good place to go cross-country to scramble up 7,292-foot Harrison Peak.)

From here it's a mere ¼ mile to the lake, although it's the steepest part of the hike. It's worth the effort.

Several overused campsites are situated near the lake, which is stocked with cutthroat trout. Early visitors are likely to find the campsites under snow in mid June.

South Route

This round trip of 5 miles is shorter than the hike above, but gains more altitude, about 1,440 feet. The same maps and information sources are applicable to both hikes.

From Sandpoint, Idaho, head north on U.S. Highway 95 toward Bonners Ferry. Drive 10½ miles, cross the Pack River bridge and turn left onto Pack River Road No. 231. Drive about 20 miles and look for the small Trail No. 271 sign at the trailhead on the right side of the road.

The trail climbs steadily, following an eroding old jeep road much of the way. It crosses at least two dependable streams for water. Large slabs of granite dominate the scenery until the lake, in its grand cirque, comes into view.

SELKIRK CREST
Proposed roadless

 # BOTTLENECK LAKE

Round trip 7 miles
Hiking time 4–7 hours or
overnight
High point 5,620 feet
Elevation gain 1,100 feet
Moderately difficult

Hikable mid July through
September
USGS Roman Nose
Information: Kaniksu National
Forest, Bonners Ferry Ranger
District

This trip is especially appealing to hikers who like to scramble up and beyond the end of a trail for lofty views of the Selkirk Crest. Bottleneck Lake itself is a sight to behold, nestled below granite cirques. But in 1987, the Forest Service was still working on a road management plan that could make or break this hike. At that time, vehicles with high clearance could drive more than halfway up the hiking route described below, making the lakes only a 1⅓-mile hike for people who wanted to drive as far as possible. (See bar across trail on map.) However, since this area has been officially designated as grizzly habitat, there's a chance the road may be blocked closer to the access road, making the lakes just a tad less accessible but vastly more enjoyable for hikers.

Drive north from Sandpoint, Idaho, on U.S. Highway 2 to Naples and bear left on Deep Creek Road. Continue north about 5 miles and turn left onto paved Snow Creek Road. Drive about 2½ miles to a Y and take the gravel road to the left. After about 10 miles, pass the Cooks Point Road on the right and continue for another ½ mile until the main road makes a switchback and two other roads split off straight ahead. Trail No. 187 officially begins here, heading up the primitive road which splits to the right up Snow Creek. (Be advised, however, that in 1987 vehicles with high clearance could still negotiate the rough road for another 2 miles.)

From the beginning of the trail, it's about 1¾ miles to a road forking to the left. This is Trail No. 185, actually an old jeep road which can be driven to within 2 miles of Snow Lake. Trail No. 187 to Bottleneck Lake makes a sharp switchback to the right up the hill. Go another ¼ mile to where it switchbacks again at Corner Creek. This is where the walking-only route begins, leading 1⅓ miles to the lake. Turn left and follow the brushy but easy-to-follow trail about a mile up to a marshy area. The trail then turns west (and wet) and climbs quickly to the shallow lake below Bottleneck Peak. Two camping areas are available. One is right at the end of the trail, but the more preferable site lies near the outflow at the end of the lakeside trail to the left.

Bottleneck Peak is most inviting and can be climbed by continuing around to the southeast corner of the lake to the bottom of the talus. Scramble up the talus to the cliff that rings the cirque and walk toward the base of the peak. Access to the ridge top is easily achieved via a narrow chute just before the peak. The fastest way to the summit is to follow

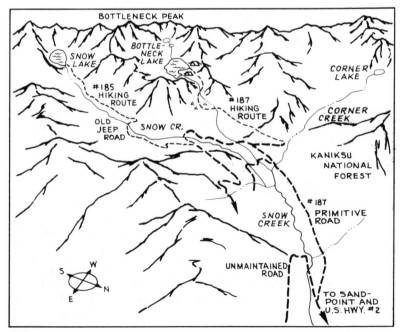

Bottleneck Lake, Idaho Selkirks. (Don Mattoon photo)

the ridge, but this involves a couple of moderately exposed maneuvers. An alternative is to go down the other side along the east face and climb the brushy slope to the more gentle south ridge. From the summit, the view of the east slope of the Selkirk Crest from Harrison Peak to Hunt Peak is impressive. Also be sure to walk south along the ridgetop for a view of Snow Lake and Roman Nose.

SELKIRK CREST
Proposed wilderness

32 BEEHIVE LAKES

Round trip 9 miles
Hiking time 6–8 hours or
   overnight
High point 6,460 feet
Elevation gain 2,010 feet
Moderately difficult

Hikable late June through
   September
USGS The Wigwams, Roman Nose
Information: Kaniksu National
   Forest, Sandpoint Ranger
   District

Roads take hikers high up toward the Selkirk Crest for reasonably easy access to these high mountain lakes. The lakes are cut into the granite shoulder of the crest and can be surrounded by snow in late

June. The lakes are stocked with cutthroat trout, which seem to cope with the area's healthy mosquito crop better than hikers who do not come equipped with repellents and long-sleeved shirts and pants.

From Sandpoint, Idaho, head north on U.S. Highway 95 toward Bonners Ferry. Drive about 10½ miles, cross the Pack River bridge and turn left onto Pack River Road No. 231. Drive about 18 miles, staying on Road No. 231, and look for the Beehive Lakes trail sign at the left side of the road. The road is rough and rocky in its upper reaches. (About 14 miles up the Pack River Road there's a good view of Chimney Rock on the Selkirk Crest to the west.)

Walk down from the road, cross the Pack River on a footbridge and head up Trail No. 279. The route begins as an old road that dwindles to a trail. Continue up, through a high meadow and into a timbered area, where the trail switchbacks up a steeper slope. Cairns and arrows help hikers navigate through rock slabs and eventually to the rocks sur-

Little Harrison Lake in Beehive Lakes area, Idaho Selkirks.
(Will Venard photo)

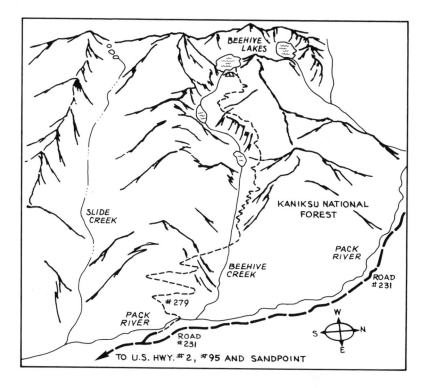

rounding the lake. The area is worth exploring, not only to see all three lakes, but also to scramble to the Selkirk Crest for a view. One must bushwhack to another one of the Beehive Lakes, better known as Little Harrison Lake.

SELKIRK CREST
Proposed roadless

33 ROMAN NOSE LAKES

Round trip 3 miles
Hiking time 2 hours
High point 6,200 feet
Elevation gain 310 feet
Moderate

Hikable June through September
USGS Roman Nose
Information: Kaniksu National
Forest, Bonners Ferry Ranger
District

This is a short, heavily used trail that gives hikers a quick-fix alpine adventure. Because it is only 1 mile from the trailhead to the first lake, one can expect company not usually associated with backcountry travel. But the terrain is captivating, with plenty of opportunities for scrambling away from the beaten track.

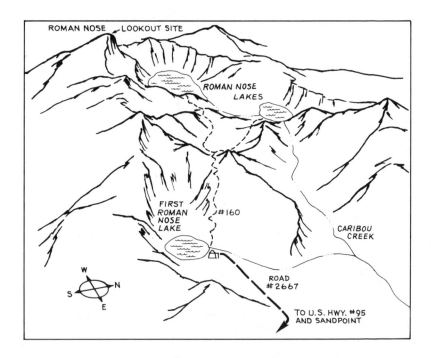

From Sandpoint, Idaho, drive to the junction with State Highway 200 and head north on U.S. Highway 95 about 29 miles toward Bonners Ferry. Turn left (west) at an intersection marked as a national forest entrance, which is ½ mile south of the Bonners Ferry Ranger Station. Drive 3 miles and turn right on Road No. 417, following the sign toward Kootenai National Wildlife Refuge and Snow Creek Road. Drive to a Y and turn left onto unpaved Snow Creek Road No. 402. Follow the road, passing Forest Road No. 2646 and going a short way past Cook's Peak Road No. 661. Then turn left onto unmarked Forest Road No. 1007 approximately 11 miles from Highway 95. (These are the road numbers shown on the 1985 Kaniksu National Forest map; numbers on old maps are different.) Follow Road No. 1007 for about 8 miles, over Ruby Pass, then turn right on Road No. 2667 and go 2 miles to the campsite and trailhead at First Roman Nose Lake. (Road No. 2667 is poorly maintained and difficult to negotiate without a four-wheel-drive vehicle. Some hikers might prefer parking near the junction of Road Nos. 1007 and 2667 and walking the 2 miles to the trailhead.)

Trail No. 160 begins about 100 yards from the first lake. There is no sign at the trailhead, but it's easy to find. Cross a small bridge over the stream flowing from the lake. The trail is pleasant, offering excellent views of the countryside as one gains elevation. Silvery snags grace the trailside together with wild rhododendron, mountain ash, alpine fir and various wildflowers.

Walk about 1 mile from the trailhead to a Y. The left fork leads about ½ mile to Upper Roman Nose Lake (the largest of the three lakes), but the trail has been neglected and could require some scrambling through

First Roman Nose Lake, Idaho Selkirks. (Tony Dolphin photo)

deadfall. The trail to the right leads about ½ mile to Lower Roman Nose Lake, which is in a picturesque alpine setting. A stream from the upper lake cascades down the headwall of the lower lake. The trail does not lead around the lower lake, but one can bushwhack to several campsites around its shores. Trout fishing can be fair in the lakes. The 1,000-vertical-foot scramble from the upper lake to the Roman Nose lookout site is worth the effort. The existing structure was built in 1955, but the mountain has had a lookout on it since 1917.

34   CHIMNEY ROCK

Round trip 5 miles
Hiking time 3–4 hours or
  overnight
High point 7,160 feet
Elevation gain 1,070 feet
Moderately difficult

Hikable July through October
USGS Mt. Roothaan
Information: Kaniksu National
  Forest, Priest Lake Ranger
  District and Idaho Department
  of Lands in Cavanaugh Bay

Chimney Rock is the most distinctive formation on the Selkirk Crest. Visible from Priest Lake and portions of U.S. Highway 95 north of Sandpoint, it is one of the few mountain features just about everyone in the region can identify. It has been a rite of climbinghood for rock climbers throughout the region since 1934, when a group of Seattle climbers led by Byron Ward made the first recorded ascent of the 360-foot rock column to the 7,124-foot summit.

There are two distinct routes to Chimney Rock. This book is featuring the route in from the Priest Lake side (west), since it is the most scenic for the hiker. However, the route in from the Pack River side (east) is also described, since it is well used, particularly by climbers coming from the Sandpoint area.

West Route

From Priest River, Idaho, drive north on Highway 57 about 21½ miles and turn right toward Coolin. Drive 5⅓ miles to Coolin and turn right on East Shore Road toward Cavanaugh Bay. Continue about 9 miles (going from pavement to gravel at Cavanaugh Bay) and take a sharp right turn onto unmarked Horton Ridge Road. (The turn is just after the road crosses Horton Creek.) Drive 7½ miles to the trailhead at the end of the road. Many logging spur roads have sprouted off this road. Stay on the main route and continue uphill. Alders are encroaching on the road in some places—rough on a good auto paint job. The last ½ mile of road across a south-facing slope is very rough, suitable only for vehicles with high clearance. By parking at the wide pullouts just before the road switches back and up this slope, one would add only 1 mile round trip to this hike.

The trail is easy to follow from the end of the road, even though it is not shown on recent USGS or Forest Service maps. The first 1½ miles are gentle, but the route becomes steep as it heads almost straight up the west ridge of Mt. Roothaan. (The mountain was named by Jesuit missionaries after a Dutchman who was once Father General of the Jesuits.) Once on top of the ridge, Chimney Rock will be in sight. Some people turn around here. Others will scramble the ridges or—if they have hauled water—there are a couple of small sites on which to camp.

To continue the remaining ¾ mile to Chimney Rock, follow the trail over the ridge. The obvious trail hugs the rocks to the right. But the best route bears slightly left and drops faintly through 20 feet of rocks before becoming obvious again. The trail plunges steeply to the bottom of a

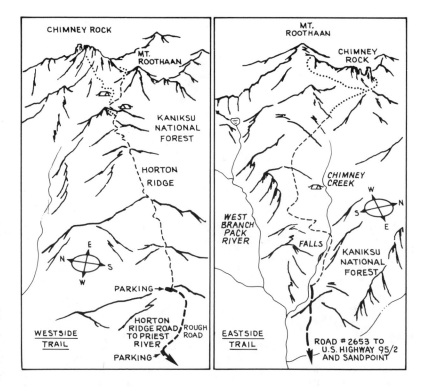

cirque. (This is a north-facing slope which can hold snow in July.) Here there are several small, fragile campsites and seeps of water. From here one basically must scramble through the talus to the base of Chimney Rock. This hike is rated moderately difficult because of steepness and route-finding after the ridge. The hike to that point is moderate.

(From the ridge at which hikers first see Chimney Rock, it's also possible to contour through the talus on the north side of Mt. Roothaan to a notch between Roothaan and the rocky ridge that forms Chimney Rock. This is an easy scramble and the fastest route from Horton Ridge to the east side of Chimney Rock.)

East Route

Round trip hiking distance is 5 moderate miles, gaining 1,880 feet. Use the Mt. Roothaan USGS map; obtain information from the Forest Service Sandpoint Ranger District.

From Sandpoint, follow U.S. Highway 95/2 north for 24 miles and turn west onto Forest Road No. 231 (Pack River Road). Follow Pack River Road 17 miles and turn west onto Forest Road No. 2653. Drop downhill, cross a bridge and go left and uphill for about 2½ miles to the end of the road. Road No. 2653 is primitive and may not be suitable for vehicles with low clearance. A good campsite is situated along the road about 1 mile before the trailhead.

Looking from the east at Chimney Rock, Idaho Selkirks. (Stan Bech photo)

From the end of the road, hike up the hill on an old logging road. Be sure to note the creek cascading down the granite slide to the left about ½ mile up the trail. A short way beyond the creek is a fork in the trail. Go to the left, following the colored flags across the bridge and up the hillside on the trail marked by flags and rock cairns. This part of the trail is another old logging road that gradually peters out as you continue up the ridge. At this point a newly constructed trail takes off, marked by more flags and cairns, going through a few switchbacks to the top of the ridge and following it through huckleberry bushes and small beargrass meadows.

The route crosses a bench, the only possible site for a camp, then heads into areas of granite slabs. After the bench, the route passes through large granite areas and the trail is hard to follow, although still heading in the same general direction marked by flags and cairns.

Finally the head of the canyon is reached, the trees are gone and a small streambed can be followed toward Chimney Rock, which is visible about ¼ mile away, standing alone at the top of the ridge. The last part is a scramble across a small rock slide. Be sure to take drinking water along; little potable water is available.

35 HUNT LAKE

Round trip 2 miles
Hiking time 2–3 hours or
overnight
High point 5,813 feet
Elevation gain 635 feet
Moderately difficult

Hikable July through September
USGS Mt. Roothaan
Information: Idaho State
Department of Lands in
Cavanaugh Bay

Don't be misled by the short mileage on this hike. One will do more hopping than walking, since the route from the trailhead to the lake weaves up a talus slope, marked by painted arrows and cairns. Many hikers will love this hike, but not if they have weak ankles.

There's an advantage to a trail through a talus slope. The Idaho Department of Lands is a timber agency, not a recreation agency. Thus, trails on state land between Priest Lake and the Selkirk Crest are rarely if ever maintained. But while other state land trails (still shown on Kaniksu National Forest maps, which cover this area) are covered with brush and blowdowns, this trail is still open.

From Priest River, Idaho, drive north on State Highway 57 about 21½ miles and turn right toward Coolin. Drive 5⅓ miles to Coolin and turn right on East Shore Road toward Cavanaugh Bay. Continue 7⅛ miles (going from pavement to gravel at Cavanaugh Bay) and turn right onto Hunt Lake Road No. 24. A flurry of logging activity in this area since

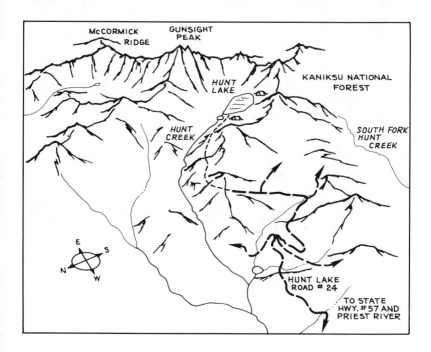

Hunt Lake. (Rich Landers photo)

1985 has produced many spur roads and route changes, making detailed directions from here impossible to publish. (The best bet is to stop at the Idaho Department of Lands office next to the airstrip at Cavanaugh Bay for a look at the latest road map.) As of 1986, one would head up Hunt

Creek Road No. 24, being careful to stay on the main route to a parking area at the end of the best-traveled road above Hunt Creek.

A post marks the trailhead and the trail runs only a few yards before it hits the boulders. Rock cairns or arrows painted on the rocks mark the trail every 50-100 feet. Only a few short stretches get down to earth in the hike up to the lake.

There are no facilities on this hike and no water until one reaches Hunt Lake, which offers fair fishing for small trout. Hikers will find two campsites at the outlet end of the lake and room for a tent or two at the far end near the inlet stream. The rest of the lake is surrounded by brush and boulders.

From the lake, hikers willing to scramble over the rocks and through shoreline brush can make their way up to Gunsight Peak, elev. 7,352 feet, and even southeast through a pass to Fault Lake in the Sundance Burn.

Some hikers might prefer to tent at the full-service campgrounds along the east shore of Priest Lake at Indian Creek or Lionhead State Park and make Hunt Lake a day trip.

LAKE PEND OREILLE
Unprotected

36 LAKE DARLING- MOUNT PEND OREILLE

Round trip 8 miles
Hiking time 5–6 hours or
overnight
High point 6,755 feet
Elevation gain 2,155 feet
Moderate

Hikable mid June through
September
USGS Mt. Pend Oreille
Information: Kaniksu National
Forest, Sandpoint Ranger
District

Hikers out for this 8-mile walk can enjoy a spectrum of attractions usually found only on multi-day backpacks. The route ranges from timbered trails to a mountain lake and up to the high open views from Mt. Pend Oreille.

From Sandpoint, Idaho, head north on U.S. Highway 95 to the intersection with State Highway 200. Continue on Highway 200 toward Clark Fork, Idaho, about 12 miles, and turn left (north) onto Trestle Creek Road No. 275. Drive about 16 miles to where the road hooks into Lightning Creek Road No. 419. Turn left onto Lightning Creek Road for about 1 mile to a sign for Trail Nos. 52 and 161. It's advisable to park here, even though the actual trailhead is 50 yards up the Gordon Creek side road to the left on a hairpin turn.

Trail No. 52 to Lake Darling has a good tread and rises gently to gain 680 feet of elevation in 2 miles. Allow about 1½-2 hours to hike to the lake, especially early in the hiking season when the last ½ mile of trail from the intersection of the South Callahan Creek Trail No. 54 may be

7/17/88 - Steve Petrusky leader. Beautiful bear grass + purple daisys. Tough day - Gordon Crk not maintained, Horrible deadfalls. Lots of macky trail all day. 11 hikers. steves goodies + Paul schroders champane at end, scratched, bitten + very sore at end of day.

107

Lake Darling. (Jim Dowell photo)

wet with snowmelt. There also is one steep section of trail in which 200 feet of elevation is gained in ¼ mile. Several campsites are available along the east shore of the lake.

Some hikers might chose to retrace their steps back to the trailhead for a round trip of 4 miles. But to complete the 8-mile loop, continue west on Trail No. 52 to the intersection with Trail No. 67. Here a Forest Service sign says it is 1½ miles to the summit of Mt. Pend Oreille. The actual distance is about ½ mile, a steady climb which one can hike in about 15 minutes. From the summit at 6,755 feet, one can see the north end of Lake Pend Oreille and Sandpoint to the south and the snowcapped peaks of the Cabinet Range to the east. The remains of an abandoned lookout tower still litter the summit.

To continue the loop, head south on Trail No. 67 toward Lunch Peak. It takes about 45 minutes to hike a little less than 2 miles to the junction with Gordon Creek Trail No. 161. Turn east and hike down the Gordon Creek Trail about 2 more miles, losing nearly 1,700 feet in elevation to the trailhead. This last 2-mile section of trail was not well maintained in 1986 and was covered with brush, requiring about 1 hour to hike.

Hikers who aren't in a big hurry can make an interesting side trip to beautiful Char Falls on the way home. From the junction of Trestle Creek and Lightning Creek roads, continue south on Lightning Creek Road about ½ mile to a large turnout on the east side of the road. (This trail is not marked; if you come to Quartz Creek, you've gone ½ mile too far.) The falls can be heard from the turnout in the road. Walk downhill

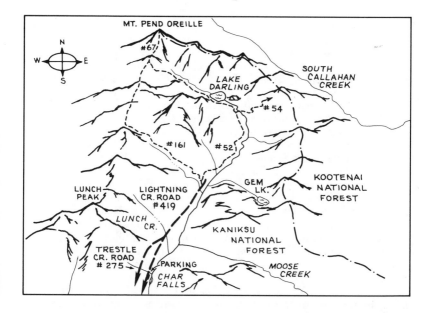

to the east on an old logging road until Lightning Creek can be seen. From there, bushwhack a short way down to the falls. Be careful; the slopes are very steep and Lightning Creek has a lightning-fast current in this area.

LAKE PEND OREILLE
Unprotected

37   LAKE ESTELLE

Round trip 5½ miles
Hiking time 3–4 hours or
   overnight
High point 5,760 feet
Elevation gain 760 feet
Easy

Hikable mid June through mid
   October
USGS Mt. Pend Oreille
Information: Kaniksu National
   Forest, Sandpoint Ranger
   District

An easy, well-maintained 2¾-mile hike from the trailhead into Lake Estelle gives daytrippers an opportunity to get into high country without much sweat or difficulty. Side trails to Blacktail and Moose lakes offer the added opportunity of sampling other small waters. Moose Lake, which is marshy and not high on the list of choice camping areas, is as easy to reach as Lake Estelle by trail but almost 400 feet lower in elevation. The Forest Service annually maintains the trails to Estelle, Moose and Blacktail lakes. The trails are heavily used, so be prepared for company on foot and on horseback. Occasionally, trail bikers go into the area, even though the Forest Service has posted signs that motorized vehicles are prohibited.

To reach the trailhead, drive north through Sandpoint, Idaho. From the junction of U.S. Highway 95 and State Highway 200 just north of Sandpoint, head east on Highway 200 toward Clark Fork, Idaho, and drive about 12 miles. Turn left (north) on Forest Road No. 275 (Trestle Creek Road) away from Lake Pend Oreille and follow it about 16 miles where it hooks into Lightning Creek Road No. 419. Continue another 1½ miles northeast (across a bridge over Lightning Creek) to Moose Creek Road No. 1022. Follow Moose Creek Road southeast for 2 miles to the trailhead.

Trail No. 237 begins in uninspired fashion in a section of forest ringed by nearby clearcuts. However, the scenery quickly improves. From the trailhead it is 2¾ miles to Lake Estelle, 2½ miles to Moose Lake and 3 miles to Blacktail Lake. About ½ mile up the trail, keep an eye out for Trail No. 24 heading right to small Blacktail Lake, elev. 5,560 feet. A little less than a mile from the trailhead, Trail No. 237 continues to Moose Lake, elev. 5,420, while Trail No. 36 bears north toward Lake Estelle.

The right fork to Moose Lake is the easiest of the two. It's about ¾ mile from the junction to Moose Lake and the trail is about as smooth and straight as a bowling lane. Moose Lake, although marshy, is worth seeing for its setting, being nestled into a large open meadow about 1 mile from Moose Mountain.

The main route heading north climbs gradually for 2 miles through old timber to Lake Estelle, a quiet alpine lake at elev. 5,760 feet sheltered on three sides by slopes of carved rock and scree. The scenic high point into the lake occurs about ½ mile past the Moose Lake junction, where the crisp and rugged ridge of hills that make up the Cabinet Mountains can be seen to the east.

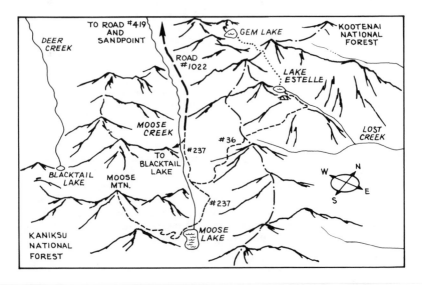

Lake Estelle. (Don Mattoon photo)

From here there is plenty of freedom to explore nearby terrain. From the campsites on the east shore of the lake, one can look across the water to a steep talus slope. It takes about 30 minutes to scramble up this slope 900 feet in elevation where one can follow a course due west (without a marked trail) about ¾ mile to Gem Lake. (There's an easier way to this more solitary lake described in Gem Lake, Hike 38.)

The trail into Lake Estelle avoids almost all the adjoining creeks or springs, so carry in enough water. Black bears occasionally are seen in the area; keep a clean camp. (Note: See Lake Darling, Hike 36, for directions to Char Falls, a side trip off of Lightning Creek Road.)

LAKE PEND OREILLE
Unprotected

38   GEM LAKE

Round trip 2½ miles
Hiking time 2 hours or overnight
High point 5,800 feet
Elevation gain 1,200 feet
Easy

Hikable mid June through mid
October
USGS Mt. Pend Oreille
Information: Kaniksu National
Forest, Sandpoint Ranger
District

Perfect for a quick overnighter or family outing, this is a short walk to a quiet lake in the Cabinet Mountains. It's not in a spectacular setting, but it offers opportunities for peaceful camping, solitude, fishing and side trips, all less than 2 miles from the access road.

From Sandpoint, Idaho, head north on U.S. Highway 95 to the intersection with State Highway 200. Continue on Highway 200 toward

Gem Lake. (Susie McDonald photo)

Clark Fork, Idaho, about 12 miles, and turn left (north) onto Trestle Creek Road No. 275. Drive about 16 miles to where the road hooks into Lightning Creek Road No. 419. Turn left onto Lightning Creek Road for a little more than 1 mile to a sign for Trail No. 554. Plenty of parking is available at the trailhead, which is 50 yards past the intersection of Moose Creek Road No. 1022.

Aside from a few rough spots, the 1¼-mile trail uphill to Gem Lake has a good tread and is reasonably easy to follow. However, it can be brushy in spots. Early in the hiking season it can be muddy from snow-melt. It is closed to motorized vehicles, but often used by equestrians. One campsite with room for four tents is situated at the west end of the

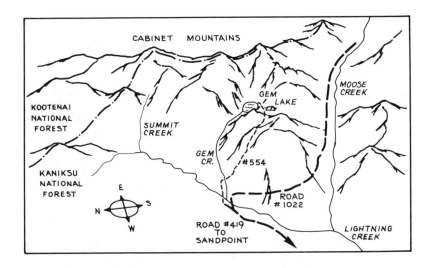

lake. Two smaller campsites can be found near the lake along the trail. The lake offers fair fishing for small trout. (Note: See Lake Darling, Hike 36, for directions to a short side trip to Char Falls.)

LAKE PEND OREILLE
Unprotected

BEE TOP RIDGE

Round trip 11 miles
Hiking time 8 hours
High point 6,212 feet
Elevation gain 3,892 feet
Moderately difficult

Hikable June through September
USGS Clark Fork
Information: Kaniksu National
  Forest, Sandpoint Ranger
  District

This dayhike north of Lake Pend Oreille offers rewarding views of the lake region for those willing to endure a major dose of uphill walking. The breeze high on the ridges can be particularly pleasing on summer days when the lowlands are hot and muggy. Forest Service archeologist Cort Sims reports that Indians once considered the high vistas overlooking Lake Pend Oreille important in communicating with spirits. As a rite of passage, an Indian youth would climb up to a high point and stay there until he received a vision from a spirit. A rock cairn was built to mark the spot where the vision was received. These cairns are fairly common in the Bee Top area. (See also Kettle Crest South, Hike 7.)

From Sandpoint, Idaho, head east on State Highway 200 toward Clark Fork, Idaho. Drive about 25 miles and turn left just before the Lightning Creek Bridge (metal truss) onto the State Fish Hatchery Road. Drive 2¼ miles, turn right onto a private road and go about 1¼ miles to an inter-

Bee Top Mountain. (Don Mattoon photo)

section. Turn right then immediately turn left onto what looks like a private drive. Drive 300 yards past a house and look for the trailhead sign on the left.

Trail No. 120 begins as an excellent footpath and heads uphill at an efficient grade. Much of the trail is in shade, which is welcome on these south-facing slopes in summer. Open sections offer increasingly better views back toward Lake Pend Oreille. Water is scarce in summer; take full water bottles. A small trickle of water usually runs across the trail at about 3,500 feet, but it's not reliable. The trail gains the skyline of a ridge at about 3 miles and leads through beargrass (spectacular when blooming in early July) ½ mile to the junction with Trail No. 63, which

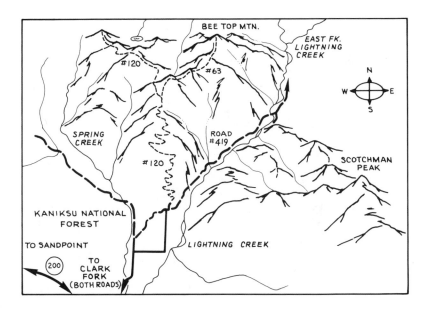

leads to Bee Top Mountain. Be alert for the Bee Top trail, since it is seldom used and the signs are not regularly maintained. Bear right onto Trail No. 63 and walk about ¾ mile to a high point for a splendid view of the area—a choice spot for a break before continuing the 1¼-mile ridge run to Bee Top's summit. The remains of a lookout burned down by the Forest Service in 1966 still can be found on the mountain.

For additional hiking, one can continue north on Trail No. 120 from the junction with Trail No. 63 for several miles of good ridge walking toward Cougar Peak.

LAKE PEND OREILLE
Unprotected

40   SCOTCHMAN PEAK

Round trip 6 miles
Hiking time 4–6 hours
High point 7,009 feet
Elevation gain 3,730 feet
Moderately difficult

Hikable late June through
  September
USGS Clark Fork
Information: Kaniksu National
  Forest, Sandpoint Ranger
  District

One has to think a bit like a mountain goat to enjoy this hike. The trail heads relentlessly uphill, but hikers are rewarded with one of the best vistas in the area, formerly the site of a Forest Service lookout. During the 30 years the lookout was used, two of its watchmen were struck and killed by lightning in separate incidents. The peak lies within a RARE II study area and a region that has been proposed for wilderness.

From Sandpoint, Idaho, take State Highway 200 to Clark Fork, Idaho. Turn left (north) on Main Street, which is marked as a national forest entrance. Follow this street, which becomes Forest Road No. 276, for slightly more than 2½ miles. Turn right on a good logging road following the signs toward Trail No. 65. Continue 1 mile and turn left. Drive just less than ½ mile and turn left again on a minor logging road. This road winds its way through a logging area and clearcuts ascending two major hills with switchbacks for 2⅛ miles. Turn left again and drive ⅛ mile to the trailhead. The roads are suitable for passenger vehicles with good clearance.

Scotchman Peak Trail No. 65 is periodically maintained by the Forest Service and is open to both hikers and horsemen, although horses generally would have difficulty on the route because of blowdowns. Take plenty of water. No dependable water sources are available late in the season. The trail ascends sharply for the first mile, then switchbacks up the broad ridge crest for 1,800 vertical feet. Long easy switchbacks cut through the alpine forest and beargrass slopes below the top of Scotchman Peak. The trail passes through south-facing meadows that are dappled with colorful wildflowers in spring and splashed with red and orange in the fall. Then it intercepts the rocky west ridge and follows it to the summit. Remains of the old lookout are evident at the top

Lake Pend Oreille from near the top of Scotchman Peak. (Jerry Pavia photo)

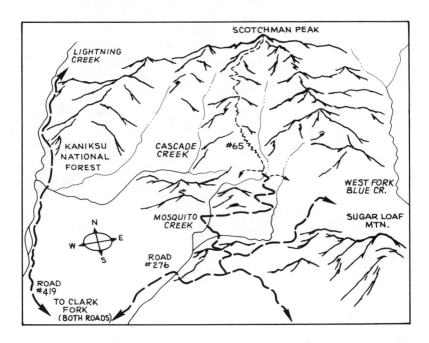

where views of the Selkirk Mountains and Lake Pend Oreille along with Cabinet Mountains peaks such as "A" Peak and Snowshoe Peak. Hikers have stacked large flat rocks to make a small wind hut just below the old lookout site.

LAKE PEND OREILLE
Unprotected

41 GREEN MONARCH RIDGE

Round trip 6 miles	Hikable mid June through
Hiking time 3–5 hours	September
High point 5,082 feet	USGS Packsaddle Mountain
Elevation gain 400 feet	Information: Kaniksu National
Moderately difficult	Forest, Sandpoint Ranger
	District

This is an undulating ridge hike that leads to a breathtaking view down an almost vertical cliff 3,000 feet above scenic Lake Pend Oreille. Big sailboats and cabin cruisers look like specks below. The town of Hope is a smudge in the distance surrounded by peaks in the Selkirk and Cabinet mountains.

From Sandpoint, Idaho, drive 25 miles northeast on State Highway 200 to Clark Fork, Idaho. Go through town, turn right at the forest access sign toward Johnson Creek Road. Cross the Clark Fork River and

Lake Pend Oreille from Green Monarch Ridge. (Rich Landers photo)

turn right on Johnson Creek Road toward Lakeview. Drive 7 miles and bear right at a Y in the road. Go 2¼ miles and turn right on Forest Road No. 278. Drive about 20 yards and turn right into a parking area, which was once a staging area for a logging operation. Park here and walk north past the slash heaps to the trailhead (which could be relocated slightly by 1987). At first the trail is a skid road crossed with ditches to prevent vehicle access. After ¼ mile, the road splits. Take the left skid road, which heads up the side of a hill. Near the top, the trail bears left into the timber. Look for surveyor's tape to help spot the trail. Once in the timber, the trail becomes a good footpath. It undulates up and down several humps in the ridge, offering only brief looks at the lake to

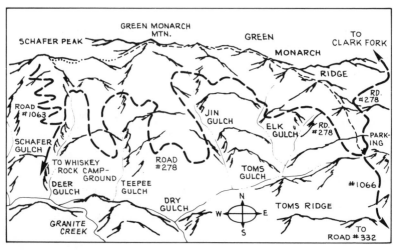

the right. Finally, just before the top of Green Monarch Mountain is an open area with a spectacular view of the northeast arm of the lake.

It's a short way farther up the trail to the top of Green Monarch Mountain and another scenic view, albeit marred by recent roads and clearcuts on the south side of Schafer Peak. This is the turn around for this hike, but the trail continues 1½ miles to Schafer Peak, where the old fire lookout was sold to a Clark Fork farmer and removed in 1976.

SPOKANE RIVER
Riverside State Park

42   SPOKANE RIVER

Round trip 5 miles
Hiking time 2–3 hours
High point 1,640 feet
Elevation gain 40 feet
Easy

Hikable April through November
USGS Spokane NW, Airway
    Heights
Information: Riverside State Park

This is a popular hike among people of all ages, beginning near the unique basalt formations known as the Bowl and Pitcher along the Spokane River just northwest of Spokane. The trail leads away from the noise of the campground and picnic area to quiet retreats along the river in Riverside State Park, which was established in 1933. Buttercups, grass widows and balsamroot are among the many plants hikers will enjoy during spring. On hot summer days, the river is always close enough for a quick dip, although one should be extremely careful around the Bowl and Pitcher and Devil's Toenail Rapids, where the water is particu-

Spokane River and a portion of Bowl and Picture rock formations, Riverside State Park. (Rich Landers photo)

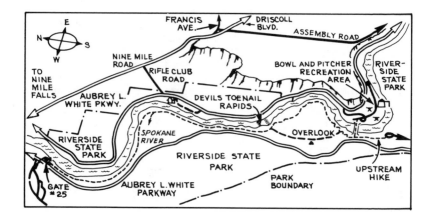

larly swift and dangerous.

From northwest Spokane, drive west on Francis Avenue to Assembly Street, where Francis becomes Nine Mile Road. Continue northwest on Nine Mile Road ¾ mile and turn left at the intersection which is well marked as an entrance to Riverside State Park. Drive ½ mile and turn left on Rifle Club Road. Go another 1½ miles to the Bowl and Pitcher Recreation Area and drive downhill to the picknickers' parking lot. Hikers should park here, walk the short way to the Spokane River and cross the suspension bridge over the frothing rapids to the trailhead.

To hike the downstream section of this trail, bear right past the picnic shelter and continue up behind the rocks that form the huge Bowl and Pitcher basalt formations along the river. The trail passes an outhouse and picnic sites before winding away from the activity. The trail becomes wide like a road; but after ½ mile it bends back toward the river, where one can hear the roar of Devil's Toenail Rapids. Bear right, off the road-like trail and onto a good footpath that leads to an overlook of the rapids. From here the trail continues downstream along the river, eventually leaving the river and paralleling Aubrey White Parkway. Then it passes the Spokane Rifle Club (across the river) and becomes wide like a road. At a Y, where the road goes left, bear right on the trail. (Trails forking to the left are horse trails that lead out to the parkway.) About ¾ mile later, the trail climbs steeply to the parkway. (The river trail ends here, but one can cross the road at Gate No. 25 and explore many miles of horse trails.) Backtrack to the suspension bridge for a round trip of 5 miles.

Although this is a river trail, it can be hot and dry. No drinking water is available beyond the Bowl and Pitcher picnic and camping area.

To hike the shorter but just-as-pleasant upstream portion of this trail, walk from the parking area, cross the suspension bridge and turn left at the picnic shelter. Follow the trail a short way and bear right as it skirts the bottom of a steep slope of scree. From here on, several horse trails intersect the river trail. When in doubt, take the trail that stays closest to the river. Trails branching away from the river will lead toward a public horse stable about a mile away. From the picnic shelter, the trail follows the river upstream 1 mile before it comes out in a large opening and connects with a road system, which includes more horse trails and a running trail leading to the Spokane Falls Community College area. Backtrack from here for a round trip of 2 miles, which can easily be walked in under two hours.

SPOKANE RIVER
Riverside State Park

43 LITTLE SPOKANE RIVER

Round trip 5 miles
Hiking time 3–4 hours
High point 2,200 feet
Elevation gain 200 feet
Moderate

Hikable April through November
USGS Dartford
Information: Washington State
   Parks Department

The Little Spokane River Valley is one of the most scenic and wildliferich areas in the Spokane area. The spring-fed river is ripe with trout (plus squawfish and carp) and waterfowl and the cover along the shores

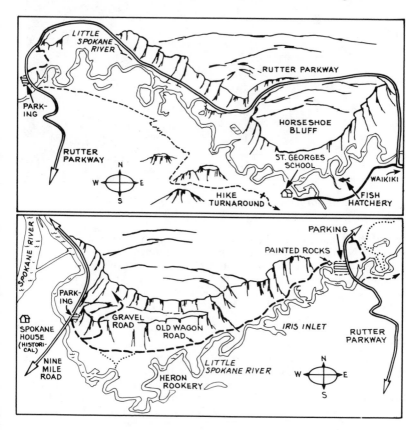

Paddlers seen from Little Spokane River Trail. (Rich Landers photo)

is still thick enough to hold white-tailed deer. But even though developers have been watching the area like circling vultures, Spokane County Parks Director Sam Angove along with river residents Morey and Margaret Haggin and others, ended 15 years of buying, swapping and negotiating in 1985 to secure a 1,500-acre preserve. The area is now managed by the state as Little Spokane River State Park.

Hikers should be gentle with the area. The Indian Painted Rocks near the trailhead hold delicate petroglyphs, waterfowl nest along the river in spring, and a fragile rookery in towering cottonwoods is a nursery for a raucous spring hatch of young great blue herons. Park rules prohibit pets, vehicles, fires and camping along the trails.

From Francis Avenue in northwest Spokane, turn north on Indian Trail Road and proceed 5 miles to Rutter Parkway. Stay to the right at a fork in the road and soon begin to head down toward the Little Spokane

River. Drive past the east trailhead, cross the bridge and park in the Painted Rocks area.

Walk back to the south side of the river and turn left (east) to the trailhead at a fence gate, which is about 200 yards from the parking area. The hike begins in a meadow and heads upstream along the Little Spokane River. The path soon enters woods from which the river can be seen intermittently. The variety in terrain makes this a pleasant hike from grassy meadows to coniferous woods to higher, drier, sunnier slopes. Then the trail becomes hard to follow on a ridge overlooking a small sand dune and St. George's School. One could continue from here to a parking area near the school, but most hikers return from here for a round trip of 5 miles.

Another easy hike, 4 miles round trip, can be made along the trail heading west from the Painted Rocks, downstream along the Little Spokane River to its confluence with the Spokane River. The hike is gentle, bordered by the river to the south and granite cliffs to the north. From March through June, hikers should give a wide berth to the heron rookery, which is about 1 mile downstream from Painted Rocks. Biologists say disturbances can frighten nesting herons and cause them to injure themselves or even to abandon their young.

The hike is colored with lupine, shooting stars, mountain bluebells and other decorative wildflowers. Occasional side trails lead toward the river, where there is a splendid display of blooming yellow iris in spring. The iris is not native. It was introduced by a river resident years ago and has spread up- and downstream. Also in the area is camas, the roots of which were once gathered as a staple by Indian tribes. About ½ mile from the end of the trail at State Highway 291, the footpath widens into an old wagon road and a gravel road heads up the hill to the north.

SPOKANE RIVER
Spokane County Parks

44 DISHMAN HILLS NATURAL AREA

Round trip 4 miles
Hiking time 2–3 hours
High point 2,300 feet
Elevation gain 100 feet
Moderate

Hikable late March through
   October
USGS Spokane NE
Information: Dishman Hills
   Natural Area Association

Thanks to a handful of people with the foresight to recognize the value of a natural preserve within an ever-growing metropolitan area, the 450-acre Dishman Hills Natural Area lives on naturally, surrounded by the burgeoning development of the Spokane Valley. Since 1966, when a newspaper story told of a high school teacher's crusade to permanently preserve a few acres adjacent to the city of Spokane, many people have hiked and enjoyed this pleasant mini-wilderness.

Tom Rogers, the father of the Dishman Hills, retired from teaching in the '70s. But in 1986, at the age of 72, he led the winning battle against the odds of raising $154,000 to secure the last 140 acres needed to keep the area intact. With the cooperation of Spokane County Parks Director Sam Angove and The Nature Conservancy, the area now is a condo-proof preserve crisscrossed with trails and blessed with wildlife. It is particularly inviting in spring, when wildflowers splash the pine-studded hills with color. Rogers has documented nearly 400 species of plants in the area and 72 varieties of mushrooms, more than 100 species of birds and 50 different butterflies.

This hike is only a sampling of the trails carved into this mini-wilderness. We have purposely left some trails uncharted so hikers can explore the Dishman Hills on their own.

Access 1: From Interstate 90 in Spokane, take East Sprague Exit No. 285 and drive east on Sprague Avenue 1¾ miles to Sargent Road. Turn right (south) on Sargent. The pavement ends after one block, but continue about ½ mile to the buildings and parking area at Camp Caro.

Access 2: From I-90, take the Argonne Exit. Go one mile south on Argonne to Sprague Avenue and turn right (west). Drive under the underpass ⅓ mile and turn left (south) on Sargent Road. Drive about ½ mile to Camp Caro.

Follow the trail from the Camp Caro parking area ⅛ mile to a T. Turn right and descend into Enchanted Ravine. The trail goes through trees and rock formations where birds are numerous and wildflowers abound in the spring. The trail loses and gains elevation several times as it meanders through the hills. After ¼ mile there will be another T. Turn right (west) to East and West Ponds which are just over a mile from the trailhead. For a shorter hike, return to the parking area from this point.

One can continue west on the trail past the ponds. At 2 miles there is a Y. The left branch returns to East and West Ponds. The right goes up a rocky slope to 2,300 feet. At 2¼ miles from the trailhead, one can see the 2,400-foot high point of the Dishman Hills ahead, which is an easy

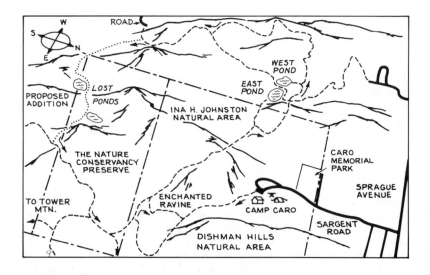

Arrowleaf balsamroot in Dishman Hills Natural Area. (Rich Landers photo)

scramble. Continue the short distance to the next Y and take the left branch to Lost Ponds. At approximately 2¾ miles the trail goes between two Lost Ponds, sometimes dry late in the season. The various ponds in Dishman Hills are tranquil spots with cottonwood trees reflected in the water.

The trail then goes through conifers and past high mossy banks. Turn right at the trail junction encountered early in the hike and walk ½ mile back to Camp Caro.

Plant and animal life is protected in the area; no fires are allowed and no pets. Camping and picnicking are permitted only at Camp Caro. No drinking water is available in the hills. Restrooms have been installed at Camp Caro and at Edgecliff Park.

For information about scheduling group outings or meetings at Camp Caro, call the Spokane County Parks Deptartment, (509) 456-4730. For more information about the Hills, write Dishman Hills Natural Area Association, E10820 Maxwell, Spokane, WA 99206. DHNA is maintained jointly by County Parks and the Dishman Hills Natural Area Association. The association still makes quarterly payments of $6,340 on the land. Contributors are welcome.

SPOKANE RIVER
Spokane County Parks

45   LIBERTY LAKE

Round trip 6 miles
Hiking time 4 hours
High point 4,200 feet
Elevation gain 2,000 feet
Moderately difficult

Hikable late May through
   September
USGS Mica Peak, Liberty Lake
Information: Spokane County
   Parks Department

Liberty Lake County Park is a popular picnicking area, with a swimming beach, cooking shelters, playground, campsites and volleyball nets. But few people realize the park extends far beyond the facilities through a timbered mountain preserve. This hike meanders up Liberty Creek and along a hillside through the park. It's a cool, quiet retreat, first through cottonwoods and Ponderosa pines, then through Douglas firs and cedars.

Drive east from Spokane on Interstate 90. Take the Liberty Lake exit. Turn right on Liberty Lake Road, then immediately turn left (east) on Mission Avenue. Drive ¾ mile and turn right (south) on Molter Street. Drive ¾ mile and turn left (east) on Valleyway. It is 2⅓ miles from here to the entrance of Liberty Lake County Park. (Note that Valleyway becomes Lakeside Road when it bends to the right around the east end of Liberty Lake Golf Course.) Turn right off Lakeside Road at the park sign.

When the park is open, June through September, hikers can drive past the toll booth straight ahead to the day-use parking area and walk to the trailhead, which is at the southeast end of the camping area near

Liberty Lake from Liberty Creek Trail. (Rich Landers photo)

RV campsite No. 21. During the months the park is closed, as in late May when spring wildflowers are at their peak, park on the hill above the park entrance by the water tower; hike down the road to the park entrance and through to the campground and trailhead.

The first portion of the trail offers easy hiking on an old road, crossing Liberty Creek on footbridges and passing several picnic sites. It's about 1½ miles to a large walk-in picnic area and campsites in a grove of cedars. Cross the creek on the footbridge to the right and start switchbacking up the hillside. From here on, the trail narrows. On the last switchback, hikers will get a glimpse of Liberty Lake before the trail heads farther up into the drainage.

The trail leads out onto the side of a ridge which is open for a view into Idaho. Hikers will climb a short stepladder up a ledge, walk through an open area and down into the woods again. The path soon works its way up to a log bridge, complete with welcome handrails, that crosses high above a cool waterfall. During spring runoff, the waterfall pounds down with considerable volume. From here the trail proceeds uphill again with numerous switchbacks through cool woods with one additional stream crossing. The trail can be vague in a few places, but it finally comes to an old cabin site and leads to an old road. Turn right on this road for a downhill return toward the campground. (Park plans call for

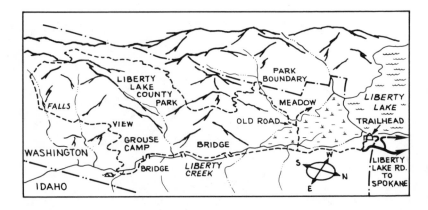

an 8-mile cross-country skiing trail to be built in this area by 1988.) Once down to the meadow area, there are two more stream crossings, then a grassy stretch before the trail returns to the trailhead.

Restroom facilities and drinking water are available only in the park campground area, with the exception of one primitive outhouse about 1¼ miles from the trailhead at the beginning of the hike.

MOUNT SPOKANE
Mount Spokane State Park

46 MOUNT SPOKANE-MOUNT KIT CARSON

Round trip 2–4 miles
Hiking time 1–3 hours
High point 5,282 feet
Elevation gain 360 feet
Moderate

Hikable mid June through
  October
USGS Mt. Spokane, Mt. Kit
  Carson
Information: Mt. Spokane State
  Park

This is an excellent dayhike in one of the highest areas around Spokane, with most of the elevation gained in a vehicle en route through Mt. Spokane State Park to the trailhead. The hike can be geared to any hiker's whim with three options on how to get to the best scenic views within a 45-minute drive of Spokane.

From U.S. Highway 2 north of Spokane, turn east on well marked Mt. Spokane Road (State Highway 206) to Mt. Spokane State Park. Pass the park headquarters and drive steeply uphill about 3 miles. At the saddle and parking area just before the road begins to go downhill to the alpine ski areas, turn left on the Summit Road. Drive up about 2 miles to Cook's Cabin (an abandoned ski lodge) and turn left off the paved road onto a gravel road. Follow the signs to the Civilian Conservation Corps Campground (about 5½ miles from the State Park entrance). Turn left again off the gravel road into the camping area. Here a log picnic shelter is equipped with a fireplace and woodstove with nearby picnic tables, pit toilets and water spigots.

The trailhead is not marked, but can be found by proceeding directly west from the picnic shelter on a well-defined path and crossing the Kit Carson Loop Road. The trail drops steeply for about ¼ mile and again crosses the Kit Carson Loop Road. Look for the trail entering the forest about 50 yards to the right.

After several hundred yards of uphill climbing, the trail forks. Here there are three options.

Option 1: A short hike requiring 40-60 minutes round trip. Bear right at the main fork. Stay on the main trail which continues up a fairly steep incline. The trail will begin to moderate and follow a rounded ridge top directly to the rocky summit of Kit Carson, elev. 5,282 feet.

Option 2: A longer loop hike requiring 60-90 minutes with a possible side trip to Day Mountain, elev. 5,057 feet. Again, bear right at the first fork in the main trail. About 150 yards up this trail is another smaller trail leading off to the right. Follow this small trail as it winds through the forest. A second fork farther along the route is signed—go left to Mt. Kit Carson, or straight ahead for the Day Mountain side trip. The left (Kit Carson) route intersects the main (Option 1) trail about 50 yards from the summit of Kit Carson. Turn right at this intersection to reach the summit.

Option 3: Another 60-90 minute loop. From the main trail, take the left fork, which actually is the remnant of an old road. The trail opens into Grouse Meadow—a large meadow dotted with wildflowers. Watch for a small trail which winds its way up through the meadow to the right (see Mt. Spokane-Day Mountain, Hike 47). Depending on maintenance schedules, the trail can vanish in the grass partway up. Continue up the slope until gaining the summit of Mt. Kit Carson—a rocky outcropping with views of the Selkirk and Cabinet mountains to the east. To com-

Grouse Meadows on the flank of Mount Kit Carson near Mount Spokane. (Gary Cassel photo)

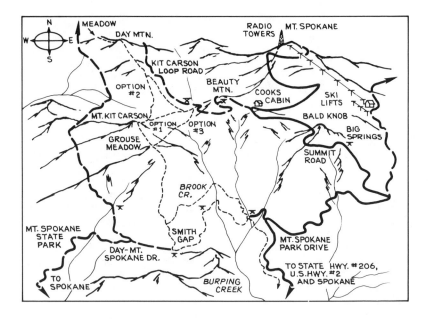

plete the hike, follow the ridge trail (Option 1) or loop trail (Option 2) back to the starting point. Be prepared for downfall on all three routes. Beargrass is abundant and especially lovely in late June and early July.

The map brochure available from the Mt. Spokane State Park office is a good guide to the roads in the park, but trails are not accurately marked. The USGS maps show some trails that are no longer maintained and omit other trails described in this hike.

MOUNT SPOKANE
Mount Spokane State Park

MOUNT SPOKANE-
DAY MOUNTAIN

Round trip 10 miles
Hiking time 7 hours
High point 5,282 feet
Elevation gain 2,060 feet
Moderately difficult

Hikable mid June to mid October
USGS Mt. Spokane, Mt. Kit
Carson
Information: Mt. Spokane State
Park

This is a long hike for those who want a top-to-bottom look at Mt. Spokane State Park, a preserve that caps one of the highest peaks in the Spokane area. It leads up a cool creek to sweeping views of the Spokane area from open meadows where grass and wildflowers can grow hip high.

From U.S. Highway 2 north of Spokane, turn east on well-marked Mt. Spokane Road (State Highway 206) to Mt. Spokane State Park. The trailhead is on the left about ½ mile past the park headquarters. Although there may not be a trailhead sign, it is easily located by the picnic table and bulletin board on the right side of the road.

The trail climbs steeply for ½ mile to a junction with a pack trail. Follow the pack trail as it gently rises and at times comes within 30 feet of the paved road heading to the summit of Mt. Spokane. The trail passes a woodland spring with trilliums and a bridge over Burping Brook, where a small but noisy waterfall runs over the rocks. The trail intersects the Day-Mt. Spokane Road at a picnic area by Burping Brook. Cross the creek on the road. The trail takes off again next to the outhouse. After a few switchbacks uphill, the trail heads westward, leaving the Burping Brook drainage and entering the Brook Creek drainage. This trail ends after a mile, intersecting with another trail that runs north from the Smith Gap picnic area. Turn right and head uphill.

The trail climbs steeply ½ mile to Grouse Meadow. The large meadow and wide view of the Spokane Valley make this a pleasant lunch spot. The trail can be faint here. Follow the meadow north and upward to a rock outcrop on the left side. This is the summit of Mt. Kit Carson. Continue ¼ mile northeast then turn due north on a trail through the trees

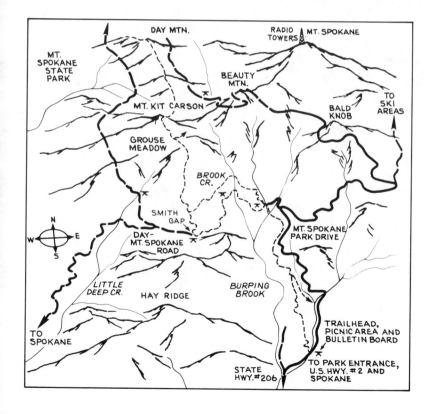

On the trail to Mount Kit Carson. (Gary Cassel photo)

to Day Mountain. Stay on top of this broad ridge as it gently drops. A small, isolated meadow on the northwest side of the mountain offers an excellent view of the Kettle Mountains in Washington, the Selkirks in Idaho and the Cabinets in Montana. Return to the trailhead by the same route.

48   MINERAL RIDGE

Round trip 3⅓ miles	Hikable April through October
Hiking time 2–4 hours	USGS Mt. Coeur d'Alene
High point 2,760 feet	Information: U.S. Bureau of Land
Elevation gain 620 feet	Management, Coeur d'Alene
Moderate	office

From humble beginnings at a picnic area on Lake Coeur d'Alene's Beauty Bay, a gentle ribbon of trail snakes its way up an arm of the mountain known as Mineral Ridge. This 3⅓-mile trail, managed by the U.S. Bureau of Land Management, is one of the prettiest hikes in the Inland Northwest, suitable for a wide spectrum of hiking abilities. One who is purely after exercise could put the trail away in less than two hours.

To reach the trailhead, drive east from Coeur d'Alene, Idaho, on Interstate 90 and turn off at Wolf Lodge Exit No. 22. At the stop sign, turn right toward Harrison. Drive 2¼ miles around the Wolf Lodge arm of Lake Coeur d'Alene and look for the Mineral Ridge parking and picnic area on the left across from Beauty Bay. Water and restrooms are open here during summer.

Guidebooks often are available at the trailhead. They are keyed to each of the 22 trailside stations and explain basic principles of tree and plant identification, forest management, geology and mining practices.

The trail gently switchbacks 1½ miles to the top of the ridge, where there's a simple shelter called Caribou Cabin and an open area with a view of Wolf Lodge Bay, perfect for a snack or picnic. The ridge is honeycombed with old, shallow mining tunnels as well as pit mines, mostly obliterated now. A side trail on the way to Caribou Cabin leads to the main entrance of a mine (now a favorite hideout for chipmunks).

From Caribou Cabin, the trail follows the ridge gently downhill to a splendid viewpoint overlooking Beauty Bay. (Hikers willing to stomp

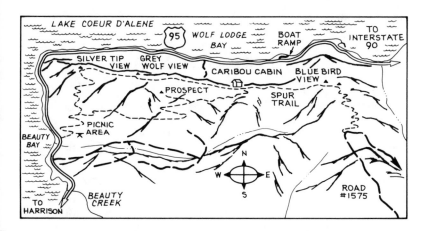

Lake Coeur d'Alene from Mineral Ridge. (Rich Landers photo)

through snow in December often can use this vista to spot bald eagles, which visit Lake Coeur d'Alene each winter to feast on spawning kokanee salmon.) From this viewpoint, the trail switchbacks steeply to the parking area.

COEUR D'ALENE RIVER
Unprotected

CHILCO MOUNTAIN

Round trip 10 miles
Hiking time 4–5 hours
High point 5,665 feet
Elevation gain 1,505 feet
Moderate

Hikable mid May to mid October
USGS Athol
Information: Coeur d'Alene
    National Forest, Fernan Ranger
    District

From the summit of Chilco Mountain, one can see Lake Pend Oreille and Lake Coeur d'Alene, mountain lakes that are as beautiful as they are big. The hike is a perfect alpine escape for people visiting one of the

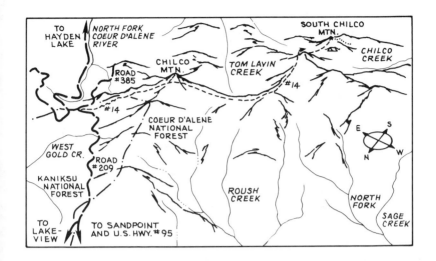

Idaho lakes. Few people hike this route to one of the most often seen but still largely unrecognized peaks in the area.

From Coeur d'Alene, head north on U.S. Highway 95 toward Sandpoint. Drive about 15 miles and turn right onto Bunco Road No. 209. (The intersection is just south of Henley Aerodrome.) Drive about 14 miles, staying on Road No. 209. Look for a trailhead sign on the right at

Chilco Mountain, Lake Pend Oreille in the background. (Sam Schlieder photo)

the junction with Forest Road No. 385. Two short concrete posts mark the entrance to Trail No. 14.

The maintained trail climbs and switchbacks through timber for 1¾ miles until it reaches the ridge running north from Chilco Mountain, one of the highest peaks in the area at elev. 5,635 feet. Here the trail splits. Left goes ¼ mile to the summit of Chilco Mountain and the right fork switchbacks down and crosses the west face of the mountain. The trail drops to a saddle and then climbs to South Chilco Mountain. (Mileage for this hike is based on returning from here, although one could continue south 1 mile to Forest Road No. 406 at the head of Chilco Creek.) Both summits offer good views of Pend Oreille, Hayden and Coeur d'Alene lakes and the Spokane Valley. No water is available along the trail, although there are sites suitable for camping in the saddle between the two summits and on top of South Chilco.

COEUR D'ALENE RIVER
Unprotected

50   INDEPENDENCE CREEK

Round trip 13 miles
Hiking time 5 hours or overnight
High point 4,600 feet
Elevation gain 1,641 feet
Moderate

Hikable mid July through mid
   October
USGS Cathedral Peak, Lakeview
Information: Coeur d'Alene
   National Forest, Fernan Ranger
   District

When the sun bears down in July and August, this is a particularly appealing hike for visitors in Upper Coeur d'Alene River country. The trail crosses Independence Creek 19 times, making sneakers the most practical footwear. Once the runoff is over in late June, it's refreshing simply to splash through the creek and keep on going. Much of Trail No. 22 follows the route of one of the first logging/mining roads in the area, where the hillsides are still studded with decaying snags from the great fire of 1910. The trail offers easy access to backcountry abundant with wildlife. Watch for signs of black bears, deer, elk, coyotes, hawks and owls. The several side trails merging into the Independence trail are used mostly by hunters in the fall.

The best access is from Interstate 90. Take Kingston Exit No. 43 just west of Kellogg, Idaho, and head north on Forest Road No. 9 (Coeur d'Alene River Road). Drive 24 miles to Prichard, where the road becomes No. 208. Continue 26 miles to where the road turns into gravel and becomes No. 6310. Continue for 3⅓ miles and turn right on Forest Road No. 3099 (just before crossing Independence Creek). Go ⅓ mile and turn left on Forest Road No. 925 to the head of Trail No. 22, where there is a camping area and pit toilet.

To reach the trail from the north via a slow, rough ride over Weber Saddle, take State Highway 95 north from Coeur d'Alene to milepost No. 446 and turn east on Bunco Road. Drive 20 miles to Forest Road No. 332

Independence Creek. (Sam Schlieder photo)

to the trailhead at the junction with Forest Road No. 904.

From the south trailhead at Independence Creek campground (elev. 3,000 feet) Trail No. 22 leads away from the creek and makes its most strenuous gain in elevation. The first ½ mile is a 200-foot climb through a forest of lodgepole pine and Douglas fir before dropping back down to the creek. From this high point, and others along the way, one has a good view of the meandering creek below. The trail follows the creek through forest and open meadows, which make ideal picnicking and camping sites.

Crossing small Trident Creek, the trail levels off and stays near Independence Creek. At 1¼ miles, pass Minor Creek and the junction with Trail No. 404. In another 300 yards, the trail crosses Emerson Creek and a junction with Trail No. 56. Continue up Independence Creek on Trail No. 22, crossing a meadow and making the first of many creek crossings. Passing the site of an old splash dam, the trail recrosses the creek twice, travels a short distance then crosses once more. (Early spring crossings could be tricky with high, fast water). Again on the north side of the creek, the trail enters a meadow then traverses the base of the canyon ridge, crosses Green Creek then Griffith Creek in succession and returns to ford Independence Creek once more.

At this point, if not before, hikers are advised to switch from boots to tennis shoes, if they have them, as the trail will cross the creek 12 times in the next 2 miles. The trail continues on level grade, crosses the creek four times in a little over ¼ mile then meets Trail No. 413 which originates on Faset Peak. Trail No. 22 continues, crosses Ermine Creek and Independence Creek eight more times and then emerges from the dense creek-side forest cover to a large meadow. This beautiful area known as Snowbird Meadows lies at about the halfway point on the trip and offers excellent camping. A road enters this spot from Hamilton Mountain; however, it is not frequently used.

From Snowbird Meadows, the trail continues up Independence Creek which it fords for the last time a short distance above the road. The trail grade is level as it crosses meadowed country scattered with huge larch snags. A mile beyond Snowbird, the trail meets Trail No. 418 from Faset Peak then enters dense spruce, lodgepole pine and Douglas fir. The trail crosses Surprise Creek and passes a junction with Trail No. 416 also from Faset Peak. The trail here swings away from Independence Creek and then meets Camp Creek where there are some good campsites. Just beyond Camp Creek, the trail passes a junction with Trail No. 3, which heads up Independence Creek for 3 miles, while Trail No. 22 begins a moderate climb out of Independence Canyon. The trail crosses rocky open slopes then enters mixed timber and slowly widens to become an old road. The trail follows this old road for about 2 miles to the north trailhead at Weber Saddle on Forest Road No. 332.

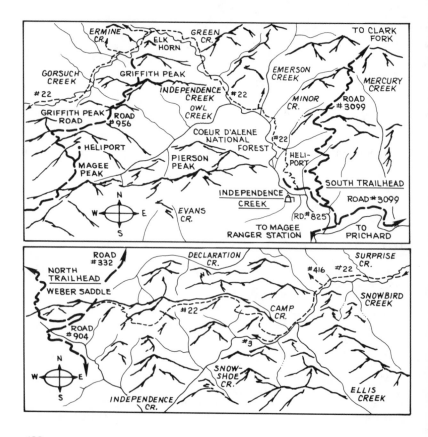

Fly fishing on the north section of the Upper Coeur d'Alene River. (Rich Landers photo)

COEUR D'ALENE RIVER
Unprotected

COEUR D'ALENE RIVER NORTH

One way 8 miles
Hiking time 4–8 hours or
overnight
High point 3,380 feet
Elevation gain 350 feet
Moderate

Hikable May through October
USGS Cathedral Peak, Jordan
Creek
Information: Coeur d'Alene
National Forest, Wallace
Ranger District

Coeur d'Alene River Trail No. 20 appeals to dayhikers, overnighters and fly fishers alike. It parallels the upper Coeur d'Alene River for about 14 miles. (Be aware that most locals still call the upper Coeur d'Alene River the "North Fork of the Coeur d'Alene River." Forest Service and USGS maps officially show the Coeur d'Alene River north of Interstate 90 as having three forks: the main stem, the North Fork and the South Fork. People who live in this region, however, refer to the Coeur d'Alene River above the South Fork as the North Fork. What the maps list as the North Fork—the stream that meets the main channel about 5 miles north of Enaville—is locally known as the Little North Fork.) Occasionally the trail comes down to the river, but for most of the way it looms several hundred feet above it. Serviceberries, huckleberries and wildflowers are profuse in some areas and the stream is full of native cutthroat trout. Anglers rugged enough to bust the brush steeply down from the trail can find excellent fishing. However, regulations don't allow anglers to keep fish in this section of the river. Anglers must use

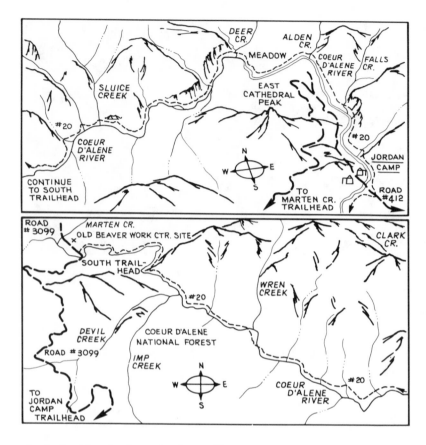

single, barbless hooks and release all trout.

The trail most logically is broken into two hikes, one beginning from the south end of the trail off Road No. 208 and heading north to Jordan Camp. (See Hike 52.) This hike, however, begins at Jordan Camp and goes to Road No. 3099 near Marten Creek. Both hikes, which pass through areas devastated by the great 1910 fire, are excellent for either dayhiking or camping.

To hike the north portion of the trail, take Kingston Exit No. 43 off I-90 (just west of Kellogg) and head north along the east side of the Coeur d'Alene River on paved Forest Highway No. 9. Drive about 23 miles to Prichard and bear left on Forest Road No. 208. About 3 miles past Avery Creek picnic area, turn right onto Forest Road No. 412 at the Shoshone Camp work center. Drive 35 miles—past Berlin Flats campground, over Jordan Saddle—to Jordan Camp campground. The trailhead is just east of the new bridge across the river. Consider shuttling another vehicle to the end of the trail on Road No. 3099 near Marten Creek.

From the Jordan Camp trailhead, the trail climbs for about ½ mile and drops a ways before becoming more gentle high above the river. The trail was reconstructed in 1978 to stay north of the river. Disregard older maps that show the trail crossing the river. From Alden Creek, the trail drops off the ridge and crosses a broad meadow. The trail here is some-what faint and boggy in the spring. Emerging from the brushy edge of the meadow, the trail meets an old road that parallels the river for ¼ mile. The route follows this road to its end then continues as a single tread trail as it rounds a bend in the river and crosses a slope of talus near Deer Creek, where some impressive rock formations loom above the river. The trail crosses loose talus then climbs gently to a point sev-eral hundred feet above the river and levels out. The slopes here are sparsely timbered allowing good views. Just before Sluice Creek, the trail passes several camping places on a flat bench near the river. More campsites can be found past Clark Creek on a forested bench across the river. The trail roller-coasters to Wren Creek, where it levels out through the forest and finally ends at Forest Road No. 3099 near the concrete foundations indicating the former location of Beaver Station work center.

COEUR D'ALENE RIVER
Unprotected

52 COEUR D'ALENE RIVER SOUTH

Round trip 11 miles
Hiking time 5–8 hours or
  overnight
High point 3,200 feet
Elevation gain 370 feet
Moderate

Hikable May through October
USGS Cathedral Peak, Jordan
  Creek
Information: Coeur d'Alene
  National Forest, Wallace
  Ranger District

The south portion of Coeur d'Alene River Trail No. 20 is 5¾ miles one way from the Coeur d'Alene River Road to Jordan Camp. (See Hike 51 for north portion.) The trail generally skirts high above the river, but one can find several places to slip down to the cool water for a dip. The river is one of Idaho's top catch-and-release fishing streams for west slope cutthroat trout.

Take Kingston Exit No. 43 off Interstate 90 (just west of Kellogg, Idaho) and head north along the east side of the river on paved Forest Highway No. 9. It's about 49 miles from I-90 to the trailhead. Follow Highway No. 9 about 23 miles to Prichard and bear left onto Forest Road No. 208 for about 26 miles. (The road passes several improved camp-grounds on the way, including Kit Price, Devil's Elbow and Big Hank.) There are two trailheads for this trip: the new trailhead just before a bridge across the Coeur d'Alene River and the old one a short way far-ther, just before the end of the pavement between mileposts 25 and 26.

The newer No. 20 trailhead was established in the late '70s. The trail leads immediately up and over some rock outcroppings and stays on the east side of the river, avoiding the need to ford. The second trailhead is the beginning of Trail No. 309 and the old source for Trail No. 20. Follow this route for about ¼ mile and bear right at the trail junction toward Trail No. 20. The trail leads over a hump and back down to the river. Several worn paths here lead to well-used campsites on the west side of

South section of the Coeur d'Alene River. (Rich Landers photo)

the river. To follow the trail and link up with Trail No. 20, one must ford the river. This is easy and pleasant after runoff, which sometimes isn't until late June or early July. It can be cold and difficult in May and sometimes well into June. From here the trail climbs high above the river, coming back close to it only twice in the remaining 4½ miles to Jordan Camp. Scenic attractions along the trail include Steamboat and Cathedral rocks which tower above the river.

Water is frequently available along the trail. Several campsites can be

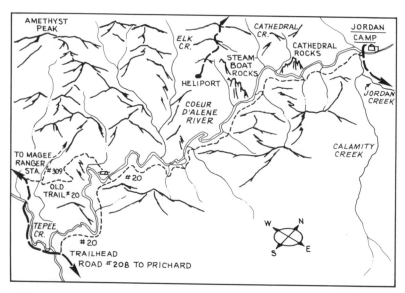

found, although they generally require a steep bushwhack down from the trail to the river. A campground and outhouse have been established at Jordan Camp.

Incidentally, Spion Knob, the unusual name of a mountain east of the trail near Jordan Camp, was named after a famous battle in the Boer War.

COEUR D'ALENE RIVER
Unprotected

53 GRAHAM MOUNTAIN

Round trip 8 miles
Hiking time 5–8 hours
High point 5,727 feet
Elevation gain 3,430 feet
Moderate

Hikable mid June through
    October
USGS Kellogg
Information: Coeur d'Alene
    National Forest, Wallace
    Ranger District

Graham Mountain is an example of hiking opportunities threatened by massive and often unjustified roading and logging planned for the Idaho Panhandle National Forests. The trail to the 5,727-foot peak has

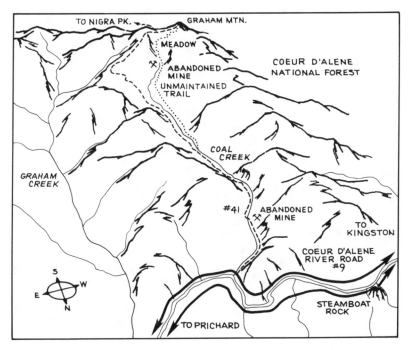

long been enjoyed by dayhikers visiting the Upper Coeur d'Alene River drainage. It was a RARE II wilderness study area. But in 1987, the Forest Service had plans for logging in what it called the Graham Mountain Planning Unit. If all goes as planned, the first clearcut would cross Trail No. 41 described below in 1988 or 1989.

From Interstate 90 between Coeur d'Alene and Kellogg, Idaho, take Kingston Exit No. 43 and head north on Forest Highway No. 9 (Coeur d'Alene River Road) toward Prichard. Drive 12½ miles to the trailhead on the right side of the road.

Coal Creek Trail No. 41 begins on the west side of the creek several hundred yards from the road. It is level for the first ¾ mile as it follows Coal Creek and leads to an abandoned mine near the creek crossing. The creek could be tricky to cross in June during runoff. The trail climbs through an old cedar grove to about 200 feet above the creek. About 1 mile after the first creek crossing, the trail comes to a fork. An unmaintained trail to Graham Mountain bears right, across the creek. The main trail stays on the east side of the creek and gains the ridge leading toward the peak. Just below the peak, the trail intersects with an unmaintained trail heading left toward Nigra Peak. Then the trail intersects with Graham Ridge Trail No. 17, which leads to the summit. From among the remains of an old lookout tower, one can see the Silver Valley and Silverhorn Ski area to the south and dozens of mountain peaks.

Heading up to Graham Mountain. (Sam Schlieder photo)

Near the summit of Mount Coeur d'Alene, looking down on Lake Coeur d'Alene. (Susan Scott photo)

COEUR D'ALENE RIVER
Unprotected

54 MOUNT COEUR D'ALENE

Round trip 10 miles
Hiking time 5–7 hours
High point 4,439 feet
Elevation gain 2,306 feet
Moderate

Hikable May through September
USGS Lane
Information: Coeur d'Alene
     National Forest, Fernan Ranger
     District

The hikers one meets on this trail usually are wonderful folks who like to hike for the sake of hiking. One who simply wants a view can drive within ⅓ mile of the summit and hike less than ⅛th the distance. The walk is pleasant, on a well-maintained trail to a point overlooking Lake Coeur d'Alene, one of the prettiest large lakes anywhere. The mountain originally was named Sticker Mountain because after the great fire of 1910, dead trees on top of the mountain gave it the appearance of being full of "stickers."

Drive east from Coeur d'Alene, Idaho, on Interstate 90 and take Wolf Lodge Exit No. 22 toward Harrison-St. Maries. At the stop sign, turn right and drive about 3 miles south on State Highway 97 to Forest Road No. 438 and go ¼ mile to Beauty Creek campground.

Caribou Ridge Trail No. 79, which leads to Mt. Coeur d'Alene, is clearly marked in the parking lot. The trail was constructed in 1982, so it does not appear on either the USGS 15-minute Lane quadrangle map or the smaller scale Mt. Coeur d'Alene topo. However, it is well-main-

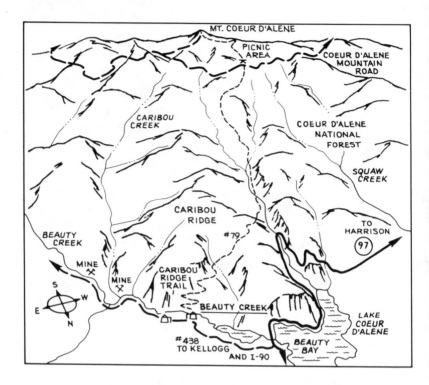

tained as it climbs a steep ridge above the campground. Hike 4⅓ miles to a picnic area, where water is available during summer, and year-round views of Lake Coeur d'Alene. From the picnic area it is only ⅓ mile to the top of Mt. Coeur d'Alene.

PURCELL MOUNTAINS
Unprotected

55   HOSKINS LAKE

Round trip 1 mile
Hiking time 45 minutes or
** overnight**
High point 3,380 feet
Elevation gain 500 feet
Easy

Hikable June through mid
** October**
USGS Bonnet Top
Information: Kootenai National
** Forest, Yaak Ranger District**

Trail No. 162 to Hoskins Lake is a very easy hike, suitable for families, to a pleasant little lake with good fishing for cutthroat trout. The most pleasant times to visit the area are right after the snow leaves (sometimes in late May) and late August or early September.

From Libby, Montana, drive north on Forest Road No. 68 (Pipe Creek

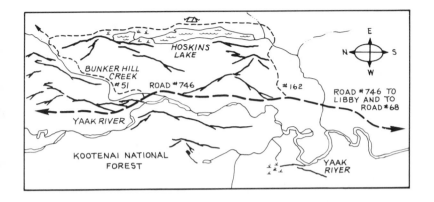

Road) about 33 miles and take the right fork onto Forest Road No. 746 (Vinal Lake Road). Drive 9 miles to the trailhead.

Trail No. 162 to Hoskins Lake is well established, with little elevation gain through a predominantly larch forest. Campsites at the lake are limited, with room for only a few tents. Expect to find mosquitoes from late June through mid August, especially at the marshy lower end of the lake. The lake has been known to produce good-sized cutthroat trout. The upper end is the most fishable, with casting room for fly fishermen along the east shore. Hikers who want to explore farther can follow the trail all the way to Bunker Hill Creek.

Cutthroat trout. (Rich Landers photo)

56   FISH LAKES CANYON

Round trip 11 miles
Hiking time 4–6 hours or
   overnight
High point 3,650 feet
Elevation gain 650 feet
Easy

Hikable late June through mid
   October
USGS Lost Horse Mountain, Mt.
   Henry, Yaak
Information: Kootenai National
   Forest, Yaak Ranger District

This is an easy but scenic hike up Vinal Creek to a chain of five lakes. With only 650 feet of elevation gain scattered over the 6 miles into the lakes, the hike is well suited for families and anglers.

From Libby, Montana, drive north on Forest Road No. 68 (Pipe Creek Road) about 30 miles and take the right fork onto Forest Road No. 746 (Vinal Lake Road). Drive 6 miles to the trailhead on the east side of the road.

Vinal Creek Trail No. 9 is easy to follow, complete with shade from cedars and larch, log bridges across the creek and plenty of water. A highlight is Turner Falls, about 3½ miles from the trailhead, where Turner Creek tumbles 50 feet into Vinal Creek. A campsite has been established here.

The first of the five lakes can become weed-choked and boggy during a dry season. Expect plenty of mosquitoes from June through mid August. The campsite at South Fish Lake, the second and largest in the chain, is spectacular. It is well used and has a picnic bench and a great view of the lake. The camping area is dry and protected, and the lake is reported to have the best fishing in the chain for cutthroat and rainbow trout. Fly fishers can find room to cast at either end of the lake.

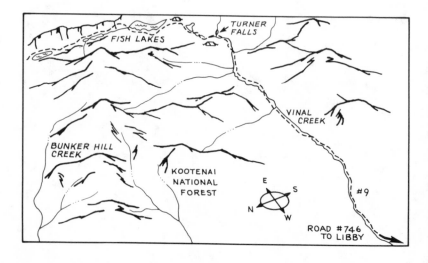

Fish Lakes Canyon. (Dale Hirschfeld photo)

Unfortunately, the Forest Service built a logging road to within about ¼ mile of this lake in 1986. Unless the road is closed, one can expect that most people will start taking advantage of the easy access and neglect the scenic trail described above.

57 TEN LAKES SCENIC AREA

Round trip 13 miles
Hiking time 8 hours or overnight
High point 7,360 feet
Elevation gain 1,500 feet
Moderate

Hikable July through early
  September
USGS Ksanka Peak, Stahl Peak
Information: Kootenai National
  Forest, Murphy Lake Ranger
  Station

The Ten Lakes Scenic Area plus an additional 35,000 acres surrounding it were proposed for wilderness designation in the 1987 Kootenai National Forest management plan. The hike from Little Therriault Lake to Wolverine Lakes, 6½ miles one way, is a beautiful hike through a high alpine area that's sinfully easy to reach. Following Bluebird Basin Trail No. 83, then Trail No. 88 to Green Mountain and Trail No. 84 to Wolverine Lakes, one hikes through forests and alpine meadows dappled with wildflowers. The peaks and ridges forming the high country around the alpine lakes are impressive. The area is ripe with other opportunities ranging from dayhikes to extended trips.

This is bear country, so keep a clean camp, be prudent in selection of food supplies that are not odoriferous, and secure food high in a tree at night.

From Eureka, Montana, travel south on U.S. Highway 93 for 9 miles and turn left onto Forest Road No. 114 (Graves Creek Road), which is marked by a sign for Therriault Lakes/Ten Lakes Scenic Area. Or, from

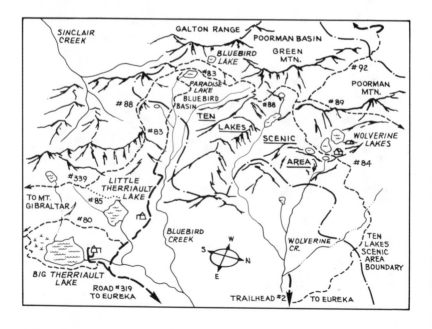

Whitefish, Montana, travel north on Highway 93 for 42½ miles and turn right onto Graves Creek Road.

Graves Creek Road is a paved two-laner which narrows after a short distance to a single-lane paved logging road with turnouts. Be on guard for logging trucks, especially on weekdays. From the highway, drive 11¼ miles and bear right at the junction with Forest Road No. 7021 (Stahl Creek/Clarence Creek Road). Continue on Road No. 114, which now becomes gravel. Just beyond mile 15 is a junction. Continue straight on to Forest Road No. 319 (Therriault Lakes Road). Keep on No. 319. At mile 30, there is a well-marked fork. The road to the left leads ½ mile to Big Therriault Lake. Take the road to the right which leads 1 mile to Little Therriault Lake. It's 1 mile farther to the end of the road, a parking area and the trailhead for Bluebird Basin Trail No. 83. (Note: In 1986, there was a trail sign at Little Therriault Lake indicating Trail No. 83 to Bluebird Basin, but the trail is no longer maintained. The trailhead has been relocated to the end of the road about 1 mile beyond the turn-in to the campground.

A Forest Service campground with nine sites is situated at Big Therriault Lake; one with six sites is on Little Therriault Lake. Both have pit toilets and hand-pump wells.

Little Therriault Lake, Ten Lakes Scenic Area. (Ida Rowe Dolphin photo)

Phlox. (Rich Landers photo)

Bluebird Basin Trail No. 83 begins at 5,856 feet and heads gradually uphill through the forest for the first ½ mile. The grade then increases and gains 800 feet in the next mile to Paradise Lake at 6,720 feet. Follow around the edge of the lake and through a meadow, where the trail becomes faint. The trail becomes distinct again as it heads north from the meadow and up another slope. At 2¼ miles, Trail No. 83 joins with Green Mountain Trail No. 88. (To see Bluebird Lake, turn left on No. 88, walk a short way and take an unsigned fork to the right (west) which leads a short way farther to the lake. Bluebird cabin, which still appears on some USGS topo maps, burned down years ago.) From the junction of Trail Nos. 83 and 88, turn right (north) toward Green Mountain. The route switchbacks up and contours around Green Mountain to approximately 7,360 feet. (Green Mountain summit is elev. 7,822 feet.) At the junction with Trail No. 84, go right, dropping down a steep, rocky slope to Wolverine Lakes.

A cabin formerly used by the Border Patrol is available at Wolverine Lakes on a first-come first-served basis. There also is ample room for camping. Wolverine Lakes are reputed to be good fishing lakes, though Bluebird and Paradise lakes are not.

Hiking parties with more than one vehicle could leave a car at the end of Trail No. 84, which leads 2½ miles from Wolverine Lakes to Wolverine Road. To drive to this trailhead, follow the road directions above onto Road No. 319 (Therriault Lakes Road) and turn right onto Forest Road No. 7091 (Wolverine Lakes Road) 3 miles before the fork to Big and Little Therriault lakes. (This turnoff to Wolverine Lakes is approximately 27 miles in from Highway 93.) Follow Road No. 7091 about 2½ miles to a fork. Turn left and drive ⅓ mile to the trailhead. (The road to the right leads to Trail No. 89, an unmaintained route to Rainbow Lake.)

Following are examples of additional hiking opportunities in the area.

Option 1: Trail No. 88, at the junction with Bluebird Lake Trail No.

Thimbleberries. (Rich Landers photo)

83, continues southeast to Therriault Pass, where one can continue to Stahl Peak or drop down to Big Therriault Lake. A lookout tower on Stahl Peak was recently repaired and is open to the public for overnight use on a first-come first-served basis. In 1986, there was no rental fee. For information, contact Murphy Lake Ranger Station.

Option 2: An ambitious hiker also could take Trail No. 339, a high scenic ridge trail south from Therriault Pass to Mt. Gibralter.

Option 3: Another possible hike near Wolverine Lakes would be up Trail No. 84 to Green Mountain and northwest on Trail No. 92, which leads through an area of mining history to the Burma Road.

CABINET MOUNTAINS
Cabinet Mountains Wilderness

58 CEDAR LAKES

Round trip 12 miles
Hiking time 5–7 hours or
  overnight
High point 5,888 feet
Elevation gain 3,108 feet
Moderately difficult

Hikable June through September
USGS Scenery Mountain,
  Treasure Mountain, Kootenai
  Falls
Information: Kootenai National
  Forest, Libby Ranger District

Hikers who don't mind the likelihood of skipping over a few horse muffins consider this one of the prettiest hikes in the Cabinet Mountains Wilderness. Cedar Lakes are nestled in the midst of towering peaks. A short climb from the lakes puts a hiker in position to see Kootenai Falls

Upper Cedar Lake, Cabinet Mountains Wilderness. (Joe Ohl photo)

on the Kootenai River and a distant look into Glacier National Park. Ambitious hikers also can extend this trip into a 16-mile loop.

From Sandpoint, Idaho, head north on U.S. Highway 95 to the junction of U.S. Highway 2 about 2 miles north of Bonners Ferry. Drive east on Highway 2 to Troy, Montana, and continue 12 miles. At milepost 27.9, turn right (south) on Forest Road No. 402 (Cedar Creek Road). Drive about 3 miles, staying on the main road, to the trailhead parking area.

Trail No. 141 climbs steadily, passing the Scenery Mountain trail junction at 1 mile and entering the Cabinet Mountains Wilderness at 3 miles. It then continues up, with a few steep pitches, another 2½ miles to Lower Cedar Lake. It leads another ½ mile to Upper Cedar Lake. The trail is well maintained and is an authorized horse trail as well as a hiking trail. According to Forest Service statistics, this trail gets the heaviest stock use of any trail in the wilderness. It is heavily forested; there's no doubt where the name Cedar Creek came from.

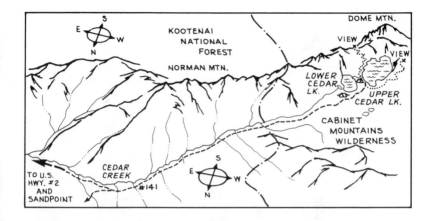

Campsites are available at both lakes and fishing in either lake can provide enough cutthroat trout for a meal. But remember, this is bear country; keep a clean camp.

Ambitious hikers can continue past Upper Cedar Lake and climb an additional 1,500 feet on a switchbacking trail heading northwest to Dome Mountain for spectacular views of hidden lakes as well as the numerous peaks surrounding the area. This is the route one could take to loop up and back to the trailhead via the Scenery Mountain trail, a high, appropriately named ridge route. However, the trail from the viewpoint above Cedar Lakes to Scenery Mountain is not regularly maintained. It would require use of map and compass.

CABINET MOUNTAINS
Cabinet Mountains Wilderness

 # SKY LAKES

Round trip 13 miles
Hiking time 8 hours or overnight
High point 6,200 feet
Elevation gain 2,500 feet
Moderate

Hikable mid June through
 September
USGS Treasure Mountain
Information: Kootenai National
 Forest, Libby Ranger District

This 6½-mile trail leads to a pair of pretty mountain lakes at the base of an unnamed 7,700-foot peak near Sugarloaf Mountain in the Cabinet Mountains Wilderness. The route is popular among both hikers and equestrians. Lower Sky Lake is forested on three sides with a rock slide on the south side. The trail is easy to follow, but it is rugged and seems longer than it is. Creek crossings are generally easy. Be sure to begin with water bottles filled, since it's a 2-mile hike from the trailhead to the first water source. To be safe, water should be treated.

From Libby, Montana, drive 1⅛ miles from the City Center sign south

Lower Sky Lake, Cabinet Mountains Wilderness. (Lance Schelvan photo)

on U.S. Highway 2 and turn right onto Shaugnessy Road (also marked with a Cabinet View Country Club sign). Drive up the hill ½ mile to a three-way intersection at the top of the hill. Bear left. Drive about ½ mile and turn right (west) onto Forest Road No. 618 (Granite Creek). Drive ¾ mile to Forest Road No. 128 (Flower Creek Road) and follow the main Flower Creek Road, a good gravel road, 5 miles to the trailhead parking area. The trailhead is about 100 yards south of the sign-in area at the parking lot.

Trail No. 137 begins in the trees about 150 feet south of the parking area. It is level or downhill for about 1 mile, then it heads steadily uphill for another mile to the creek coming down from the Hanging Valley to the left. There is a small campsite here. (Across Flower Creek is an un-maintained angler's trail which heads steeply up to the Hanging Lakes.) This is the last easy place to get water for about 3 miles. The trail continues through timber and huckleberries in and out of meadows with head-high brush. One could see bears in this area in late July and August. The trail breaks into an open meadow at about 5 miles and turns to the left at the base of Sugarloaf Mountain for the last ascent to Sky Lakes. Again, this section of trail can be brushy and occasionally muddy. The lower lake itself is surrounded by timber and brush. It has several

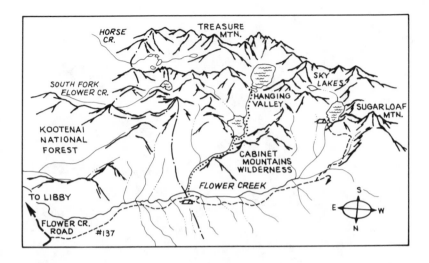

campsites east of the outlet. A faint footpath on the west side of the lake leads to Upper Sky Lake.

The area is ripe for higher exploration north to Sugarloaf Mountain and Minor Lake.

CABINET MOUNTAINS
Cabinet Mountains Wilderness

60   GRANITE LAKE

Round trip 12 miles
Hiking time 6–8 hours or
    overnight
Elevation gain 1,400 feet
High point 4,605 feet
Moderate

Hikable late June through
    September
USGS Little Hoodoo Mountain,
    Treasure Mountain, Snowshoe
    Peak
Information: Kootenai National
    Forest, Libby Ranger District

This hike has a number of attractions worthy of a dayhike in themselves. They begin 2 miles up the trail with scenic Granite Falls. The trail winds through heavy timber of the Cabinet Mountains Wilderness for the first 4½ miles before breaking into open, brushy country and spectacular views of "A" Peak. The hike offers good camping and plenty of alternatives for further exploration.

From Libby, Montana, drive 1⅛ miles from the City Center sign south on U.S. Highway 2 and turn right onto Shaugnessy Road (also marked with a Cabinet View Country Club sign). Drive up the hill ½ mile to a three-way intersection at the top of the hill. Bear left. Drive about ½ mile and turn right (west) onto Forest Road No. 618 (Granite Creek). Follow Road No. 618 about 10 miles to the trailhead parking area, which

Granite Lake, Cabinet Mountains Wilderness. (Tom Horne photo)

is about ½ mile past a parking area for trailers and a horse-loading ramp.

Trail No. 136 is a well-marked, well-traveled trail that follows Granite Creek 6 miles to Granite Lake. The trail crosses the creek at four points where hikers must ford or cross using deadfall. These crossings require extra care early in the hiking season during high water. Dense brush makes off-trail hiking unpleasant; few campsites are available between the trailhead and the lake.

Several campsites can be found at the north and west sides of the lake, plus a couple at a small pond just below the lake. "A" Peak to the south dominates scenery. The main feed for Granite Lake is melt from the Blackwell Glacier that comes 1,500 feet down an almost solid black slab

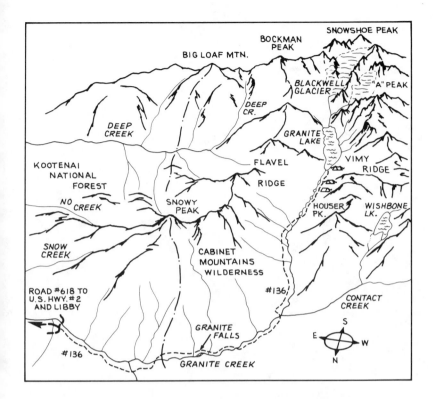

of rock to the south of "A" Peak. Expect plenty of mosquitoes in late June and July.

For a side trip, consider bushwhacking up to Vimy Ridge, west of the lake. Going up the forested slope, hikers will find lots of deadfall along with acres of huckleberries, which usually are prime in late July and early August.

CABINET MOUNTAINS
Cabinet Mountains Wilderness

61 LEIGH LAKE

Round trip 3 miles
Hiking time 3 hours or overnight
High point 5,250 feet
Elevation gain 884 feet
Moderate

Hikable June through September
USGS Snowshoe Peak
Information: Kootenai National
  Forest, Libby Ranger District

It's almost sinful that such a stunning area is so easy to reach. Leigh Lake is a spectacular alpine area accessible to virtually anyone who can walk. Problem is, this easy access has made it one of the most popular

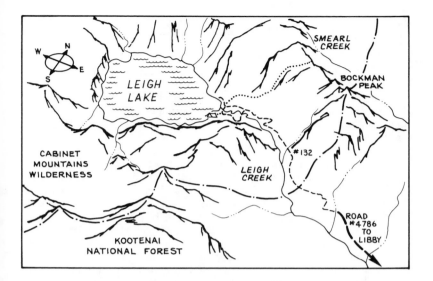

and overused areas in the Cabinet Mountains Wilderness. In July and August, despite its beauty, this is a place seekers of solitude will want to avoid. (According to Forest Service officials, a Cabinet Mountains Wilderness Plan developed in 1987 was to propose a ban on camping within 500 feet of the lake. This could essentially make this a day-use trail, since potential for campsites away from the lake is limited.)

From the City Museum in Libby, Montana, head south on U.S. Highway 2 about 6½ miles and turn right (west) onto Forest Road No. 278 (Bear Creek Road). The road bends south just less than 3 miles to a T at Forest Road No. 867 (Cherry Creek). Turn right (west), drive 4⅓ miles, bending south again, to Forest Road No. 4786 (Leigh Creek). (If you pass over the Leigh Creek Bridge, you have driven 100 yards or so too far.) Turn right (west) on Road No. 4786 and drive 2 miles to the trailhead at the end of the rough, narrow road.

The hike on Trail No. 132 is a moderate-to-steep, switchbacking climb into the Cabinet Mountains Wilderness up Leigh Creek, which is distinguished by many small waterfalls. It is very well maintained. About 1 mile from the trailhead, the trail crosses Leigh Creek and heads up more switchbacks to the lake where there are campsites on the east and west sides. The lake also holds some rainbow and brook trout and is the starting point for one approach to the summit of Snowshoe Peak, elev. 8,738 feet. Two faint, unmaintained trails lead up toward ridges below Bockman and Snowshoe peaks.

Left: Leigh Lake, Cabinet Mountains Wilderness. (Steve Weinberger photo)

62   ROCK LAKE

Round trip 8 miles
Hiking time 5–6 hours or
  overnight
High point 4,958 feet
Elevation gain 2,000 feet
Moderate

Hikable mid June through
  September
USGS Elephant Peak
Information: Kootenai National
  Forest, Cabinet Ranger District

Rock Lake offers a relatively easy access to a remote and scenic high alpine mountain lake area on the border of the Cabinet Mountains Wilderness. The trail is just outside the Cabinet Mountains Wilderness, but the lake is protected within the wilderness boundaries.

From Sandpoint, Idaho, head east on State Highway 200. About 1¾ miles past the turnoff to Noxon, Montana, (51 miles from Sandpoint) cross a bridge over the railroad tracks and turn left onto graveled Rock Creek Road. Drive ⅓ mile and bear right onto Forest Road No. 150 along Rock Creek. Follow the road, which slowly deteriorates, 5½ miles and turn right onto Forest Road No. 150-A (East Fork Rock Creek). This road, recommended only for four-wheel-drives or vehicles with high clearance, winds uphill about 1 mile to a gate, where there's room for parking and camping.

The first part of the hike continues up this old mining road, passing a campsite at 2 miles and a larger campsite with an outhouse at 2½ miles. (Since there is only one campsite at Rock Lake itself, these group campsites are recommended, leaving only a dayhike of less than 2 miles up to

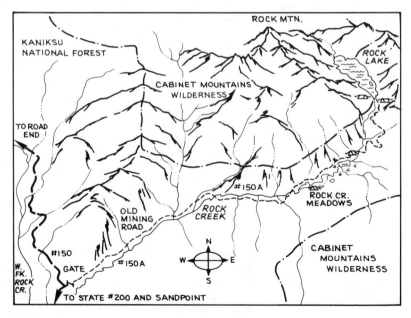

Rock Lake, Cabinet Mountains Wilderness. (John Roskelley photo)

the lake.) At about 3 miles, the trail is posted with a Trail No. 935 sign. The trail then leads to an abandoned mine and Rock Creek waterfall before leaving the old road grade and heading to the right and uphill. The trail to Rock Lake (labeled "Main Trail") forks to the right about 100 feet before reaching the Heidelberg Mine. Camping at the lake is limited to one designated site to the right of the outlet stream, although a makeshift campsite is available to the left of the outlet. Water is frequently available along the trail. The lake is bordered mostly by steep rock slides high above timberline and offers scramblers access to several peaks.

CABINET MOUNTAINS
Cabinet Mountains Wilderness

 63 # WANLESS LAKE

Round trip 18 miles
Hiking time 2 days minimum
High point 6,400 feet
Elevation gain 3,500 feet
Moderately difficult

Hikable July through September
USGS Howard Lake, Goat Peak,
  Noxon Rapids Dam
Information: Kootenai National
  Forest, Cabinet Ranger District

Hikers who simply want to get quickly to a mountain lake won't appreciate this hike. Many other lakes in the Cabinet Mountains Wilderness are easier to reach. But this hike is worth the effort, with lofty views, good-sized trout and less competition for a campsite than the more accessible areas. The area does, however, attract quite a few horse

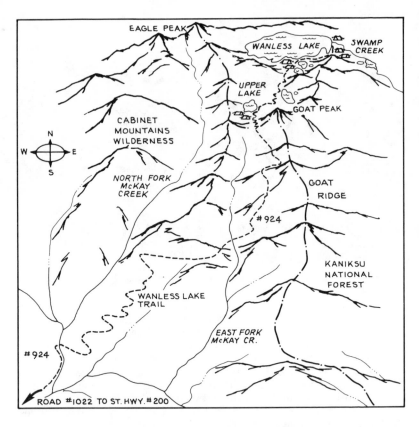

packers. The trail begins at 2,900 feet and reaches its highest point, elev. 6,400 feet, at Goat Peak Ridge for a gain of 3,500 feet.

From Sandpoint, Idaho, drive east on State Highway 200 into Montana to Noxon. From the Clark Fork River bridge that leads to Noxon, continue 3 more miles on Highway 200 and turn left onto Forest Road No. 1022 (McKay Creek Road) at the intersection with Noxon Dam Road. Drive about 4 miles to the trailhead at the end of the road.

Trail No. 924 begins at 2,900 feet, where it might be cool. But be sure to begin with full water bottles, since the next dependable water source is 6 miles up the trail at Upper Lake. From the trailhead, the route is a long series of switchbacks 5 miles uphill to the Cabinet Mountains Wilderness boundary just east of Goat Peak. The first 3 miles are through coniferous forest before the trail breaks into beautiful high alpine country for the remaining 2 miles to the boundary. The trail reaches its high point, both physically and visually here at elev. 6,400 feet. The trail then descends a steep series of switchbacks ¾ mile to Upper Lake, at 5,900 feet. Fit hikers can make it here in about 4 hours. Two good campsites can be found just off the trail next to the lake. Some hikers might choose to camp here and dayhike the remaining 3 miles to Wanless Lake.

The trail continues on from Upper Lake past three smaller unnamed

Wanless Lake, Cabinet Mountains Wilderness. (Steve Weinberger photo)

On the trail to Wanless Lake, Cabinet Mountains Wilderness. (Steve Weinberger photo)

lakes. The second lake, about 1½ miles from Upper Lake, has another good campsite, large enough for several tents. It's all downhill from here to Wanless Lake, at 5,090 feet, but plan on about 1½ hours of hiking. At least three good campsites can be found on Wanless, which holds good numbers of large cutthroat trout. Remember, however, this is bear country. Prudent hikers will keep a clean camp.

CABINET MOUNTAINS
Cabinet Mountains Wilderness

64 GEIGER LAKES

Round trip 7 miles
Hiking time 4–5 hours or
  overnight
High point 5,360 feet
Elevation gain 1,695 feet

Easy
Hikable June through September
USGS Howard Lake
Information: Kootenai National
  Forest, Libby Ranger District

This is a popular hike—a perfect and painless introduction to an alpine scenic area in the Cabinet Mountains Wilderness. As one might expect, easy access to a lake framed by stunning granite walls is likely to attract plenty of company. The Forest Service documented 2,500 user-days at these lakes in 1986.

From Libby, Montana, head east on Highway 2 for 24 miles and turn right on Forest Road No. 231. Follow this road for 5½ miles and turn left on Road No. 2332. Go ½ mile to the Lower Geiger Lake sign and turn left onto Road No. 6748. (One could continue straight to Lake Creek campground.) Follow Road No. 6748 for 1¾ miles to the trailhead parking area.

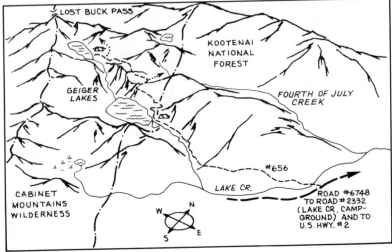

Moose near Lower Geiger Lake, Cabinet Mountains Wilderness. (Steve Weinberger photo)

The Lake Creek Trail leads hikers over 2 miles of gentle uphill to Lower Geiger Lake, a pretty spot surrounded by rocky slopes. Continue up the trail 1½ slightly more steep miles to the upper lake. One can continue beyond the lake 1¼ miles to Lost Buck Pass for a good view. Campsites are available at both lakes, although some have been closed by the Forest Service to allow them to recover from overuse.

65   REVETT LAKE

Round trip 4 miles
Hiking time 3 hours or overnight
High point 5,600 feet
Elevation gain 500 feet
Easy

Hikable mid July through
  September
USGS Burke, Cooper Gulch
Information: Coeur d'Alene
  National Forest, Wallace
  Ranger District

This is a short, easy hike to a clear mountain lake above an area that was heavily mined beginning in 1882 when gold was discovered in Prichard Creek. The hike is especially popular with beginning backpackers and families. Some cutthroat trout are stocked in the lake and huckleberries begin to ripen in the area in late July.

From Interstate 90, take Kingston Exit No. 43 just west of Kellogg, Idaho, and head north on Forest Highway No. 9 (Coeur d'Alene River Road). Follow this paved road 24 miles past Babins Junction to the little town of Prichard and bear right, staying on Highway 9. Continue on through Murray, where the pavement ends. (Murray is the remains of a boom town which once crammed thousands of people into the narrow valley. Consider paying a visit here to the historic Skragpole Bar/Museum.) This Highway No. 9 is a well-maintained gravel road that winds about 10 miles along acres of dredged creek bottom up to

Revett Lake. (Liz Escher photo)

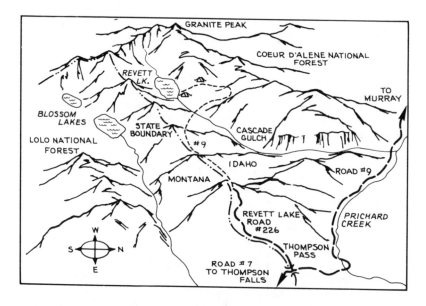

Thompson Pass, which is on the Montana-Idaho border. Revett Lake Road is at the top of the pass to the west. Drive to the end of the road where Revett Lake Trail No. 9 begins. No camping or water is available at the trailhead parking area.

To reach the trailhead from Wallace, Idaho, head north past the historic railroad depot and under the soon-to-be-built I-90 bypass onto Forest Road No. 456 toward Dobson Pass. This road is windy and steep, but paved. Drive over the pass and continue to Babins Junction. Turn right onto Forest Road No. 9, bearing right at Prichard and heading up to Thompson Pass, which is 39 miles from Wallace. To reach the trailhead from Thompson Falls, Montana, use paved Forest Road No. 7, clearly shown on Lolo National Forest maps.

Trail No. 9 to Revett Lake starts at the end of a short spur road and immediately dives into the alpine forest. The route curves around the ridge that divides Idaho from Montana, passing beneath steep, rugged talus slopes. In autumn, the rocky slopes are ablaze with mountain ash and huckleberry, contrasting with the deep greens of hemlock, alpine fir and spruce. The trail is well graded, wide and easy to follow. It winds through stands of mature forest, crossing a lovely creek (Cascade Gulch) at about ¾ mile on a split log bridge. A miniature waterfall can be seen here off to the left through the trees. The route then begins to climb gradually to the north, turning back to the south at its one and only switchback in a large talus slope. Passing in and out of trees and rocks, the trail finally gains the lip of the hanging valley where the lake lies in a bowl, surrounded by steep slopes. The outlet stream is to the left of the main trail in a swampy meadow. Camps are strung out along the outlet side of the lake, the better ones in the trees above the lake. The shoreline is rocky, with thick brush and trees in most places. The trail ends near a small, swampy beach littered with driftwood.

66   STEVENS LAKES

Round trip 5 miles
Hiking time 4 hours or overnight
High point 5,553 feet
Elevation gain 1,550 feet
Moderate

Hikable late June through mid
   October
USGS Wallace
Information: Coeur d'Alene
   National Forest, Wallace
   Ranger District

Popular among weekend campers, this hike quickly leads from Interstate 90 to an area of quiet alpine lakes in the western reaches of the Bitterroot Mountains. The lakes are situated just at the brink of timberline below Stevens Peak and just a ridge west of St. Regis Lakes described in Hike 68. Stevens Peak was named in the 1800s by Captain John Mullan for Isaac Stevens, territorial governor of Washington Territory and later a general in the Civil War.

Heading east on I-90 from Wallace, Idaho, take East Mullan Exit No. 69. Drive north over the freeway to State Highway 10 and head east past the Lucky Friday Mine to Shoshone Park junction. Turn south, taking the overpass across I-90, and drive to a parking area at the abandoned railroad right of way. (Note: This trailhead has been plagued by vandalism in recent years. Hikers should never leave anything valuable in their vehicles, especially here.)

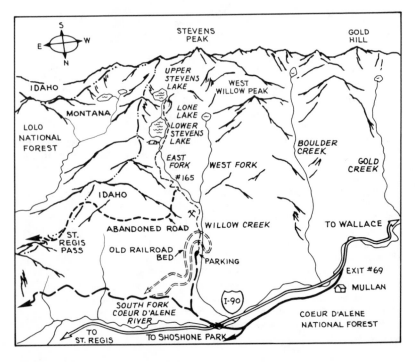

Stevens Lake. (Rich Landers photo)

Hike across the trackless railroad bed and bear left onto a spur road about ½ mile to a small mining operation. Continue up the road about another ½ mile to the second switchback and look for the trailhead on the right. Vandals rip off the trail signs as fast as the Forest Service can put them up, so keep a sharp eye out for a trail that might not be signed.

East Fork Willow Creek Trail No. 165 begins at elev. 4,000 feet and heads up a steep slope, across a rock slide and into the forest. Less than a mile later, it breaks out of the timber into a large basin surrounded by precipitous slopes and a stunning waterfall, which is powered by water from Stevens Lakes. The trail leads across East Fork Willow Creek and climbs steeply up the hillside, rising 350 feet in ¼ mile to Lower Stevens Lake, where several campsites can be found. The trail continues along the west shore and climbs a small rise to Upper Stevens Lake and several more campsites. Small rainbow trout can be caught in both lakes and the alpine scenery is better than one should expect for so little effort. Expect to see pockets of snow in the shadows of treeless spires well into July. Hikers often scramble up the ridge to the west of the lakes to 6,826-foot Stevens Peak for spectacular views of other lakes in the region.

IDAHO-MONTANA DIVIDE
Unprotected

 67 # BLOSSOM LAKES

Round trip 5 miles
Hiking time 3 hours or overnight
High point 5,695 feet
Elevation gain 950 feet
Easy

Hikable July to mid September
USGS Cooper Gulch
Information: Lolo National
    Forest, Thompson Falls Ranger
    District

An easy 5-mile round trip to Lower Blossom Lake can be extended into a longer hike of moderate difficulty to Pear Lake (7¼ miles round trip) and Glidden Ridge. These lakes are off the beaten track of hikers heading to more glamorous areas in the Idaho and British Columbia Selkirks to the north and the Cabinet Mountains to the east. But they have their own quiet charm.

From Interstate 90 west of Kellogg, Idaho, take Kingston Exit No. 43 and head north on Forest Highway No. 9 (Coeur d'Alene River Road). Drive about 24 miles to Prichard and bear right, staying on Highway No. 9 about 6 miles to Murray. From the end of the pavement at Murray, drive 10 miles of good gravel road to Thompson Pass. On the Montana side of the pass, the road becomes paved Forest Highway No. 7. Go a little more than ½ mile and watch for the trailhead sign on the south side of the road. Go a short way farther and turn right on a spur road. The road parallels the highway for about 50 yards, doubling back to the west to a dead end at a little campsite hidden from the highway by the brush. Walk up the hill. Trail No. 404 begins just across a logging road and heads into the trees. (The trailhead also can be reached from Wallace, Idaho, via Dobson Pass and from Thompson Falls, Montana, via Forest Highway No. 7.)

Glidden Gulch Trail No. 201 starts from the road near Cooper Pass, but soon intersects Trail No. 404 at Glidden Pass. The trail then follows the ridge, dropping down steeply into Pear Lake. Cooper Pass is approximately 12 miles by road from Wallace.

Trail No. 404 crosses, then parallels a logging road for about ¼ mile

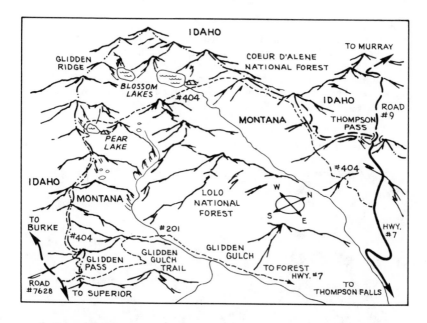

before climbing up through the trees on the side of a broad ridge. The forest consists of small, subalpine timber, mainly hemlock with some white pine, whitebark pine, lodgepole pine, Sitka spruce, Douglas fir, western larch and alpine fir. The trees are small and thick, so views are scarce. After climbing most of the 950-foot gain to Lower Blossom Lake in two gradual steps, this remarkably straight trail curves around to a view, about ¼ mile short of the lake. Standing on glacier-carved bedrock, the hiker can look out toward the northeast and the heavily forested ridges of Driveway Peak. The trail soon begins to contour above a creek set in a narrow, precipitous, rocky gorge, only a short way from Lower Blossom Lake.

The trail passes through good campsites on the northeastern side of the lake. Looking over to the western side of the lake, the ridge rises up to 6,629 feet, a wall of broken talus, cliff bands, scattered trees and brush. The eastern and southern edges of the lake are heavily wooded. One lonely camp sits high on a rocky knoll above the western side of the outlet stream with a lovely view of the lake. There is no trail to Upper Blossom Lake, although one can bushwhack through heavy brush and rock outcropping to reach it.

A dam was built at Lower Blossom Lake in 1883 to store water for placer mining operations at Murray. Near Lower Blossom Lake, the trail crosses an old diversion canal, which was dug by Chinese laborers. This canal, which was never used, can be traced all the way to Thompson Pass.

Hikers who want to extend the trip can stay on the trail, which climbs steadily up the side of a hogback ridge, again through thick timber and past rock outcroppings for about 1 mile, topping out at about 6,240 feet. The trail then drops down to a narrow, rocky basin where tiny Pear Lake nestles under a sheer 500-foot cliff. The only decent camp at Pear Lake is at the northeast end of the lake on a weedy beach. The lake basin, sitting as it does on a shadowy north slope, could hold snow for a long time in a cool year. The lake looks rather stagnant, although one small inlet creek gurgles down a talus slope at the southwest end of the lake.

From here, the trail climbs steeply up to the ridge, topping out close to 6,600 feet. The trail follows the ridgeline, dropping slowly down, until it intersects with Trail No. 201 at Glidden Pass.

Lower Blossom Lake. (Liz Escher photo)

68   ST. REGIS LAKES

Round trip 6 miles
Hiking time 3–4 hours or
overnight
High point 5,600 feet
Elevation gain 1,000 feet
Moderate

Hikable mid June through
September
USGS Saltese
Information: Lolo National
Forest, Superior Ranger
District or Coeur d'Alene
National Forest, Wallace
Ranger District

Easy access off Interstate 90 makes this a popular weekend trip to a scenic mountain lake area. The hike is easy, except for the fairly steep last ½ mile up to the main St. Regis Lake. The round-trip distance can be shortened to about 4 miles if one wants to drive as far as possible. But most visitors prefer to walk the rough road along the upper St. Regis River. This is huckleberry country; bring an extra "empty" water bottle in late July and early August.

From I-90 on the summit of Lookout Pass (Montana-Idaho border), take Exit No. 0. Turn right at the stop sign and head south. At the junction with the ski area road, turn left away from the ski area and head down, paralleling an old railroad grade on Old Mullan Road about ½ mile, where the road turns right and then another ½ mile to a hairpin turn to the left. Just into the hairpin turn, look for a dirt road to the right, which leads to a couple of undeveloped camping spots.

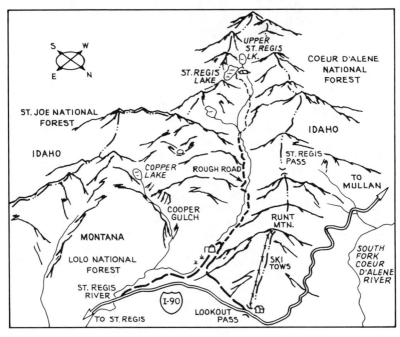

Huckleberry. (Rich Landers photo)

From the campsites, hike up the creek to the abandoned railroad right of way. Follow the railbed to the left a few hundred feet to pick up the trail along the south side of the creek (not Forest Service maintained), or follow the railbed to the right several hundred feet to pick up the rough road that heads up the north side of the creek. The trails join about ¾ mile upstream (the north trail crosses the creek on an old road). Both trails are in fairly good condition, although the south trail is better hiking. Both trails have spurs that lead down to the creek.

From the junction of the two trails, continue on an old road along the south side of the creek for about ½ mile and look for a poorly marked trail junction to the right just before the road starts to climb steeply. Some people actually drive to this point. Take the trail to the right and drop down to the creek. Cross the creek and continue west ¾ mile to the base of a headwall. From here the trail climbs steeply with a couple of switchbacks for ½ mile to the main lake. This lake is brushy, with only a couple of campsites on the north shore. The upper lake is small and boggy. The main lake has a good population of hungry brook trout.

69   HUB LAKE

Round trip 6 miles
Hiking time 5 hours or overnight
High point 5,700 feet
Elevation gain 1,720 feet
Moderate

Hikable July through September
USGS Haugan, St. Regis
Information: Lolo National
  Forest, Superior Ranger
  District

A perfect quick weekend trip or an outing for families, the 3-mile trail to Hub Lake is reasonably gentle and pleasant. The trail dips through cedar groves. It follows Ward Creek for 1¼ miles and crosses other small creeks most of the way to good campsites at the lake. One can take the trail beyond the lake, too, and climb to excellent viewpoints at Ward or Eagle peaks.

On Interstate 90, drive east of DeBorgia, Montana, 7½ miles and take Exit No. 26. (Unfortunately, drivers westbound out of St. Regis, Montana, will not find Exit 26. They must take Exit 25, then go back on the freeway eastbound 1 mile to Exit 26.) Once off the freeway, drive south on Ward Creek Road No. 889 about 6½ miles until it crosses Ward Creek. The trailhead is on the right side of the road just before it crosses the creek. The only available parking is a wide spot in the road.

Trail No. 262 follows Ward Creek about 1¼ miles up to the junction with Hazel-Hub Lake Trail No. 280. The trail is fairly gentle for the next mile to a 100-foot spur trail heading south to Hazel Lake. This lake holds

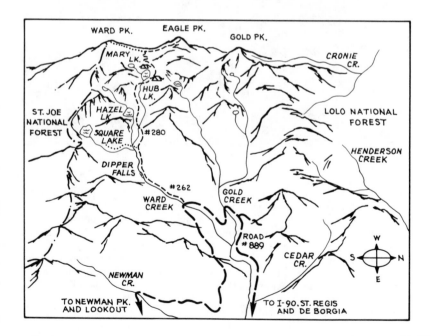

Hub Lake. (Nancy Smith photo)

fish, but it is brushy. Trail No. 280 climbs more steeply for the last mile up to Hub Lake. It passes through a flower-studded meadow flanked by Ward and Eagle peaks. The trail, which occasionally becomes faint through the meadow, traverses northeast through a draw for ¾ mile to the lake's outlet.

Several places are suitable for camps, including the outlet area, where one can still find the remains of an old mining cabin. Late in the season, the meadows at the upper end of the lake dry up enough for camping.

One can kill time by fishing for the lake's cutthroat trout, or follow the faint trail to the saddle between Ward and Eagle peaks.

70   HEART LAKE

Round trip 6 miles
Hiking time 3–4 hours or
   overnight
High point 5,790 feet
Elevation gain 1,130 feet
Moderate

Hikable mid June through
   September
USGS Straight Peak NW, Hoodoo
   Pass
Information: Lolo National
   Forest, Superior Ranger
   District

Some backpackers consider this the ideal hike to the largest alpine lake in this western portion of the Bitterroot Mountains, in an area proposed as part of the Great Burn Wilderness. Walk a reasonably easy 3 miles to a high lake, make camp and behold the opportunities for a scenic sidetrip to the lofty, rocky ridge above without the heavy pack. The trip also can be extended to visit Pearl or Dalton lakes or into a loop trip that would include a visit to Hoodoo Lake.

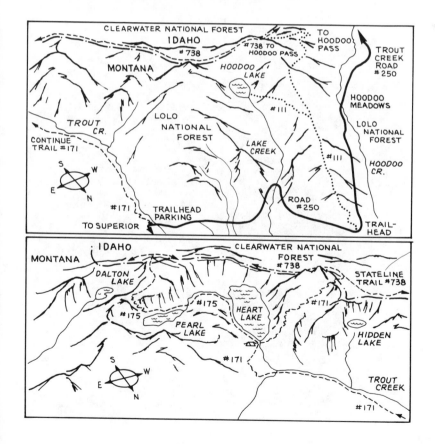

From Interstate 90, exit at Superior, Montana, and head east on State Highway 257, which runs parallel to the south side of I-90. (The pavement ends at a large saw mill and becomes Trout Creek Road No. 250.) It's about 20 miles from Superior to the well-marked Heart Lake trailhead on a switchback in the road. Parking is available for five or six vehicles.

Well-used Trail No. 171 follows the South Fork of Trout Creek and crosses several small tributary streams in the drainage. The Forest Service built corduroy log crossings in 1985, but be prepared for fancy footwork or wet boots. The hike is reasonably gentle, gaining 1,130 feet in 3

Heart Lake from the Montana-Idaho divide. (Clyde Blake photo)

miles through timber and grassy meadows. The undergrowth is thick, but the trail usually is well brushed. Heart Lake has several good campsites, and anglers generally have little trouble catching small trout.

For a worthwhile dayhike, follow the trail up the steep, rocky headwall west of the lake, switchbacking up 900 vertical feet to the ridge and Stateline Trail No. 738. This is the border between Idaho and Montana. At points the trail is faint and difficult to locate, but the ridge is distinctive. Look for rock cairns marking the trail. From above at elevations ranging from 6,700 feet to nearly 7,000 feet, one is rewarded with a fantastic view of Montana to the east and Idaho to the west. Although there is water all the way to Heart Lake, the ridge above the lake is dry.

One can hike the Stateline Trail back along the ridge toward the road, coming out at Hoodoo Pass. Along the way, there's a good view down onto Hoodoo Lake. It is possible to make a complete loop, hiking down to Hoodoo Lake along a newly built trail northeast of the Hoodoo overlook. No good campsites are found around the lake. One would have to continue out, following a good trail from the lake about 1 mile back to the Trout Creek Road. Total distance from the Stateline Trail to Trout Creek Road is about 2 miles. It would be 1½ miles down Road No. 250 from the Hoodoo Lake trailhead to the Heart Lake trailhead, making the entire loop about 8 miles.

LITTLE NORTH FORK CLEARWATER RIVER
Unprotected

71   SNOW PEAK

Round trip 10 miles
Hiking time 6 hours or overnight
High point 6,760 feet
Elevation gain 1,240 feet
Moderately difficult

Hikable July through September
USGS Bathtub Mountain,
  Montana Peak
Information: St. Joe National
  Forest, Avery Ranger District

This hike offers not only good views of the beautiful Mallard-Larkins roadless area (proposed for wilderness), but also the chance to see elk and a notorious band of mountain goats. This trail (along with others in this region) attracts large numbers of hunters in the fall, but it is lightly used in summer.

Take the St. Regis, Montana, exit off Interstate 90. Head northwest on the Camel Hump road just north of the freeway about ¾ mile and turn south, crossing over I-90, on Little Joe Road. Drive about 29 miles (the gravel road turns to pavement when it enters Idaho) to the St. Joe River and turn left on Forest Road No. 218 toward Red Ives. Drive 8 miles to Beaver Creek campground. Turn right at the campground onto Forest Road No. 303 and cross the St. Joe River. Drive about 7½ miles on the dirt road to the junction with Forest Road No. 201 and turn right toward Pineapple Saddle. Go another 8 miles to the trailhead on the south side of the road at the road junction to Bathtub Mountain. Parking is avail-

Snow Peak and lookout. (Tony Dolphin photo)

able for a few cars. There is a campsite here with a spring a few hundred feet to the west. (This area also is accessible via Avery, Idaho. See Hike 76.)

Trail No. 55 is a lovely walk through forest for about 4 miles before breaking uphill out of the trees the last mile to the summit of Snow Peak. The trail roller-coasters along a ridge, gaining and losing considerable elevation in some cases but offering occasional glimpses of the peaks to the east into Montana as well as the Hoodoo Range to the west. About 1 mile from the trailhead, a spur trail along Lightning Ridge takes off to the south. (This trail dead-ends after 3 miles.) Walk a few hundred yards farther on Trail No. 55 for a good look at Snow Peak, distinguished from surrounding mountains by its tall granite face. At about 4 miles, the trail breaks into an open area on a saddle for another dramatic view of the peak and its lookout tower. Spotted Louis Trail No. 104 branches off to the northwest at this saddle, but this trail is primitive and is a challenge to follow down to the Little North Fork of the Clearwater River. A trail also branches off to the south from the opening, heading to a meadow below the rocky north face of the peak. This area makes a good campsite, although the only dependable water would come from two boggy lakes. (Carry either water or a water filter and purifying tablets.) This area also is a choice spot for a stand from which to watch for mountain goats that frequently roam the cliffs. To continue up the ridge to the lookout atop Snow Peak, bear right at the fork in the trail. The last mile to the summit gains 1,240 feet, but the view is worth it.

The mountain goats can be curious and almost tame one day and elusive and shy the next, but evidence of their presence is always abundant. Please take care not to disturb them. This is NOT a hike on which the family dog should join the group. The Idaho Fish and Game

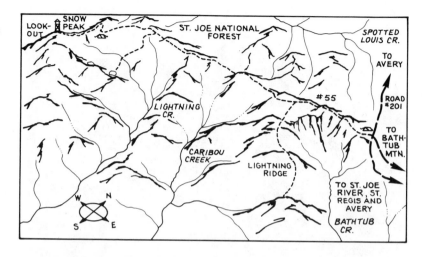

Department occasionally traps goats from the prolific Snow Peak group for relocation in other parts of the state.

Two possible side trips are the Lightning Ridge spur, and a short 1½-mile round-trip hike to Bathtub Mountain along the road beginning across from the Snow Peak trailhead.

LITTLE NORTH FORK CLEARWATER RIVER
Proposed wilderness

72   GRANDMOTHER AND GRANDFATHER MOUNTAINS

Round trip 8 miles
Hiking time 4–5 hours or
  overnight
High point 6,369 feet
Elevation gain 1,040 feet
Moderate

Hikable late June through
  September
USGS Grandmother Mountain
Information: St. Joe National
  Forest, St. Maries Ranger
  District

There's nothing geriatric about the hike to Grandmother and Grandfather mountains. The trail rocks hikers to sleep with gentle ridgetop terrain before bringing out the creaks in their legs with steep sections to the summits. Grandmother, at elev. 6,369 feet, and Grandfather, at 6,306 feet, have stood for generations above one of the few roadless areas remaining in northern Idaho. The Forest Service has proposed the area for wilderness management.

The Grandfather Mountain trail leaves what was the Old Montana Trail, formerly a route used by the Indians, at Marks Butte. The Marble Creek drainage to the north was logged between 1916 and 1932. At one time it was said to contain the largest stand of uncut white pine in the

Overlooking Crater Lake near Grandfather Mountain. (Don Crawford photo)

country. But no more. Disease took its toll among the trees and the evidence of early day logging is everywhere. Skeletons of steam engines, logging camps, flumes, trestles and log chutes abound.

From St. Maries, Idaho, drive south on State Highway 3 to Clarkia. At Clarkia, head east on Forest Road No. 301, climbing steeply 13½ miles to the trailhead at Freezeout Saddle. (The last 3 miles are very rough and dusty.) The trail heads north from an extra-wide turnout at the saddle.

In 1987, Trail No. 275 to Grandfather and Grandmother mountains was unmarked, but easy to locate. The trail climbs briefly up and across the shoulder of Marks Butte before descending and following an open ridge 2 miles to Grandmother Mountain. Along this ridge halfway between Marks Butte and Grandmother Mountain, hikers will pass an intersection with Trail No. 251 coming up the ridge above Gold Center Creek from the Marble Creek drainage. A short way farther up Trail No.

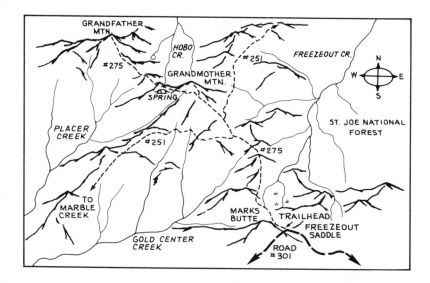

275 is another junction at which Trail No. 251 heads north around the east side of Grandmother to the Cornwall Creek drainage. Continue on Trail No. 275. Hikers enjoy good views of the Freezeout Creek drainage to the east and Gold Center Creek to the west. An abundance of huckleberries in August will help keep a hiker's mind off the dusty trail.

From a short spur trail heading to the summit of Grandmother Mountain, the trail descends to a spring and nice campsite before continuing through thick, twisted timber. The last ¼ mile to Grandfather Mountain is steep, but the 360-degree summit view of the Marble Creek drainage and Clarkia is worth the effort.

LITTLE NORTH FORK CLEARWATER RIVER
Proposed wilderness

73 MALLARD-LARKINS LOOP

Round trip 24½ miles
Hiking time 3–4 days
High point 6,541 feet
Elevation gain 4,150 feet
Moderately difficult
Hikable July through September

USGS Mallard Peak, Buzzards
Roost, Bathtub Mountain,
Montana Peak
Information: St. Joe National
Forest, Avery Ranger District

Hikers who have the time and enthusiasm to explore great hiking and fishing areas will find this trip to be one of the best in northern Idaho. The route is rugged, climbing to high ridges and plunging deep into river valleys. But behold! This is Idaho!

Take the St. Regis, Montana, exit off Interstate 90. Head northwest on

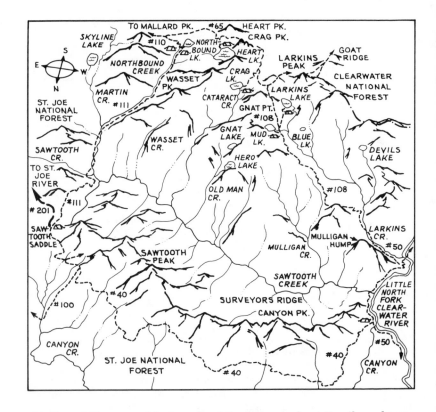

the Camel Hump road just north of the freeway about ¾ mile and turn south, crossing over I-90, on the Little Joe Road. Drive about 29 miles (the gravel road turns to pavement when it enters Idaho) to the St. Joe River and turn left on Forest Road No. 218 toward Red Ives. (This area is also accessible via Avery, Idaho. See Hike 76.) Drive 8 miles to Beaver Creek campground. Turn right at the campground onto Forest Road No. 303 and cross the St. Joe River. Drive about 7½ miles on the dirt road to the junction with Forest Road No. 201. Turn left and drive to Sawtooth Saddle, where there is plenty of parking. The road is primitive and rough in spots; vehicles with low clearance could have trouble.

The route begins on Northbound Creek Trail No. 111 and immediately drops 1,400 feet in the first 2 miles to Sawtooth Creek. Ford the creek and head up the Northbound Creek drainage. The trail crosses Northbound Creek three times and is quite marshy in places. About 4 miles farther and 1,400 feet higher, one will come to Northbound Lake at elev. 5,436 feet. The first campsite has the most scenic view of the lake, but it is an overused and abused horsepackers' camp. There is another campsite just across the creek along the trail, and another off the trail at the head of the lake.

From Northbound Lake, Trail No. 111 switchbacks ½ mile up to the top of the ridge where it intersects Heart Pass Trail No. 65 at elev. 5,671 feet. Go right on this well-maintained trail following the ridge toward

Mountain goats, Mallard-Larkins proposed wilderness area. (Rich Landers photo)

Heart Lake. The trail junction to Heart Lake is about 1 mile up the ridge; it is another ½ mile down this trail to Heart Lake, which is larger than Northbound Lake. It offers limited campsites because it is surrounded on three sides by steep cirque walls.

The high point on the trip, Heart Pass at 6,541 feet, is ½ mile beyond the junction to Heart Lake on the Heart Pass trail. (Snow often covers the trail in the cirque above Heart Lake until early August.) Many breathtaking views of the lake and mountains are visible along this stretch of trail. From Heart Pass, the trail is easy walking as it leads gently downhill. Walk ¾ mile past the junction of the trail heading steeply down to Crag Lake. Go ¼ mile to another trail junction and bear right on Larkins Lake Trail No. 108. Larkins Lake can be seen tucked beneath Larkins Peak to the left of this trail. Walk another mile to where the trail branches in three directions. Downhill and to the left is Larkins Lake. Uphill and to the right is Mud Lake. Despite its name, Mud Lake is a picturesque mountain lake nestled in a cirque. (Perhaps someone shared the intentions of the Vikings, who named an icy, forbidding land as Greenland, while they named a beautiful, more temperate place they hoped to keep for themselves as Iceland.) There are two very nice campsites—one at the mouth of Mud Lake and another farther along the north side.

Skyland Lake from Mallard Peak, Mallard-Larkins proposed wilderness area. (Rich Landers photo)

From Mud Lake, follow Larkins Creek Trail No. 108 downhill to the Little North Fork Clearwater River. It's downhill all the way, losing 3,000 feet in 5 miles. (It seems longer.) The slope is gentle initially and the trail leads through a stand of giant cedars. Most of this area was burned in a fire in 1910, with only a few pockets of trees such as these surviving.

After the cedar grove, the trail begins to lose elevation sharply following the Larkins Creek drainage. As you approach the Little North Fork, the trail crosses an open slope high above the creek. At this point, about 4½ miles from Mud Lake, it intersects Clearwater Trail No. 50. Go right, up a short distance to get over the base of Mulligans Hump and then down ½ mile to Sawtooth Creek. Again, the creek must be forded. It's another ½ mile from the creek to Surveyors Ridge Trail No. 40.

Just beyond this intersection, the Clearwater Trail drops down to the mouth of Canyon Creek, which empties into the Little North Fork. A meadow suitable for camping and an old trappers' cabin can be found here. Unfortunately, like Northbound Lake, this spot has been abused; signs of people abound. The Little North Fork is an excellent native cutthroat trout stream.

The last day is an arduous uphill hike up Surveyors Ridge Trail about 8½ miles to Sawtooth Saddle. Even though the trail gains 2,000 feet, packs should be light by now and the grade is evenly spread over the entire 8½ miles. Water is available along the trail, which crosses many small drainages. But it is best to do this section in the morning, before the hot afternoon sun bears down on this south-facing slope.

LITTLE NORTH FORK CLEARWATER RIVER
Proposed wilderness

74 MALLARD-FAWN LAKES

Round trip 14 miles
Hiking time 6–10 hours or
    overnight
High point 6,090 feet
Elevation gain 390 feet
Moderate

Hikable late June through
    September
USGS Pole Mountain, Mallard
    Peak
Information: St. Joe National
    Forest, Avery Ranger District

This is a gentle hike with no demanding ups or downs, to a secluded lake off the paths beaten regularly to the more popular lakes in the Mallard-Larkins Pioneer Area. The Forest Service has recommended the Mallard-Larkins area for wilderness status. It is home for a large elk herd, which is why it also is popular with hunters during fall.

Take the St. Regis, Montana, exit off Interstate 90. Head northwest on the Camel Hump road just north of the freeway about ¾ mile and turn south, crossing over I-90, on the Little Joe Road. Drive about 29 miles

Picking huckleberries between Mallard Lake and Mallard Peak, Mallard-Larkins proposed wilderness area. (Rich Landers photo)

(the gravel road turns to pavement when it enters Idaho) to the St. Joe River and turn left on Forest Road No. 218 toward Red Ives. (This area is also accessible via Avery, Idaho. See Hike 76.) Drive 8 miles to Beaver Creek campground. Turn right at the campground onto Forest Road No. 303 and cross the St. Joe River. Drive about 7½ miles on the dirt road to

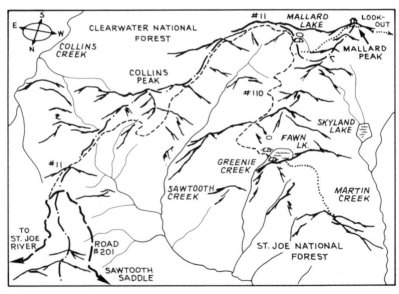

the junction with Forest Road No. 201 and turn left. Drive 7¾ slow, rough miles to the signed trailhead, where small turnouts before and after the trail provide parking for two or three vehicles. Parking and camping also are available ¼ mile before the trailhead at Table Camp Meadow.

Trail No. 11 roller-coasters gently as it contours the headwater bowl of Sawtooth Creek for 5 miles to the junction with the trail to Mallard Lake. Mallard is ⅛ mile south of Trail No. 11. This is a good place to make a base camp for huckleberry picking or a dayhike 2 miles up to the refurbished fire lookout on nearby Mallard Peak. (The ground-level lookout, which is on the National Register of Historic Places, was restored in the early 1980s by lookout buff Ray Kresek of Spokane.) To get to Fawn Lake, stay on Trail No. 11 and walk just past the Mallard Lake turnoff before bearing north on Trail No. 110. From here it is less than 2 miles on a pleasant pathway to Fawn Lake, which has several well-used campsites at 5,912 feet. The lake is periodically stocked with cutthroat trout.

ST. JOE RIVER AREA
Proposed wilderness

75   BEAN-BACON LOOP

Round trip 24 miles
Hiking time 3–4 days
High point 6,600 feet
Elevation gain 2,600 feet
Difficult
Hikable July through September

USGS Bacon Peak, Illinois Peak,
  Chamberlain Mountain,
  Simmons Peak
Information: St. Joe National
  Forest, Avery Ranger District

This is a loop with many rewards for backpackers up to the test of a few steep grades, river fords and a little bushwhacking to reach off-trail lakes. The route crosses the pristine waters of the St. Joe River, along with several of its tributaries, and runs high into one of the more remote areas of the proposed Mallard-Larkins Wilderness Area. The alpine lakes are high and secluded and stocked with trout. Hikers should consider carrying wading shoes to ford the St. Joe.

Take the St. Regis, Montana, exit off Interstate 90. Head northwest on the Camel Hump road just north of the freeway about ¾ mile and turn south, crossing over I-90, on the Little Joe Road. Drive about 29 miles (the gravel road turns to pavement at the pass when it enters Idaho) to the St. Joe River and turn left on Forest Road No. 218 toward Red Ives. (This area is also accessible via Avery, Idaho. See Hike 76.) Drive almost 10 miles to Red Ives Ranger Station, cross Red Ives Creek and turn left on Forest Road No. 320. Follow this rough, rocky road (negotiable for passenger cars with good clearance) 7 miles and take a nearly 180-degree right turn toward Needle Peak. The trailhead is 1 mile farther on the right, with a slight widening in the road offering parking for three vehicles. Go another 300 yards to the end of the road for more parking

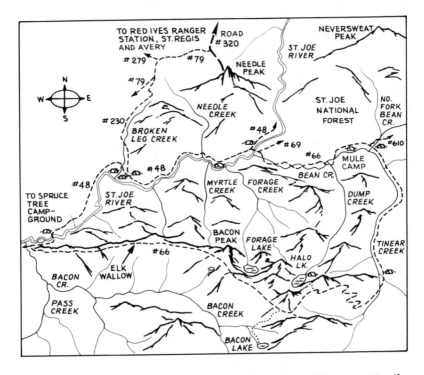

and a turn around area. (Follow the trail from this parking area ½ mile to the old Needle Peak lookout site for a view across the St. Joe drainage to the Bacon Peak area described below.)

Begin walking down Trail No. 79. Go about 1 mile to the junction with Trail No. 279 and turn left, continuing on Trail No. 79 for ¼ mile to another junction. Bear left on Broken Leg Trail No. 230 and walk down 3 miles to St. Joe River Trail No. 48. Water is abundant and three large campsites are available near this junction. Nearby is the rotted foundation of a ranger station built in 1911, one of the first in the St. Joe National Forest.

Continue the loop by turning left on Trail No. 48, which soon begins to hug the shore of the St. Joe River. Go 2¾ miles upstream and turn right at Bean Creek onto Bacon Loop Trail No. 66. (Incidentally, historical accounts indicate that Bean and Bacon creeks were named by hungry prospectors.) Walk ¼ mile to a large campsite and ford the St. Joe River. This leg-numbing ford can be difficult in late June and early July, depending on runoff. Wading shoes and an improvised wading staff are recommended.

From the river, it's about 7 miles to Halo Lake. The first 5 miles of Trail No. 66 follow Bean and Tinear creeks up the valley bottom, fording Bean Creek several times. Several good campsites and plenty of water are found in this stretch. The observant hiker can spot evidence of turn-of-the-century mining, such as hand-placed rocks along the stream. Decades ago at a large meadow called Mule Camp, an old-timer stuck a gold pan in a small pine which has since grown up around the pan. The last good campsite and the last water source other than the lakes is near the Tinear Creek crossing just before the steep trail climbs up the last mile to Halo Lake. The lake cannot be seen from the trail; one must scramble up from the last switchback and look over the ridge. No trail leads to the lake and it is a steep bushwhack down to the very limited camping area near the outlet.

The trail becomes faint as it contours around the ridge south of Halo Lake. One can continue along the ridge to the steep cliffs that plunge down to Forage Lake on the right. The trail is easy to pick up in the saddle south of Forage Lake as it begins to head up Bacon Ridge. From here it is a ½-mile bushwhack south to Bacon Lake, which cannot be seen from the trail. One must walk farther on the trail to drop safely into the outlet end of Forage Lake. Again, few campsites are available.

No dependable water sources are available along the scenic Bacon Ridge as it leads gently back 5 miles to the St. Joe River. (Many St. Joe National Forest maps list this part of the loop as Trail No. 70, but it was changed in 1981 to No. 66.) About 1 mile above the river, the trail runs through a huge elk wallow. This is a dirt patch, rank with elk urine, the size of two volleyball courts, where elk come to dust and lick the ground for minerals—a very likely area to see elk. Trail No. 66 is the small and brushy track exiting on the downhill side of the wallow. Keep an eye out

Forage Lake on Bean-Bacon Loop, Mallard-Larkins proposed wilderness area. (Rich Landers photo)

for the trail blazes, since the elk trails often look more substantial.

After fording the St. Joe River, bear left through the packers' campsite onto a trail that leads ¼ mile to St. Joe River Trail No. 48. From here it is about 1½ miles back to the mouth of Broken Leg Creek to complete the loop plus another 4 miles back up to the trailhead.

ST. JOE RIVER AREA
Proposed wilderness

76   ST. JOE RIVER

One way 17 miles
Hiking time 2–3 days
High point 4,690 feet
Elevation gain 890 feet
Moderate

Hikable June through mid
   October
USGS Bacon Peak, Simmons
   Peak, Illinois Peak
Information: St. Joe National
   Forest, Avery Ranger District

This is an excellent route for hikers who like a good footpath, plenty of wildlife and one of Idaho's best fishing streams for a constant companion. The St. Joe is the highest navigable river in the country, according to the Forest Service. One can expect to see elk and camp within the soothing rush of a federally designated Wild and Scenic River. The name St. Joe is a shortened version of St. Joseph, the name given to the stream in 1842 by Jesuit missionary Father Peter DeSmet. The river is 133 miles long from its origin at St. Joe Lake to its mouth at Lake Coeur d'Alene.

Take the St. Regis, Montana, exit off Interstate 90. Head northwest on the Camel Hump road just north of the freeway about ¾ mile and turn

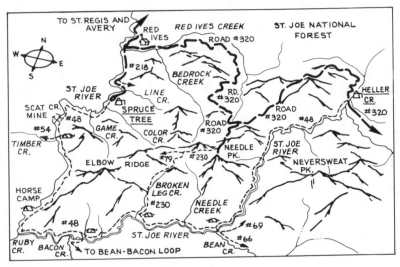

St. Joe River. (Rich Landers photo)

south, crossing over I-90, on the Little Joe Road. Drive about 29 miles
(the gravel road turns to pavement when it enters Idaho) to the St. Joe
River and turn left on Forest Road No. 218 toward Red Ives. Drive almost 10 miles to Red Ives Ranger Station. From here it's another 2 miles
to Spruce Tree campground and the well-marked trailhead at the south
end of the campground loop road.

From Lewiston, Idaho, head east on U.S. Highway 12, turn left on
State Highway 3 and drive to St. Maries, Idaho. Turn right on the St. Joe
River Road toward Avery. Drive upriver on a slow, winding road 74
miles to Gold Creek and bear right. From here it is almost 10 miles to
Red Ives. (Note: The route through Avery was scheduled for massive
construction and upgrading in the late 1980s.)

To get to the Heller Creek trailhead, cross Red Ives Creek just past the
Red Ives Ranger Station and turn left on Forest Road No. 320. Follow
this rough, rocky road (negotiable for passenger cars with good
clearance). Pass the road leading to Needle Peak on the right 7 miles
from Red Ives and continue another 4 miles to the junction with Forest
Road No. 346. Turn right and drive to the trailhead just south of Heller
Creek campground.

The hike requires little explanation. From Spruce Tree campground,
St. Joe River Trail No. 48 follows an old road up to the old Scat Creek
garnet mine. Past Timber Creek, horse trails meander back and forth
across the river, but the hiking trail stays on the north side. About 5
miles up the river, one will pass a horse-packing concession operated by
St. Joe Lodge. Beyond here, there are many good campsites, particularly
at the points where side trails intersect the St. Joe River Trail. The trail
has its ups and downs, but generally it is an easy route which is usually
well maintained. The trail also offers access to the Bean-Bacon area (see
Hike 75) and Five Lakes Butte (see Hike 79). Fishing on this section of
the St. Joe is governed by special rules requiring the use of single barbless hooks. Check Idaho's fishing regulations carefully.

77 ST. JOE LAKE

Round trip 11 miles
Hiking time 6 hours or overnight
High point 7,100 feet
Elevation gain 1,500 feet
Moderate

Hikable late June through
  September
USGS Illinois Peak
Information: St. Joe National
  Forest, Avery Ranger District

St. Joe Lake, headwaters of Idaho's beautiful St. Joe River, is a high
alpine lake surrounded by steep ridges with snowfields, even in summer.
This trail follows the river—a small stream at this point—to the lake,
which holds small cutthroat trout. Open ridges above beckon the hiker
to explore miles of additional trails on the Idaho-Montana border. Indians once called the lake Swallowing Lake. Legend has it that an Indian once disregarded a tradition of not drinking from the lake. He was
subsequently chased up to the Bitterroot Divide and swallowed by the
waters. The lake was renamed St. Joseph by a Jesuit priest, Father
Peter DeSmet.

From St. Maries, Idaho, drive west of town ½ mile and take the St. Joe
River Road about 50 miles to Avery, mostly on paved roads scheduled for
major construction in the late 1980s. Continue to Red Ives. Immediately
after crossing the Red Ives Creek bridge, turn left on Road No. 320. This
is a very rough road not suitable for vehicles with low clearance. Drive
up and past Heller Creek campground to Medicine Creek. The trailhead
is just across the Medicine Creek bridge. (Many established Forest Ser-

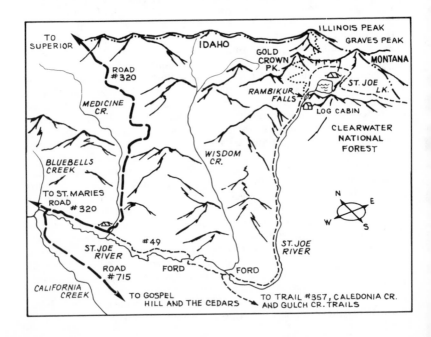

vice campgrounds are scattered along the St. Joe River east of Avery.)

From Superior, Montana, drive 2 miles east on State Highway 257 parallelling Interstate 90. Turn right on Road No. 320 up Cedar Creek. Drive 28 miles to the state line, where Road No. 320 then becomes rougher and drops down along Medicine Creek. As the road approaches the St. Joe River, it bends right and crosses Medicine Creek. The trailhead is just before the Medicine Creek bridge.

From the trailhead, where water and campsites are available, follow St. Joe River Trail No. 49. For several miles the trail follows an old road bed which winds through a scenic valley of grassy meadows. (This road is shown on Forest Service maps published in the '70s.) The trail crosses the St. Joe River twice. During high water, which can last until the end of June, hikers will have to wade the river. Later in the year, one can jump across at narrow spots.

After the first crossing, look across a wide meadow for a silver-colored diamond marker on a tree. The trail begins to gain elevation approximately ¼ mile above Wisdom Creek Trail. Pass the junction of the trail to Bostonian Creek. Continue up the river about 2 miles as the trail opens into a high valley resplendent with wildflowers. Remnants of early-day mining activity can be seen along the trail. Several hand-dug water diversion ditches cross the area around Wisdom Creek. These ditches can be mistaken for the trail if one isn't watching for the blazes and markers. Rambikur Falls highlights the features at the head of the valley. Above the falls, a log cabin still remains in substantial condition. From the cabin, the trail climbs steeply for ¼ mile to the lake. Hikers who become confused at any point should simply remember that the trail generally follows the river all the way to the lake.

A number of campsites can be found on the northeast side of the lake.

St. Joe Lake. (Don Hutchings photo)

Hiking the ridge above the cirque of the lake provides a vista into Montana and additional trails to Illinois Peak and other nearby peaks. On the divide, hikers will find Stateline National Recreation Trail No. 738. The best route to the Stateline Trail branches from Trail No. 49 near the old cabin and climbs to the saddle between Gold Crown Peak and Illinois Peak. This trail is a little steep in spots, but is easier than trying to follow the trail toward Graves Peak. (Stateline Recreation Trail is also accessible from the Cedar Creek-Medicine Creek Road, which it crosses.) Additional side trips besides Stateline Trail are the Missoula Lake Trail and the Oregon Lakes Trail, both in Montana, but accessible from Cedar Creek Road near the state line.

ST. JOE RIVER AREA
Unprotected

78   GIANT WHITE PINE

Round trip 3 miles
Hiking time 1–2 hours
High point 3,200 feet
Elevation gain 400 feet
Easy

Hikable late April through
   October
USGS Emida
Information: St. Joe National
   Forest, St. Maries Ranger
   District

This is an enjoyable walk through some of the few ancient and awesome white pines remaining in northern Idaho. A pleasant Forest Service campground is situated at the trailhead. Interpretive signs edu-

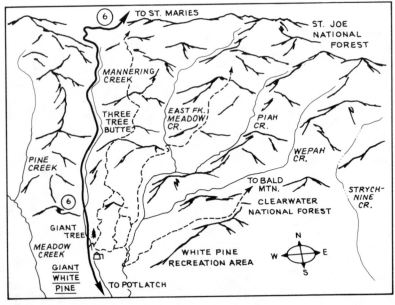

Giant white pine in White Pine Recreation Area. (Rich Landers photo)

cate the hiker at stations along the route. The hike is particularly pleasant in spring, combined with a drive north through St. Maries on State Highway 3, where lakes along the lower Coeur d'Alene River attract a variety of waterfowl.

From Coeur d'Alene, drive south on U.S. Highway 95 to the junction with State Highway 6. Turn east toward Potlatch and drive about 17 miles to the Giant White Pine campground on the east side of the highway. Plenty of parking is available along with campsites, drinking water and pit toilets. Mannering Creek flows along the area.

The 3-mile loop trail starts at the north side of the campground near a large white pine about 6 feet in diameter and 200 feet high. The marker says the tree was just a seedling when Columbus made his first voyage in 1492. The trail is well kept and easy to follow. About ½ mile from the trailhead it leaves Mannering Creek and heads east, climbing gently for ½ mile to a junction with a trail going to Three Tree Butte. Continue east and start descending to the East Fork of Meadow Creek about ½ mile. The wet bottomland gives the trees a rain forest quality as the trail heads south ½ mile to the junction with the trail to Bald Mountain. To return to the campground, the trail climbs moderately for ½ mile then drops for ½ mile to the trailhead.

ST. JOE RIVER AREA
Proposed wilderness

79   FIVE LAKES BUTTE

Round trip 6 miles
Hiking time 4–5 hours or
   overnight
High point 6,713 feet
Elevation gain 1,500 feet
Moderate

Hikable July through September
USGS Bacon Peak, Chamberlain
   Mountain
Information: Lolo, Clearwater
   and St. Joe national forests

This hike leads to a high rocky butte pocked with five lakes and a view overlooking the St. Joe River drainage. It is an outstanding route for those who like exploring high alpine areas and camping near small, secluded lakes.

From Interstate 90, exit at Superior, Montana, and head east on State Highway 257, which runs parallel to the south side of I-90. (The pavement ends at a large saw mill and becomes Trout Creek Road No. 250.) From Superior, drive about 38 miles and turn right on Forest Road No. 720. Drive 14 miles and bear right on Road No. 715 about 5 miles to the well-marked trailhead and well-used camping area. (Note: One needs to purchase a Lolo National Forest map, which shows most of the road access to this hike. Some of the roads and the trails are shown on the Clearwater forest map, while some of the trails coming in from the north are shown on the St. Joe forest map.)

Follow the old road, now Trail No. 233, to the west, climbing 600 vertical feet in 1½ miles to a large open meadow. The trail leads to tiny Tin Lake with Copper Lake tucked behind a small knoll a few hundred yards beyond. Copper Lake is known to have a few resident moose, which deserve to be undisturbed. Both lakes are periodically planted with cutthroat trout. The area has plenty of open areas, but the ground is marshy and not the best for camping except at the south end of the meadow. Expect clouds of mosquitoes during summer.

Silver Lake on Five Lakes Butte. (Don Mattoon photo)

Continue on the trail another ¼ mile, gaining 200 vertical feet up a rocky slope to Silver Lake, which is full of Eastern brook trout. This lake has good campsites away from the shoreline. The trail leads gently another ½ mile to Gold Lake, where one will find the best campsites and a lake stocked with rainbow trout.

Although there is no trail, one can easily complete the hike by heading south up to the ridge, and continuing north for a 900-vertical-foot scramble to the summit of Five Lakes Butte. Here one will find the best view in the area. As an extension, one could contour gradually up and

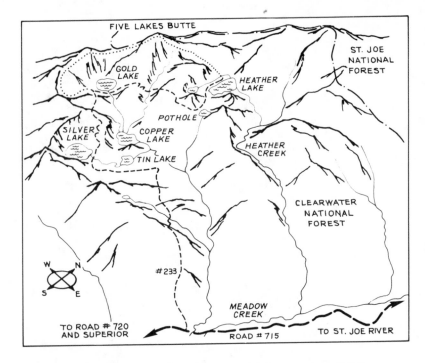

north 1 mile to the pass between two rocky buttresses and follow up a draw to Heather Lake, which is stocked with brook trout. To make a loop, go up to a small pothole and head southwest above timberline back to Gold Lake.

KELLY CREEK
Unprotected

 # PETE OTT LAKE

Round trip 3 miles
Hiking time 3–4 hours or
overnight
High point 6,300 feet
Elevation gain 580 feet
Moderate

Hikable July through mid
September
USGS Elizabeth Lake
Information: Clearwater National
Forest, North Fork Ranger
District

This is a pleasant hike along a ridge trail to several lakes full of brook trout and cutthroats. The road, however, is suitable only for vehicles with good clearance. Only four-wheel-drives might be able to make it the last mile to the trailhead, although the road is easy to walk. Pete Ott and other nearby lakes are nestled in trees below rounded, timbered mountains. Pete Ott Lake is named after a former Forest Service trail foreman who died in 1921.

From Interstate 90, exit at Superior, Montana, and head east on State Highway 257, which runs parallel to the south side of I-90. (The pavement ends at a large saw mill and becomes Trout Creek Road No. 250.) From Superior, drive 53 miles over Hoodoo Pass, through the North Fork of the Clearwater River's Black Canyon to the Kelly Forks intersection. (Serious fishermen should allow an extra day or two to drive this road, which follows the North Fork's excellent cutthroat and rainbow fishery for more than 15 miles.) Turn right at the junction, continuing past the Kelly Creek Ranger Station on Road No. 250 and drive 2⅓ miles to Cold Springs work center. Turn right toward Mush Saddle on Road No. 711. Drive 1½ miles and turn right on unmarked Ice Creek Road. Drive 2⅓ miles up the switchbacks and turn right again. Drive 3¼ miles and turn right yet again, this time through a gate that is scheduled to be open from June 15 through September 15. From here the road can be rough, with deep water drainage ditches for about a mile before it enters the timber. Hikers without four-wheel-drive vehicles might make it this far, but probably should park their vehicles at the last switchback before entering the timber. The road becomes steep and rutted for about ¾ mile (this road still is shown as a trail on 1980 Clearwater National Forest maps) before leveling off at the saddle where the trail begins on the left near an overused campsite. (One also can reach this area via forest roads from Pierce, Idaho.)

From the trampled campsite, follow the blazes to the good foot path of Trail No. 176 for about 1⅔ miles up and down along a ridge to the Pete Ott-Ice Lake junction. Turn right down Trail No. 440-455. At about 200 yards, a trail leads to the left and switchbacks down to Ice Lake, which

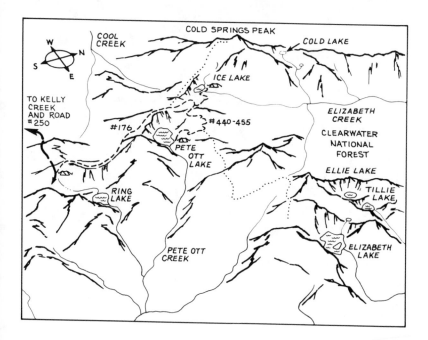

has several small campsites, but they can be boggy until August. Continue on the main trail a short way farther to a trail leading to the right and down ¼ mile to Pete Ott Lake, which has a large campsite. No water is available along the trail.

For further exploration, one might continue on an unmaintained trail to Elizabeth Lake. However, the trail is faint and/or steep in some places, and it's a rugged semi-bushwhack down to the lake. A better side

Ice Lake. (Rich Landers photo)

trip would be to continue on Trail No. 176 from the Pete Ott-Ice Lake trail junction about ¾ mile to Cold Springs Peak, for a good view of the area.

KELLY CREEK
Proposed wilderness

81 KELLY CREEK

Round trip 18 miles
Hiking time 2–3 days
High point 3,830 feet
Elevation gain 630 feet
Moderate
Hikable mid June through October

USGS Gorman Hill, Toboggan Ridge
Information: Clearwater National Forest, North Fork Ranger District

This trail leads into a roadless area, proposed for wilderness, along Kelly Creek. The stream was named after a prospector and now is nationally known because of its excellent fly fishing for native cutthroat trout. It has special regulations requiring anglers to use single, barbless hooks and release all fish caught. The trail is gentle, leading into coun-

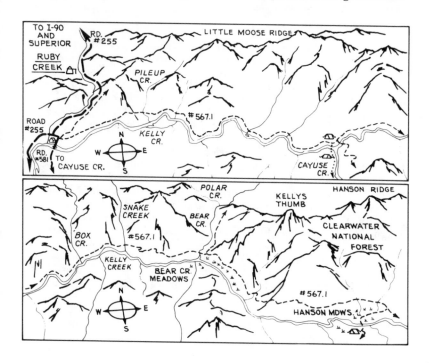

Kelly Creek. (Rich Landers photo)

try full of deer, elk, moose and black bear. The Forest Service was doing major reconstruction on the trail in 1985-87, with long-range plans for a hiker's dream-come-true: a plan that will link the Kelly Creek trail with Stateline Trail No. 738 to make a 21-mile route all the way to Hoodoo Pass at the Montana-Idaho border. When this route is completed, a hiker would be able to spend a week en route, exploring and fishing all the way to the border. But the Kelly Creek trail to Hanson Meadows will always be a splendid hike in itself.

From Interstate 90, exit at Superior, Montana, and head east on State Highway 257, which runs parallel to the south side of I-90. The pavement ends at a large saw mill and becomes Trout Creek Road No. 250. From the end of the pavement, drive 20 miles to Hoodoo Pass. From the beginning of the pavement on the Idaho side of the pass, drive 14½ miles to the junction of Road Nos. 250 and 255. Turn left onto Road No. 255 at a sign that says "Pierce, Idaho, via Kelly Creek." (One who misses this junction will continue down the North Fork of the Clearwater toward Hidden Creek campground.) Follow this road to Deception Saddle, continuing on Road No. 255 south down Independence Creek and Moose Creek to the junction with Road No. 581 at Kelly Creek. (Look up the hill to the left: the large bare area is a mineral lick, where deer and elk come to eat dirt for minerals required in their diets.) The trailhead is just left of the road junction. There's ample parking for dozens of cars, but rarely more than a few there. (One also can reach this area via forest roads from Pierce, Idaho.)

Kelly Creek Trail No. 567.1 follows up the north side of the creek, often ranging high above it. The first 3½ miles of trail to the confluence with Cayuse Creek are gentle with a good view of the creek. The trail is on an open, unshaded south-facing slope which can be hot during mid-day. The creek is broad with occasional deep holes and there are a few places to camp along gravel bars in this section. The Cayuse Creek-Kelly Creek Junction campground is well used, but attractive. (The trail heading up Cayuse Creek is not maintained, but there is a campsite on the south side of Kelly Creek along Cayuse Creek.)

From the Cayuse junction, Kelly Creek trail climbs into the forest, with occasional views of the creek's falls and boulder gardens below. It leads 3½ miles before heading down to camping areas at Bear Creek and Bear Creek Meadow. The trail again retreats from the creek for another 2 miles to good camping areas at Hanson Meadows. The trail in this section is through light forest with abundant huckleberries.

KELLY CREEK
Unprotected

 # 82   CAYUSE CREEK

Round trip 8 miles
Hiking time 3–6 hours or
  overnight
High point 3,650 feet
Elevation gain 150 feet
Moderate

Hikable July through September
USGS Gorman Hill
Information: Clearwater National
  Forest, North Fork Ranger
  District

This hike is especially appealing to hikers who never like to be far from a clear mountain stream, and fly fishers interested in blue-ribbon waters far away from the crowds. The trail runs along Cayuse Creek, a protected catch-and-release native cutthroat stream and tributary to another famous trout stream, Kelly Creek (see Hike 81). The hike leads to good camping areas near Pony Flats, a perfect base camp for dayhiking and fishing. The hike is easy, except for three fords of Cayuse Creek, which can be tricky as late as mid July. Cayuse Creek was named by two trappers in 1887 when they dropped into the drainage and found a pony, or cayuse, that had wintered there.

From Interstate 90, exit at Superior, Montana, and head east on State Highway 257, which runs parallel to the south side of I-90. The pavements ends at a large sawmill and becomes Trout Creek Road No. 250. From the end of the pavement, drive 20 miles to Hoodoo Pass. From the beginning of the pavement on the Idaho side of the pass, drive 14½ miles to the junction of Road Nos. 250 and 255. Turn left onto Road No. 255 at a sign that says "Pierce, Idaho, via Kelly Creek." (One who misses this junction will continue down the North Fork of the Clearwater toward Hidden Creek campground.) Follow this road to Deception Saddle, continuing on Road No. 255 south down Independence Creek and Moose Creek to the junction with Road No. 581 at Kelly Creek. (From here it is 8¾ miles to the Cayuse Creek trailhead.) Turn left on Road No. 581 and cross Kelly Creek. Bear left at the Y and head up, over East Saddle and down to the Cayuse aircraft landing field. The trailhead is just across the Cayuse Creek bridge and to the right. (This road can be rough, but usually it is navigable by passenger cars with good clearance. When muddy, however, it can be passable only to four-wheel-drives.) Several good car-camping areas are scattered around the landing field area. The airstrip is rarely used, but one still wouldn't be wise to pitch a tent on it. (One also can reach this area via forest roads from Orofino, Idaho, or the Lolo Pass area off U.S. Highway 12 southwest of Missoula, Montana.)

Head southwest on Trail No. 532 paralleling Cayuse Creek. At 1 mile, deteriorating Field Creek Trail No. 532 heads up to the left toward Lunde Peak. Continue on Trail No. 532, which is well maintained for 2½ miles to the first crossing of Cayuse Creek. From here, one might have to follow a faint tread, blazes and cut logs to keep on the trail. The route crosses the creek two more times before all but disappearing near Monroe Creek near Pony Flats, a large, gravely burned area. The route passes several good campsites and, of course, water is plentiful.

Although only a handful of people visit Cayuse Creek each year, fly fishers from across the nation have written the Clearwater National

Cayuse Creek. (Rich Landers photo)

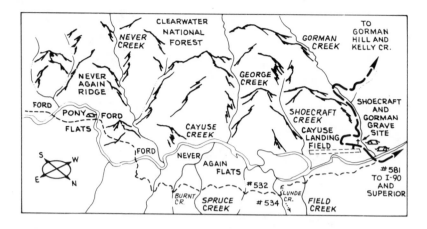

Forest in the early 1980s to protest the proposed Toboggan Creek timber sale, which could destroy part of this hiking trail and seriously threaten the fish-producing water quality of Cayuse and Kelly creeks. More than 700 letters opposing the logging plan poured into the Forest Service in 1984-85, including a strong protest from the Idaho Fish and Game Department. As of 1986, Forest Service officials still had not totally dismissed plans to cut the area, although there were indications the plans could be changed in the forest plan scheduled for release in 1987.

KELLY CREEK
Unprotected

83 GOAT LAKE

Round trip 7 miles
Hiking time 3-4 hours or
** overnight**
High point 7,318 feet
Elevation gain 915 feet

Moderate
Hikable July through September
USGS Rhodes Peak
Information: Clearwater National
** Forest, Powell Ranger District**

Goat Lake is a surprisingly scenic, pristine and lightly used alpine lake surrounded by steep, open cliffs and slopes. It offers many good campsites and fishing. Elk, deer and mountain goats are likely to be seen if one is hiking early or late in the day, although the goats tend to stay in the craggy areas of Williams Creek to the north.

From Missoula, Montana, drive south on U.S. Highway 93 to Lolo. Turn right onto U.S. Highway 12 toward Lewiston, Idaho. Drive 45 miles (over Lolo Pass and into Idaho) and turn right onto Parachute Hill Road No. 569. (This turn is ¼ mile before the turn to Lochsa Lodge and Powell Ranger Station.) From this junction, drive 7 miles to Papoose Saddle. Stay on the main road; don't turn off on the many spur roads.

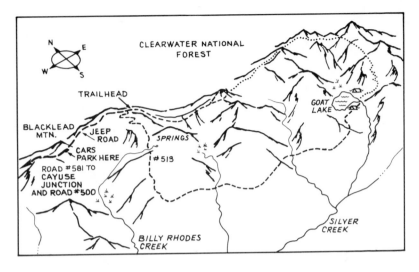

(Also note that the road number changes to No. 500 just before Papoose Saddle at Powell Junction.) From Papoose Saddle, drive 11½ miles to Cayuse Junction. Turn right onto Road No. 581 and drive 8 miles to a road junction marked by a sign reading "Deer Creek Trail No. 513." Turn right onto this rough road and drive 1 mile up to Blacklead Mountain. Hikers without four-wheel-drive vehicles should park here.

If driving to the area from west of Missoula, exit Interstate 90 at Superior and head east on State Highway 257, which runs parallel to the

Goat Lake. (Rich Landers photo)

south side of I-90. The pavements ends at a large sawmill and becomes Trout Creek Road No. 250. From the end of the pavement, drive 20 miles to Hoodoo Pass. From the beginning of the pavement on the Idaho side of the pass, drive 14½ miles to the junction of Road Nos. 250 and 255. Turn left onto Road No. 255 at a sign that says "Pierce, Idaho, via Kelly Creek." (One who misses this junction will continue down the North Fork of the Clearwater toward Hidden Creek campground.) Follow this road to Deception Saddle, continuing on Road No. 255 south down Independence Creek and Moose Creek to the junction with Road No. 581 at Kelly Creek. (From here it is 8¾ miles to Cayuse Creek. See Hike 82.) Turn left on Road No. 581 and cross Kelly Creek. Bear left at the Y and head up, over East Saddle and down to the Cayuse landing field. (The road up to East Saddle can be rough, but usually it is navigable by passenger cars with good clearance. When muddy, however, it can be passable only to four-wheel-drives.) From the Cayuse Creek Bridge, drive 17⅓ miles on Road No. 581 up Toboggan Ridge to the turnoff toward Deer Creek Trail No. 513 and Blacklead Mountain.

From the top of Blacklead Mountain, begin hiking north along a jeep road down the open ridge for ½ mile, where the road ends in a saddle. Trail No. 513 heads off the ridge to the east, switchbacking down the steep slope. Soon the trail levels off and contours around through timber and open slopes about 3 miles to the lake.

For hikers who aren't opposed to a little cross-country walking, an excellent loop trip can be made by following the ridges to Goat Lake. From the end of the jeep road, a trail can be seen heading straight up the ridge to the northeast. This tread leads up to an unnamed 7,514-foot peak. From here, stay to the left of the ridge, crossing talus and heading up a slope of scattered timber to another unnamed peak, elev. 7,497 feet. From here, one can see the lake and several tarns above it. Rock cliffs make it tricky to go straight down to the lake. The best route is to follow the ridge farther, swinging east and down another ridge just north of the lake and coming down a grassy slope to the outlet. Return via Trail No. 513 to complete the loop.

KELLY CREEK
Unprotected

 # LOST LAKES

Round trip 6 miles
Hiking time 3–4 hours or
   overnight
High point 6,970 feet
Elevation gain 860 feet
Moderate

Hikable late June through
   September
USGS Cayuse Junction
Information: Clearwater National
   Forest, Powell Ranger District

This hike won't appeal to everyone. The lakes are in a valley, surrounded by timber and trampled by the feet of elk. But it's a peaceful walk into the heart of big game country and the headwaters of what be-

Lost Lakes. (Rich Landers photo)

comes a great fishing stream called Cayuse Creek.

From Missoula, Montana, drive south on U.S. Highway 93 to Lolo. Turn right onto U.S. Highway 12 toward Lewiston, Idaho. Drive 45 miles (over Lolo Pass and into Idaho) and turn right onto Parachute Hill Road No. 569. (This turn is ¼ mile before the turn to Lochsa Lodge and Powell Ranger Station.) From this junction, drive 7 miles to Papoose Saddle. Stay on the main road; don't turn off on the many spur roads. (Also note that the road number changes to No. 500 just before Papoose Saddle at Powell Junction.) From Papoose Saddle, continue west on Road No. 500 3¾ miles to the trailhead, which is at a pullout to the right as the road comes up to a timbered ridge. The only sign marking the trail is a credit-card-sized aluminum marker with "Lolo Trail" scratched into it. The Lolo Trail is the historic route used by generations of Indians and also by the Lewis and Clark Expedition. It's notable that while the expedition nearly starved as it traveled through this area, the region is now filled with elk that weren't to be found here a century ago.

Trail No. 13 has a good tread maintained primarily by elk, hunters and erosion. The Forest Service maintains it about every other year. It climbs gently at first, then follows a pleasant open ridge for about ¼ mile. Then it plunges steeply down for ¼ mile before becoming gentle again. It crosses Cayuse Creek, which is an easy ford at this elevation, except in late June when hikers are likely to get wet over their boots. From here it is about ½ mile to the lower lake and the junction with Lost Lake Trail No. 35. A few campsites can be found around the lakes, the largest of which is just west of the middle lake, but this is a licensed outfitter's camp. Backpackers should be courteous and camp away from this site. All of the lakes have catchable-sized fish. This area could be a bit on

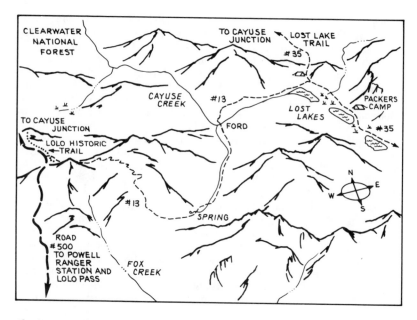

the buggy side in July and early August. Perhaps it is at its prettiest in September, when the brush is ablaze with red.

Beyond the lakes, the trail heads down into the Boulder Creek drainage.

SELWAY RIVER
Selway-Bitterroot Wilderness

85 SELWAY CRAGS-COVE LAKES

Round trip 13 miles
Hiking time 2 days minimum
High point 7,000 feet
Elevation gain 1,840 feet
Difficult
Hikable mid July through
September

USGS Fenn Mountain, Fog Mountain
Information: Nez Perce National Forest, Moose Creek Ranger District

This is a rugged but rewarding hike that roller-coasters into one of the most scenic—and popular—areas of the 1.8-million acre Selway-Bitterroot Wilderness. The crags, as one might guess, is an alpine area of sky-scratching peaks pocked with lakes. This trip is but an introduction to trails that offer many extensions into the heart of the wilderness. The area is fragile and off-limits to pack animals. Hikers, too, must respect the area by camping at least 200 feet away from the lakes.

From Lewiston, Idaho, drive east on U.S. Highway 12 about 95 miles to Lowell, a small resort area situated where the Selway and Lochsa rivers meet to form the Middle Fork of the Clearwater. Turn southeast, cross the bridge over the Clearwater and follow the road upstream for about 17 miles, keeping to the left of the Selway River. (Information is available from the Fenn Ranger Station, clearly visible on the left side of the road about 7 miles up from the Clearwater bridge, or farther up the road at the Selway Falls Ranger Station.) After crossing Gedney Creek turn left onto Fog Mountain Road. (The turnoff is signed, but can be missed.) This road leaves the Selway River canyon and switchbacks steeply up ridges and slopes for about 14 miles, gaining 4,100 feet, to the trailhead at Big Fog Saddle. The road is rocky, rutted and slow even for vehicles with good clearance. Vehicles with low clearance probably can make it, but at a snail's pace. It is especially hazardous when wet. Big Fog Saddle offers the highest elevation vehicle access to the Selway Crags. There is plenty of parking space.

From the saddle, take the western most trail (a section of Trail No. 693) toward Cove Lakes. Beginning at 5,850 feet, the trail heads northwest through trees and brush, dropping as low as elev. 5,160 feet as it crosses two forks of Canteen Creek. It then climbs brushy slopes along poor trail, which becomes steep and gullied. In places, footing is loose. These few miles are the most difficult en route to Cove Lakes. The trail tops out at 7,000 feet in a pleasant subalpine meadow with wildflowers and trickles of water. After traversing the meadow, the trail drops to a ledge at 6,600 feet that looks north to the central part of the Crags with the two Cove Lakes below. From here, the trail drops quickly to the lakes as shown on the USGS maps. Campsites are on the two moraines, one at the lower end of each cirque lake. There's a good site north of the upper lake.

Cove Lakes are a good introduction to the Crags, but not necessarily a good base camp from which to explore. It's a tough pull out of the lakes to get into the South Three Links area and the base of beautiful Fenn Mountain. But many hikers make this excursion as a daytrip from Cove Lakes.

During the Pleistocene, these mountains were covered with a small

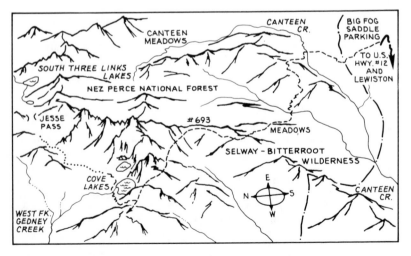

Fenn Mountain and the ridge above Three Links Lakes in the Selway Crags. (Tom McMaster photo)

ice cap that sent short valley glaciers radiating outward in all directions. Glacial activity has carved numerous subalpine basins, cirque lakes, horns, and arêtes into granite bedrock of the Idaho Batholith. Cove Lakes sit at the southern edge of this rugged and rocky area. Fenn Mountain, at elev. 8,021 feet, is the highest point. Huckleberries are abundant and moose, elk, deer and other wildlife can be seen in this relatively remote and unvisited area. Many of the lakes in the Crags are stuffed with brook trout; a few have been stocked with cutthroats. The area north of Cove Lakes is managed as a pristine area, which means trails are not maintained and signs are not posted.

86 TUCANNON RIVER- DIAMOND PEAK LOOP

Round trip 21 miles
Hiking time 2 days minimum
High point 6,325 feet
Elevation gain 2,700 feet
Moderately difficult

Hikable June through early
October
USGS Stentz Spring, Diamond
Peak, Panjab Creek
Information: Umatilla National
Forest, Pomeroy Ranger
District

This loop provides a vigorous two-day, or a more leisurely two-and-a-half-day, backpacking trip. Because of the scenic vistas, it's a good introduction to the Wenaha-Tucannon Wilderness.

From U.S. Highway 12 about 4 miles west of Pomeroy, Washington (or 8 miles east of Dodge), turn south on Linville Gulch Road. Follow the signs for Camp Wooten and Tatman Mountain, joining the Tucannon River Road after 9 miles. Turn south on Tucannon River Road and drive 13 miles, passing Camp Wooten, to the Tucannon River bridge at the junction with Panjab Creek. Numerous camping areas are available along the Tucannon River. Just before the bridge, turn left onto Forest Road No. 4712 and parallel the Tucannon River east 4½ miles to the end of the road. To make the loop easier, shuttle a car (or leave a bicycle) back at the Tucannon River-Panjab Creek junction.

From the trailhead, follow Trail No. 3135 about 4¼ miles along the Tucannon River to the confluence with Bear Creek. This is an easy walk that passes several good campsites. This section of trail is not inside the Wenaha-Tucannon Wilderness boundaries, but has remained relatively undisturbed. Beyond the Tucannon River crossing, ¼ mile above Bear Creek, the trail becomes Trail No. 6144 and gains a whopping 1,000 feet

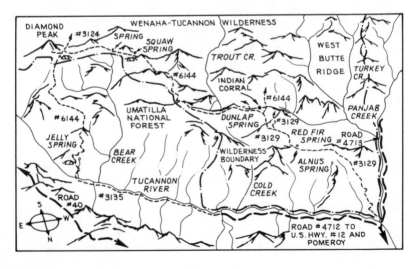

Tucannon River Canyon, Wenaha-Tucannon Wilderness. (Rich Landers photo)

of elevation in 1 mile. The ridge near Jelly Spring (a reliable water source and a good campsite) is reached at 5¼ miles from the trailhead. It offers the hiker the first scenic vistas. Similar wide-angle views are available frequently for the rest of this loop hike.

At 8½ miles, Trail No. 6144 joins with Trail No. 3124 at elev. 6,100 feet on Diamond Peak. Here one must decide whether to camp or to continue west on Trail No. 6144 to an excellent campsite at Squaw Spring 2¼ easy miles away. Check on water quality in Diamond Spring, about 200 yards south of the trail junction before making the decision. (Unless one enjoys stinging nettles and crashing through dense alder to get to a muddy elk wallow, forget about Sheephead Spring, which is midway between Squaw Spring and Diamond Spring.)

From Squaw Spring, continue west on Trail No. 6144 (Mt. Misery Trail) to the junction with Trail No. 3129, which is 7¼ miles west of Diamond Peak. Nearby Dunlap Spring is a reliable water source and a good campsite. At the junction with Trail No. 3129, turn right, heading north on Trail No. 3129. Pass campsites at Red Fir and Alnus Springs at 2 and 3 miles respectively from Indian Corral. The trail between Diamond Peak and Alnus Spring is easy, straying little from an elevation of about 5,500 feet. After Alnus Spring, it descends steeply, dropping 2,300 feet in the last 2 miles to the road at the confluence of the Tucannon River and Panjab Creek.

87 OREGON BUTTE SPRING

Round trip 4½ miles
Hiking time 3 hours or overnight
High point 6,200 feet
Elevation gain 700 feet
Easy

Hikable early June through
** October**
USGS Oregon Butte
Information: Umatilla National
** Forest, Pomeroy Ranger**
** District**

This is an easy out-and-back hike which can be extended into a down-hill overnighter to the Tucannon River. It is especially appealing to parties that can leave a shuttle vehicle at the end of the trail. Oregon Butte, an old Forest Service lookout site, offers a high vantage over the rugged Wenaha-Tucannon Wilderness. The lookout cabin, abandoned in 1973, still stands.

From U.S. Highway 12 about 4 miles west of Pomeroy, Washington (or 8 miles east of Dodge), turn south on Linville Gulch Road. Follow the signs for Camp Wooten and Tatman Mountain, joining the Tucannon River Road after 9 miles. Turn south on Tucannon River Road. About 2 miles past Camp Wooten, turn right onto Forest Road No. 4620. Drive 4 miles and turn left on Forest Road No. 46 (Skyline Road). Continue south on Skyline Road for 14 miles and turn left onto Road No. 4608 at the Godman Spring Guard Station. Continue east 6 miles to the end of the road at Teepee campground, elev. 5,500 feet.

Follow Trail No. 3143, heading east for 2¼ miles to Oregon Butte Spring, generally through old-growth timber on shady north slopes. The spring is right on the trail, with campsites up the hillside 50 yards farther. More exposed tent sites, offering a spectacular sunrise view of the northern part of the wilderness area, can be found 400 yards beyond the spring and above the junction with Trail No. 6144.

Near Oregon Butte, Wenaha-Tucannon Wilderness. (Rich Landers photo)

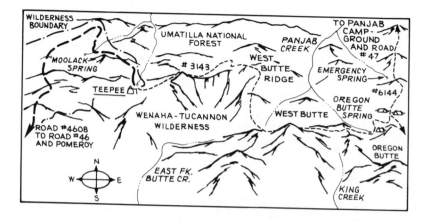

Interesting side trips include hikes to the summits of West Butte and Oregon Butte (with its old lookout cabin). The first 2 miles heading south on Trail No. 6144 are open and studded with numerous springs, wildflowers and huckleberries. This area is very popular with nesting hummingbirds as well as a variety of hawks that glide effortlessly in the updrafts.

Hiking parties with more than one vehicle can shuttle a car to the campground at the confluence of Panjab Creek and the Tucannon River on Forest Road No. 47, where they will end up after a delightful hike that drops 3,200 feet in elevation in about 8 miles. From Oregon Butte Spring, head north on Trail No. 6144, following ridges about 3 miles to the junction at Indian Corral (about 5½ miles from Teepee campground). There's a good campsite at nearby Dunlap Spring, a short way down Trail No. 3100. From the Indian Corral junction, head north, descending on Trail No. 3129 past good campsites at Red Fir Spring (1½ miles from Indian Corral) and Alnus Spring (3 miles from Indian Corral) to the trailhead at Panjab campground.

BLUE MOUNTAINS
Wenaha-Tucannon Wilderness

SQUAW SPRING

Round trip 5 miles
Hiking time 3–4 hours or
    overnight
High point 6,379 feet
Elevation gain 400 feet
Easy

Hikable early June through
    October
USGS Diamond Peak
Information: Umatilla National
    Forest, Pomeroy Ranger
    District

This is an uncommonly easy hike into the rugged Wenaha-Tucannon Wilderness. It avoids the radical ups and downs of other routes and is suitable for families. It can be done as a daytrip or as an overnighter and

Rocky Mountain elk in Wenaha-Tucannon Wilderness. (Rich Landers photo)

has several options for side trips.

From Pomeroy, Washington, head south on State Highway 128 about 7½ miles and make a 90-degree left turn. Drive 2 miles to the end of the pavement and continue straight onto Forest Road No. 40, driving about 21 miles from the left turn to Misery Spring. Turn right onto Forest Road No. 4030 and drive to its end at Diamond Peak.

From the parking area, walk south up a short, steep path less than 200 yards to the well-used Misery Diamond Trail. Turn right (west), entering the wilderness and walking past the north side of Diamond Peak to a junction with Trail No. 6144, ¼ mile from the trailhead. Continue west on this easily followed trail past Sheephead Corral at 1½ miles. This

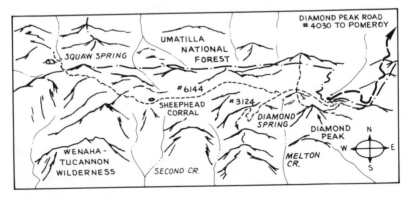

could be a good campsite, except it has poor access to water. Squaw Spring is reached at 2½ miles, where one will find a good wind-sheltered campsite with clear-flowing (but not necessarily safe) water.

Side trips on this route include a scramble to the summit of Diamond Peak, which is about a 200-foot elevation gain above the main trail. Also, Trail No. 6144 north from Diamond Peak trailhead offers good views of the upper Tucannon River drainage, and Trail No. 3124, heading south from Trail No. 6144, offers a good overlook of the Melton Creek drainage from its first switchback.

BLUE MOUNTAINS
Wenaha-Tucannon Wilderness

89 DIAMOND PEAK-WELLER BUTTE LOOP

Round trip 39 miles
Hiking time 4–5 days
High point 6,379
Elevation gain 4,000 feet
Difficult
Hikable early June through early
   October

USGS Diamond Peak, Stentz
   Spring, Panjab Creek, Oregon
   Butte
Information: Umatilla National
   Forest, Pomeroy Ranger
   District

This circuit encompasses about one-quarter of the Wenaha-Tucannon Wilderness of southeastern Washington's Blue Mountains. The route is as rugged as the steep canyon-scarred wilderness itself, but it is a rewarding trip for hikers in good physical condition. Water is scarce; filtering devices are recommended to procure water from springs.

From Pomeroy, Washington, head south on State Highway 128 about 7½ miles and make a 90-degree left turn. Leave the pavement after 2 miles and continue straight onto Forest Road No. 40, driving about 21 miles from the left turn to Misery Spring. Turn right onto Forest Road No. 4030 and drive to its end at Diamond Peak.

From the parking area, walk south, up to the Mount Misery-Diamond Peak Trail. Turn right and walk to the junction of Trail Nos. 6144 and 3124 at ½ mile. Turn left (south) onto Trail No. 3124, which switchbacks frequently as it descends 3,600 vertical feet over approximately 10 miles to the Melton Creek crossing just above the junction with Crooked Creek. A good campsite is situated just east of the Melton Creek crossing, although it is preferable to continue south another mile to campsites at (or 300 yards south of) the First Creek crossing. This first day is 11½ miles of rather rugged canyon-land scenery and a definite test for a hiker's legs.

On Day 2, load up with water and head up the pack trail that crosses Crooked Creek 400 yards south of the First Creek crossing. (There also is an unmaintained trail heading up a small trickle known as Coyote Creek. The trail joins the main trail.) Follow this trail steeply up the ridge for 1¾ miles, gaining 1,600 feet of elevation. Here the trail enters

221

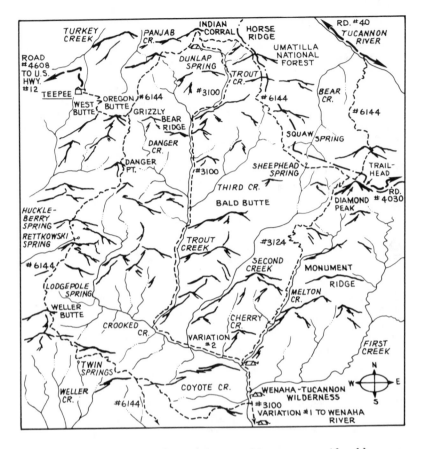

grassy parklands and Ponderosa pines, and becomes considerably more moderate. Hike another 2¼ miles, gaining another 1,000 feet, to the junction with Trail No. 6144. (Hikers who didn't fill at least two water bottles at the beginning of the day probably will be dry at this point, with no water available for yet another 2 miles at Twin Spring.) Bear right onto Trail No. 6144, continuing west about 2½ miles to Weller Butte. Head north from the butte 1½ miles, crossing two saddles, to Lodgepole Spring. Camp here for a total day's distance of 10 miles and an elevation gain of more than 3,000 feet.

Day 3 is a much easier 10 miles, with only 1,000 feet of elevation gain. Continue north on Trail No. 6144 past Rettkowski Spring and Huckleberry Spring toward Oregon Butte. The last 2 miles of trail south of Oregon Butte offer outstanding views, with ripe huckleberries available in late July and early August. (One could make it a 7-mile day and camp at Oregon Butte, where there's a lookout cabin and a spring on Trail No. 3143 about ½ mile from Oregon Butte Summit.) Continue north, heading down from Oregon Butte to Camp No. 3 at Dunlap Spring, which is about a hundred yards south of Trail No. 6144 on Trail No. 3100. Look to the right.

From Dunlap Spring, Day 4 is relatively easy. Walk back up to Trail No. 6144 and head east for a rolling 7½-mile hike over open ridges. The trail exposes one to great views to the south (the country covered the first three days) at Sheephead and Squaw Springs before making the complete loop to the trailhead on the north slope of Diamond Peak.

Here are a few variations to consider.

Option 1: Make this a five-day trip by continuing south on Trail No. 3100 the second day, reaching the Wenaha River at 4½ miles, then turning west onto Trail No. 3106. Camp at the plane wreckage below the junction of Trail No. 3106 and Trail No. 6144 for a 7½ mile day or continue up Trail No. 6144 another 1½ miles to a campsite at Soap Spring. (There's another campsite ½ mile farther at Mud Spring.) The USGS Eden quadrangle map is useful for this variation.

Option 2: Make this an easier four-day trip. Ascend Crooked Creek on Day 2 via Trail No. 3100 about 9 miles and spend the night at an excellent campsite at a stream junction located at the bottom center of Section 35 on the Wenaha-Tucannon Wilderness map prepared by the Umatilla National Forest. Then continue north for a short 3½-mile day to Dunlap Spring and finish the loop to Diamond Peak as described above.

Option 3: This loop and any of the above variations can be done by starting at Teepee campground. (See Oregon Butte Spring, Hike 87 for directions to the trailhead.) Add 4½ miles to the total distance of the loop, since Teepee campground is 2¼ miles from Trail 6144. Hikers should travel clockwise (north from Oregon Butte) on the first day to avoid ascending rather than descending the steep and sunny, bone-dry 10 miles and 3,600 feet of elevation between Diamond Peak and Crooked Creek. On Day 1, camp at Squaw Spring (10½ miles from Teepee campground), then follow directions for the standard route described above.

Mule deer in Wenaha-Tucannon Wilderness. (Rich Landers photo)

90 TWIN BUTTES- WENAHA RIVER LOOP

Round trip 18½ miles
Hiking time 2 days
High point 5,400 feet
Elevation gain 2,800 feet
Moderately difficult
Hikable early June through October

USGS Godman Springs, Wenaha Forks, Elbow Creek, Oregon Butte
Information: Umatilla National Forest, Pomeroy Ranger District

This is the trip for the fit hiker who has only two days in which to see the best of the Wenaha-Tucannon Wilderness. Typical of this vertical country, hikers will encounter some steep trails up and down the canyons.

From U.S. Highway 12 about 4 miles west of Pomeroy, Washington (or 8 miles east of Dodge), turn south on Linville Gulch Road. Follow the signs for Camp Wooten and Tatman Mountain, joining the Tucannon River Road after 9 miles. Turn south on Tucannon River Road. About 2 miles past Camp Wooten, turn right onto Forest Road No. 4620. Drive 4 miles and turn left on Forest Road No. 46 (Skyline Road). Continue south on Skyline Road for 14 miles to the turnoff for Godman Spring Guard Station. Pass the turnoff, continuing south 6 miles, and turn left

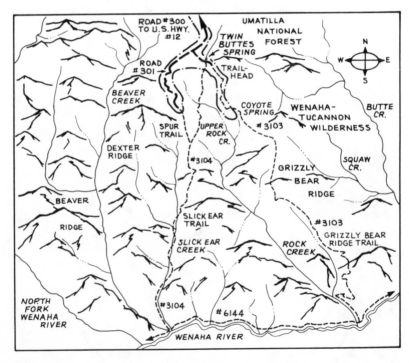

Grizzly Bear Ridge in the Wenaha-Tucannon Wilderness. (Richard Rivers photo)

onto Forest Road No. 300. Drive 5 miles to a parking area at Twin Buttes Spring. The trailhead is just beyond the spring to the south.

Trail No. 3104 (Slick Ear Trail) starts on a ridge, drops 300 feet to cross upper Rock Creek, then regains the elevation before descending a semi-open ridge for 1 mile. It then drops steeply to Slick Ear Creek. The first 1½ miles of this trail are not maintained by the Forest Service. (Trail crews do maintain the spur trail that connects Slick Ear Trail with the end of Forest Road No. 301.) The trail follows the creek to the Wenaha River, 6 miles from the trailhead. At the Wenaha River, turn left onto Trail No. 6144, which follows the river 4¾ miles downstream to Rock Creek and the junction with Trail No. 3103. Camp at any one of several sites near this junction.

On Day 2, load up with water and ascend Trail No. 3103, known as the Grizzly Bear Ridge Trail even though there are no grizzlies in the Wenaha-Tucannon Wilderness. After 1 mile, the trail reaches the ridge. Here, with wind-whipped fir snags in the foreground and miles of Wenaha River leading the eye to distant gorge walls, is one of the best photographic viewpoints in the area. About ½ mile farther, the trail enters a grassy parkland of scattered Ponderosa pines, an ecosystem as unique as it is striking in its beauty. Along with the eastern slopes of Smooth Ridge (10 miles to the east), this is one of very few virgin Ponderosa pine-grass parklands to escape the chain saws in Washington. The grasslands here serve as summer home to two of the most colorful birds of the Northwest, the Audubon warbler and the western tanager.

From here, the trail continues at a more gradual incline up Grizzly Bear Ridge, generally in the shade of towering firs and pines. It is 8 miles from the Wenaha River to Twin Buttes Spring with no water easily available in between. In the region of Coyote Spring (easily missed) the trail seems to disappear in several open areas, leaving the hiker on any one of numerous elk trails, which themselves then vanish. There is a deceptive old motor vehicle road near the ridge top, which also vanishes. Trust your topo map and compass and stay well to the west and below the ridge during the last 1½ miles of this trail.

BLUE MOUNTAINS
Wenaha-Tucannon Wilderness

WENAHA RIVER

One way 21 miles
Hiking time 2–4 days
High point 4,950 feet
Elevation gain 2,500 feet
Difficult

Hikable June through October
USGS Eden, Elbow Creek,
  Wenaha Forks
Information: Umatilla National
  Forest, Pomeroy Ranger
  District

This excellent hike takes one along the shores of the Wenaha River through a variety of terrain, from forest and alpine meadows to dry rocky canyon lands. The best way to enjoy the hike is to leave a shuttle vehicle at the east end of the hike and begin the walk from Elk Flats. Beware, however, that early-season hikers could have some difficulty in crossing the Wenaha toward the end of the hike. Hikers also should be on the lookout for rattlesnakes, which are known to inhabit this area.

From Troy, Oregon, drive south on the main road ⅓ mile and turn right. Continue west 2¼ miles to another fork in the road and bear right onto Forest Road No. 62. Drive 19 miles to Elk Flats campground.

If possible, shuttle a car 8 miles back down Road No. 62, turning left onto Road No. 6212 and driving 4⅓ miles to the head of Hoodoo Ridge Trail No. 3244 north of Long Meadows.

The hike begins on the Elk Flats-North Fork Wenaha River Trail No. 3241 at 4,950 feet and plunges down a total of 2,800 feet in 5 miles to the North Fork. Actually, the trail is fairly steep at first with several switchbacks; then it levels off after 3 miles and becomes gentle for a mile as it heads through a dark old forest. The last 2 miles of trail offer magnificent views of the Wenaha's headwaters.

The trail first crosses via a few toppled logs to the north side of the South Fork, where signs of several well-used horse camps can be seen. Hike ½ mile farther to the North Fork. The best crossing in 1986 was about ¼ mile downstream from the trail over a fairly large log. (The easiest way to get to it was to hike parallel to the river, about 100 feet away, through sandy areas among the heavy undergrowth.) Once across the North Fork, hikers will be on the Wenaha River Trail.

Continue hiking downstream. After several miles, the trail alternates from following the edge of the river to skirting up the canyon wall. Several good flat campsites can be found when the trail comes close to the

Wenaha River, Wenaha-Tucannon Wilderness. (Richard Rivers photo)

river. Rattlesnakes have been seen in this area. Continue hiking east along the river. Note the gradual change in vegetation. The farther east one travels, the drier the canyon becomes. The junction with the Cross Canyon Trail is at mile 14. This is an alternate exit from the Wenaha Canyon which should be noted, especially early in the season when the river is high. A large log makes this a dependable place to cross the river for an exit to the south.

At mile 16, the trail passes the wreckage of a downed plane, where one will find a good campsite. About 4 miles farther east, the trail crosses a flat, wide meadow. A wooden sign on a tree marks the crossing for the Hoodoo Ridge Trail. Walk straight past the sign to the river where it is

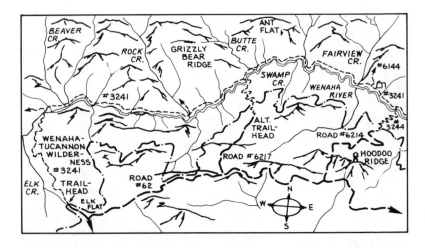

wide and shallow. The only way to cross here is to wade. (Sneakers come in handy.) The trail starts on the other side of the river at 2,100 feet and heads upward immediately. About 15 switchbacks lead up the mile from the river to the trailhead, a gain of 1,800 feet.

WALLOWA MOUNTAINS
Eagle Cap Wilderness

92 ICE LAKE

Round trip 16 miles
Hiking time 2 days minimum
High point 7,920 feet
Elevation gain 3,220 feet
Moderately difficult

Hikable early July through late
 October
USGS Eagle Cap
Information: Wallowa-Whitman
 National Forest, Wallowa Lake
 Ranger Station

Ice Lake is a popular destination in the Eagle Cap Wilderness even though many hikers might be discouraged by a long series of switchbacks to its perch in the granite slopes of the Hurwal Divide. The lake is at timberline below Sacajawea and the Matterhorn, the two highest peaks in the Wallowas.

From Enterprise, Oregon, drive south on State Highway 82 to Joseph. Follow the clearly marked signs through Joseph leading to Wallowa Lake, and continue driving approximately 4 miles around the east side of the lake. At the south end of the lake there is a fork in the road. The trailhead is straight ahead 1 mile at the end of the road by a power substation. (By bearing right at the fork, one would end up at Wallowa Lake State Park, where overnight camping accommodations and hot showers are available during the summer season.) Pitching tents at the trailhead is not permitted. The state park campground operates on a reservation system from Memorial Day through Labor Day weekend. Reservations can be made beginning in January by mail. Contact Wallowa Lake State Park, Route 1, Box 323, Joseph, OR 97846, telephone (503) 238-7488.

A sign showing the various trail systems into the lakes is situated at the trailhead. Follow the signs onto West Fork Wallowa River Trail No. 1820 toward the Lake Basin. This is one of the most popular trails in the wilderness, beginning at elev. 4,700 feet. Hike about 2¾ miles, gaining 900 feet in elevation and turn right at the junction with a trail heading uphill to the west toward Ice Lake. From here, much of the horse and foot traffic continues south toward the heavily used Lake Basin (see Hike 95), but there's no shortage of diehards willing to head up to Ice Lake. Cross a bridge and be prepared to start heading steadily up; make sure you have plenty of water. This well-graded trail makes 37 switchbacks in 5¼ miles to the lake. This is the steepest part of the hike, but it's also the most beautiful. Look for a good lunch stop near a breathtaking view of a waterfall between switchbacks 22 and 23.

Ice Lake is a cold, refreshing, blue-green lake with several good camp-

Ice Lake and Eagle Cap Peak, Eagle Cap Wilderness. (Chuck Kerkering photo)

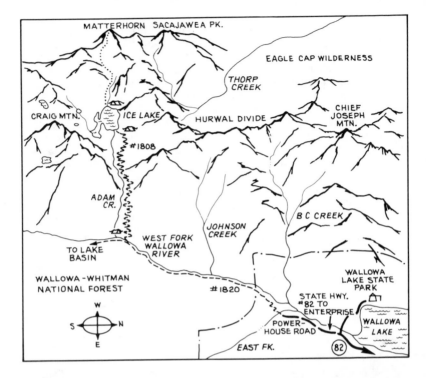

sites to the right (north) of the trail as it approaches the lake. It is possible to scramble to the top of both the Matterhorn and Sacajawea Peak following a trail that starts from the far west end of the lake near the inlet stream.

WALLOWA MOUNTAINS
Eagle Cap Wilderness

93 SWAMP LAKE

Round trip 18 miles
Hiking time 2 days minimum
High point 8,400 feet
Elevation gain 2,800 feet
Moderate

Hikable late July through
  September
USGS Eagle Cap
Information: Wallowa-Whitman
  National Forest, Eagle Cap
  Ranger District

Swamp Lake is a small, picturesque lake off the beaten track of the more popular Lakes Basin. It is not swampy in the sense of a shallow lake. Instead, one end of the lake is dotted with tiny grass islands in shapes that have the appearance of a finely arranged Japanese garden.

From Enterprise, Oregon, drive northwest on State Highway 82 about

10 miles to Lostine. As the highway through town bends right, watch for a white-steepled church on the left and a green sign indicating the Lostine River. Turn left onto Lostine Canyon Road No. 8210 and proceed south about 17 miles to Two Pan campground. The first 7 miles of this road are paved, then the gravel road gradually becomes narrower and more rocky. Drivers in vehicles with low clearance should be very careful. Plenty of parking is available at Two Pan campground, along with a bulletin board that usually has trail information.

From the bulletin board, follow the trail to the left for ¼ mile to a junction and head right onto West Lostine River Trail No. 1670. This trail, the main route to Minam Lake, climbs gradually beside the Lostine River through dense forest. Hike 2¾ miles and head right on Copper Creek Trail No. 1656, crossing the Lostine River. The trail crosses at a shallow spot, but there is no bridge. Walk 100 yards upriver where a fallen log might still be spanning the stream.

The trail follows the north side of Copper Creek. Finding water is no problem. The trail crosses Copper Creek three or four times. Crossings can be treacherous often through July. Again the trail is of moderate steepness, going from dense forest to more sparsely forested terrain, finally into open meadows about 2½ to 3 miles from the turnoff. This is a trail on which one keeps thinking the lake is "just over the next ridge." The trail continues by Copper Creek through some rocky meadows that are filled with flowers during much of the hiking season. Several good campsites can be found in this area. When the creek starts to peter out, fill water bottles as this is the last water until reaching the lake.

After winding through sparsely timbered meadows and numerous

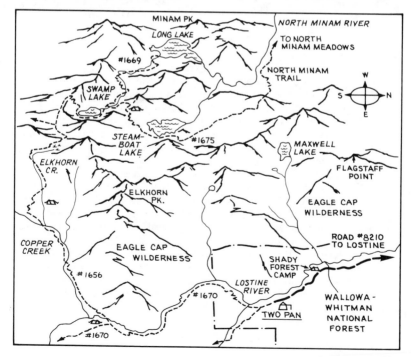

Swamp Lake, Eagle Cap Wilderness. (Mary Weathers photo)

false hopes for reaching the lake, one reaches a high rocky plateau with beautiful views into the Minam River valley and beyond. Below to the right, Swamp Lake comes into view, nestled in a picturesque basin. The trail traverses the plateau at 8,400 feet, then meets a junction with Trail No. 1676 to Upper Minam River at 5 miles past the Copper Creek turnoff. Continuing toward Swamp Lake, the trail descends a steep embankment via switchbacks to the south end of the lake at 7,700 feet and closeup views of the "Japanese garden."

The lake is surrounded by small meadows and rocky slopes. Following the trail a short way past the north end of the lake, one encounters the junction of the trails to Long Lake and Steamboat Lake. Since campsites must be 200 feet from lakes, an example of a good place to camp is reached by following the Steamboat Lake Trail for a short distance to the pass betwen the lakes. Here one will find a pond with good views.

It is an easy 1¾ miles to Steamboat Lake at 7,300 feet. The lake's terrain is similar to Swamp Lake and takes its name from a rock island in the center. The trail to Long Lake, though shorter (1 mile), descends in a steep, rough, unmaintained path. Long Lake is surrounded by trees with plenty of campsites. Both of these lakes make good side trips; all are periodically stocked with trout.

94 MIRROR LAKE

Round trip 13 miles
Hiking time 2 days
High point 7,600 feet
Elevation gain 2,000 feet
Moderate

Hikable July through early
October
USGS Eagle Cap
Information: Wallowa-Whitman
National Forest, Eagle Cap
Ranger District

This is a popular route to the heart of Eagle Cap Wilderness and a lake which often reflects the stunning image of 9,595-foot Eagle Cap Peak.

From Enterprise, Oregon, drive northwest on State Highway 82 about 10 miles to Lostine. As the highway through town bends right, watch for a white-steepled church on the left and a green sign indicating the Lostine River. Turn left onto Lostine Canyon Road No. 8210 and proceed south about 17 miles to Two Pan campground. The first 7 miles of this road are paved. From there, the road gradually becomes narrower and more rocky. Drivers in vehicles with low clearance should be very careful. Plenty of parking is available at Two Pan campground, along with a bulletin board that usually has trail information.

From the bulletin board, follow the trail to the left for ¼ mile to a junction and bear left onto East Fork Lostine River Trail No. 1662. The first 2 miles or so are fairly steep, switchbacking through boulders and tall stands of spruce and fir. The trail gradually straightens and continues to climb for about 1 mile before entering a big meadow, which marks the beginning of the upper valley. Water is plentiful en route.

The next 2 miles of trail are fairly gradual through a classic U-shaped glaciated valley. The trail meanders through small open stands of tim-

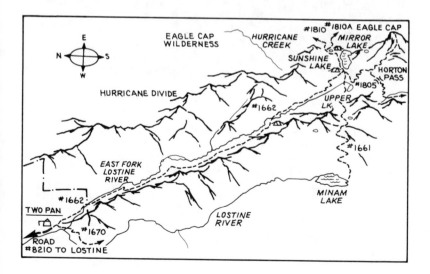

Mirror Lake and Eagle Cap Peak (Chuck Kerkering photo)

ber and boulder fields. The mystical half-dome shape of Eagle Cap Peak looms at the head of the valley.

At about 5½ miles, the trail reverts once again to a series of short steep switchbacks up to the rim above Mirror Lake. As the lake begins to come into view, there is a junction where a trail heads off to Horton Pass. Bear left and hike a short way to Mirror Lake. Outcrops of brilliant marble-like granite hang above the lake. Talus slopes and steep granite slabs meet the south shore of the lake and drop to invisible depths. Camp at the obvious spots on the flat benches above the north shore, making sure to keep a minimum of 200 feet from the water. Generally the best (and legal) sites are to the north (left) of the trail as one hikes east along the lake.

For a good dayhike from a base camp at Mirror Lake, consider scrambling to the summit of Eagle Cap. Walk back to the trail junction and head south toward Horton Pass on Trail No. 1805 for about 1 mile. Watch for an obvious trail branching left (east) and follow it about 1 mile steeply to the top of Eagle Cap. From the summit, one can enjoy sweeping views of Hurricane Canyon, the towering white Matterhorn, Lostine Canyon, Glacier Lake to the southeast and much more. Remember to fill water bottles in camp before attempting this hike.

WALLOWA MOUNTAINS
Eagle Cap Wilderness

95 LAKE BASIN LOOP

Round trip 50 miles
Hiking time 6 or 7 days
High point 8,450 feet
Elevation gain 4,400 feet
Difficult

Hikable late July through early
  September
USGS Eagle Cap, Cornucopia
Information: Wallowa-Whitman
  National Forest, Eagle Cap
  Ranger District

This is a classic week-long, 50-mile loop trip that weaves below, around and through the sky-scraping peaks of Oregon's Eagle Cap Wilderness. The route leads through deep valleys, along sparkling streams and past dozens of alpine lakes, a concentration of which is known as the Lake Basin in the shadow of 9,595-foot Eagle Cap Peak.

For ease in identification, many of the recommended camping areas described below are near lakes. Please be aware the Forest Service enforces a regulation that prohibits camping within 200 feet of any lake within the wilderness. Hikers should do their share in minimizing the heavy impact around these fragile lakes by considering the many choice campsites along creeks and ridges away from their shores. For example, instead of zeroing in on lakes, one will find good campsites in the meadows along East Eagle Creek, on the bench ½ mile above Mirror Lake (a fabulous site with water), on the meadow benches between Glacier and Frazier lakes, and at the headwaters of the South Fork Imnaha River just south of Hawkins Pass.

From LaGrande, Oregon, drive 31 miles southeast on State Highway 203 to a spot on the map called Medical Springs. Continue to the crossroads and bear left, following the signs to Tamarack campground. Drive about 2 miles and bear left on Forest Road No. 67. At Tamarack campground, drive past the left turn toward Boulder Park and continue on the main road (now Forest Road No. 77) along Eagle Creek. Turn left on Forest Road No. 7740 (East Fork Eagle Creek) and drive to the end of the road.

Note: In 1986, the road ended at a washed-out bridge near Kettle Creek as shown on the Eagle Cap Wilderness map published in 1980.

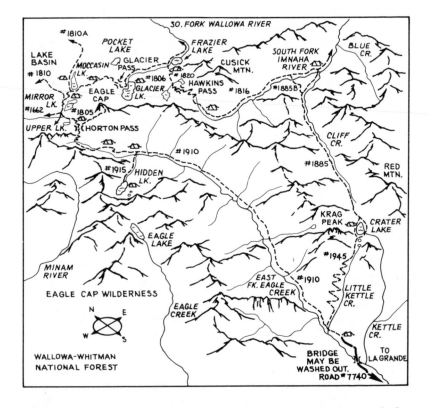

Previous maps show the road extending about 2 miles farther north. In 1987, the Forest Service had plans to rebuild the bridge, which would enable visitors to drive north to the mouth of Little Kettle Creek. Play it safe. Expect the bridge to be washed out and prepare to ford the creek and walk 2 miles on the road to the actual trailhead at Little Kettle Creek.

From the mouth of Little Kettle Creek, head north on Trail No. 1910 up East Fork Eagle Creek through a deep valley once filled with a 13-mile-long glacier. The trail gains elevation moderately but steadily. Water is abundant, but campsites are few among the granite boulders strewn about the valley. The best bet for the first night's camp is Hidden Lake, about 9 miles from the trailhead, including a 2-mile climb up from East Eagle Creek. Trail No. 1915 to Hidden Lake is a little steeper and more strenuous, but well marked and maintained. Like many of the lakes nestled in the bowls among the Wallowa Mountains, this lake offers good trout fishing. Also like other lakes in the wilderness, lakeshores have been protected by a requirement to keep campsites at least 200 feet from the water. Be sure to check with the Forest Service for current regulations.

On Day 2, return to the East Eagle Creek trail and continue north, up the valley about 8 miles to the top of steep, rocky Horton Pass, elev. 8,000 feet. The trail is well maintained, but snow is a possibility any time of year. Hikers should refer to their maps often in this area. From the top of the pass, the trail passes the route to the summit of Eagle Cap Peak and drops into the Lostine River Valley on Trail No. 1805. After about 1 mile, bear right onto Lake Basin Trail No. 1810-A. The areas around Upper Lake, Mirror Lake and Moccasin Lake are just a few of the good choices for Camp No. 2. The Lake Basin is a 2- by 4-mile plateau dotted with lakes and endless campsites. This is a perfect area for a layover day and a possible scramble south from Mirror Lake to the summit of Eagle Cap. (See Mirror Lake, Hike 94 for details.) Hikers not interested in bagging a summit can explore some 20 lakes in a day. Moccasin Lake, about ¾ mile east of Mirror Lake, is one of the deepest and most scenic lakes in the area.

To continue the loop on Day 3, follow Trail No. 1806 southeast from Moccasin Lake over the highest point of the loop, Glacier Pass, elev. 8,450 feet, and into the West Fork Wallowa River drainage. Just south of the pass, at about 3 miles, Glacier Lake makes a good lunch stop. From here it's another 3 miles to good campsites near Frazier Lake, which is a short way east of Trail No. 1806 on Trail No. 1820. While hiking between Glacier and Frazier lakes, listen for a waterfall.

On Day 4, backtrack west from Frazier Lake a short distance to Trail No. 1820 and head south toward Hawkins Pass, elev. 8,390 feet, and South Fork Imnaha River. The drop into the South Fork valley is one of the most spectacular on the loop, an observation one will find hard to believe during the first few days of the trip. A crystaline mountain on the shoulder of Hawkins Pass and a great glacial cirque filled with flowers are sights to behold. Continue down the valley to clearings just north of the confluence of Cliff Creek and the South Fork, where one can call it

Moccasin Lake in Lakes Basin, Eagle Cap Wilderness. (Loren Johnson photo)

quits for the day after 7½ miles. Beware of overly friendly deer.

On Day 5, head across the South Fork Imnaha River (the bridge was out in 1986) and head southwest on Trail No. 1885. The trail leads into deep woods along Cliff Creek. Watch for one giant tamarack about 15 feet off the trail, and don't be surprised if a few deer are following quietly and curiously behind. The trail leads over an unnamed pass. Carefully follow the signs to Crater Lake, where good fishing might make it worthwhile to make camp after a 4½-mile day.

On Day 6, head west from the west side of Crater Lake on Trail No. 1945, making a long, steep descent down Little Kettle Creek. Be sure to get on the right trail. The USGS Eagle Cap quadrangle incorrectly shows a trail down Kettle Creek; this trail has been abandoned. Be sure to head down "Little" Kettle Creek. After many switchbacks and about four distinct climate zones, the trail joins familiar territory in the East Fork Eagle Creek valley. At the junction with Trail No. 1910, turn left and walk about 2½ miles back to the trailhead, for a total day of about 8 miles.

CANADIAN SELKIRK MOUNTAINS
Kokanee Glacier Provincial Park

96   SILVER SPRAY CABIN

Round trip 8 miles
Hiking time 8 hours or overnight
High point 7,858 feet
Elevation gain 3,335 feet
Moderately difficult

Hikable early July through early October
Canadian topo Slocan 82F/NW or 82F/14
Information: British Columbia Parks, Nelson District

No getting around it, this is a groaner that gains more than 3,000 feet in elevation in 4 miles. But the views of jagged peaks in the Kokanee Glacier Provincial Park area of the Canadian Selkirks is worth the sweat. Besides, miners used to do it laden with picks, shovels and beans —and the beans weren't freeze dried, either.

From Nelson, British Columbia, follow Highway 3A northeast to Balfour, bearing north onto Highway 31 to Ainsworth Hot Springs, a total of about 30 miles. (The hot springs provide a soothing sidetrip after the hike.) From Ainsworth, continue 4 miles and turn west on the Woodbury Creek access road. This gravel road is steep at its beginning and can at times be dangerously icy or muddy. (For an alternate access, continue 2½ miles farther north on Highway 31.) From the highway, drive 7 miles to a junction and turn right on a road that descends sharply. Drive 1¼ miles to the trailhead parking area, which has picnic tables and an outhouse.

The first portion of the trail is used for both this hike and Woodbury Creek Basin, Hike 97. It is a good path, originally constructed in the 1920s to service lead and silver mines. Follow the trail 1½ miles to an old log cabin and a trail junction. Turn right (north) here and get into

Silver Spray Cabin, Kokanee Glacier Provincial Park. (John Carter photo)

low gear for a steep climb. It takes about an hour to climb the mile to another old cabin and, just beyond, a crossing of Silver Spray Creek. This is a good place for a rest and, in the right season, a feast of huckleberries. The trail soon breaks out of thick woods into an open, flower-covered subalpine forest, up past the remains of yet another old cabin and into Clover Basin. Crossing open meadows, small brooks and rock outcroppings below Sunrise Mountain, the trail continues up the ridge before

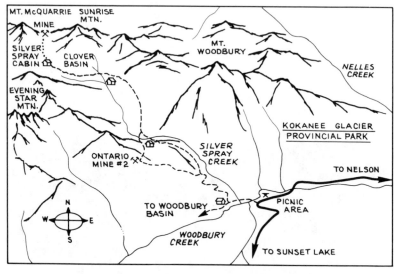

topping the rise and terminating at Silver Spray Cabin.

The historic cabin is maintained by British Columbia Parks and sleeps eight. Wood, rare and precious at this elevation, is provided for heating only; a backpacking stove is a necessity for overnighters.

Silver Spray is a marvelously preserved 1920-vintage high-elevation mine. Because of its backcountry location, little was salvaged from the mine when it closed, and the high elevation has delayed deterioration of the buildings. The cabin originally was the bunkhouse for the Violet Mine, offering shelter to the miners who dug lead and silver from the surrounding peaks. For a worthwhile side trip and a spectacular view, follow the trail up the rocky hillside above the cabin to the old mine site at the pass between Sunrise Mountain and Mt. McQuarrie. Although the mine has collapsed, a wood building, which served as a blacksmith shop, is virtually intact. The mine and the cabin are a priceless heritage; please treat them as such. Leave everything in its place.

CANADIAN SELKIRK MOUNTAINS
Kokanee Glacier Provincial Park

97 WOODBURY CREEK BASIN

Round trip 10 miles
Hiking time 8 hours or overnight
High point 7,000 feet
Elevation gain 2,700 feet
Moderately difficult

Hikable mid June through early
  October
Canadian topo Slocan 82F/NW or
  82F/14
Information: British Columbia
  Parks, Nelson District

This trail—the only route up the Woodbury Creek drainage—travels through a luxuriant forest cut by numerous open avalanche paths into the subalpine basin below Woodbury Glacier in Kokanee Glacier Provin-

Woodbury Glacier, Kokanee Glacier Provincial Park. (John Carter photo)

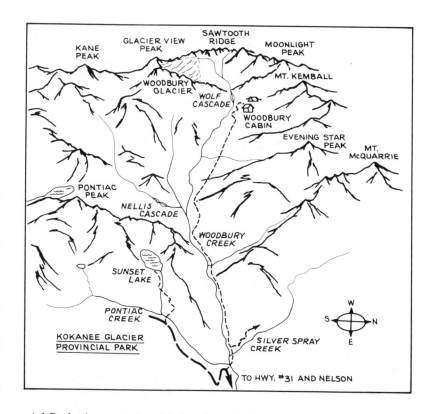

cial Park. A mountain cabin has been built here to accommodate up to 12 hikers and climbers. The semi-open forest, with its abundance of food and cover, makes the valley an ideal refuge for both black and grizzly bears. Mountain goats roam the peaks of the upper reaches.

From Nelson, British Columbia, follow Highway 3A northeast to Balfour, bearing north onto Highway 31 to Ainsworth Hot Springs, a total of about 30 miles. (The hot springs provide a soothing side trip after the hike.) From Ainsworth, continue 4 miles and turn west on the Woodbury Creek access road. This gravel road is steep at its beginning and can at times be dangerously icy or muddy. (For an alternate access, continue 2½ miles farther north on Highway 31.) From the highway, drive 7 miles to a junction and turn right on a road that descends sharply. Drive 1¼ miles to the trailhead parking area, which has picnic tables and an outhouse.

The first portion of the Woodbury Creek Trail also is used for Silver Spray Cabin, Hike 96. It is a good path, originally constructed in the 1920s to service lead and silver mines. Follow the trail 1½ miles to an old log cabin and a trail junction. Bear left at the junction to find the trail that leads up Woodbury Creek. For the next mile, the trail is disrupted by muddy and rocky sections remaining from mining in the early 1970s. Little by little it is being improved by trail crews. Beyond this poor section, the 2½-mile hike up the valley is pleasant.

241

Woodbury Creek Basin nestles on the eastern flank of the rugged Sawtooth Ridge while the Woodbury Glacier sprawls down the side of Glacier View Peak to the south. Just below the basin, Wolf Cascade tumbles down the headwall. The trail continues above the basin and quickly reaches the new Woodbury Cabin, a stone and wood-frame chalet. The cabin, which accommodates up to 12 persons, is a welcome sight at the end of the trail. Additional tent pads are situated around the cabin. Several unmaintained mining trails continue above the hut toward several summits, which offer spectacular views of Kokanee Glacier to the south and high summits of the Selkirks and Purcells to the north and northeast. Travel on the Woodbury Glacier should only be attempted by those who have the proper equipment—ropes, ice axes and crampons—and the skills to use them.

CANADIAN SELKIRK MOUNTAINS
Kokanee Glacier Provincial Park

98 JOKER LAKES

Round trip 5 miles
Hiking time 5–6 hours or
   overnight
High point 6,600 feet
Elevation gain 1,800 feet
Difficult

Hikable late June to early
   October
Canadian topo Slocan 82F/NW or
   Slocan 82F/l4
Information: British Columbia
   Parks, Nelson District

This short but strenuous trail leads to a fishable mountain lake and excellent views of the Purcells, Kokanee Glacier and possibly mountain goats. Like the other hikes in Kokanee Glacier Provincial Park, the trail goes through an old subalpine burn that has produced good grizzly habitat. It is not unusual for this trail to be closed for about a month beginning sometime in August. At any time spring through summer, be alert, keep a clean camp and follow the guidelines explained in the introduction under "Hiking in Grizzly Country."

From Nelson, British Columbia, take Highway 3A east to Balfour where it becomes Highway 31 and heads north to Kaslo. (Note: Ainsworth Hot Springs, a great place for an after-hike soak, is along this highway just south of Kaslo.) At Kaslo, drive east on Highway 31A toward New Denver for 4½ miles and turn left on South Fork Kaslo Creek Road. (Drivers who come to the yellow highway closure gates on Highway 31A have gone 500 feet too far.) Drive 15 miles up the Keen Creek drainage to the Joker Millsite trailhead at the end of the narrow and bumpy, but adequately maintained road. (About 8 miles up this road, a new logging road bears off to the right. At this point be sure to bear left; do not go up this new road.)

This area was once known as a haven for porcupines, which would chew on wood and leather and seemed to have a peculiar fetish for rubber tires and radiator hoses! But in 1987, park officials said they hadn't had a report of porcupine damage in years.

Joker Lake, Kokanee Glacier Provincial Park. (George Neal photo)

A wide trail leaves the parking area just behind the bulletin board, which shows maps of the area. Walk about 100 feet up the trail and take the left fork. (See Kokanee Glacier, Hike 99 for description of the other fork.) The trail climbs steadily into an ever-better panorama of the Sawtooth Range to the left and Kokanee Glacier ahead. The trail becomes gentle for a while in the main Joker Creek valley before heading up 13 steep switchbacks to the lakes.

Joker Lakes are evidence of an odd quirk of nature. Although only a few yards apart, the two lakes are completely different colors. The lower lake is a milky turquoise, typical of lakes filled with glacial silt in the Canadian Rockies. Meanwhile, the upper lake is a clear, deep blue. Geologists say the glaciers above apparently flow over different types of rock, with runoff from one type flowing into the lower lake and runoff from the other type flowing into the upper lake. A campsite is situated between the two lakes.

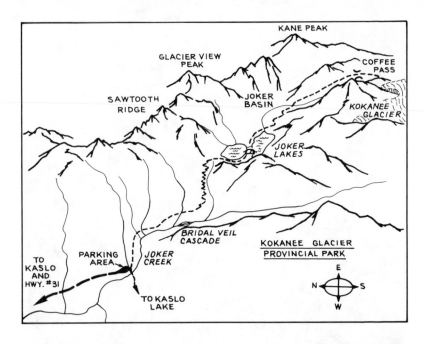

Allow two hours for the 2-mile round trip walk southeast and up 1,100 feet to Coffee Pass, at 7,700 feet. Begin from the west (downstream) end of the upper lake and continue up the main trail ¾ mile to the decaying Mansfield Mine cabin. Continue another ¼ mile through a canyon, snow, boulders and alpine tundra to Coffee Pass. Here the views of the Purcell Mountains to the east are superb, and a sharp eye often can find a mountain goat on the cliffs above.

CANADIAN SELKIRK MOUNTAINS
Kokanee Glacier Provincial Park

99   KOKANEE GLACIER

Round trip 12 miles
Hiking time 9 hours or overnight
High point 6,600 feet
Elevation gain 1,500 feet
Moderate
Hikable July through early
  October

Canadian topo Slocan 82 F/14 and
  Kokanee Peak 82 F/11
  (1:50,000), or Kokanee Glacier
  Park (1:25,000)
Information: British Columbia
  Parks, Nelson District

Kokanee Glacier Provincial Park is an exciting hiking and climbing area north of Nelson, British Columbia. The following hike and alternate route lead to Slocan Chief Cabin and campground in the alpine area at the base of Kokanee Glacier. The area offers many side trips, including an easy climb to 8,500 feet above the glacier for those who bring in glacier climbing gear. This is grizzly country; hike and camp accordingly. Especially in August, hikers should contact the Parks Branch to get reports on bear activity.

From Nelson, head northest on Highway 3A about 12 miles. After passing Redfish and Sandspit campgrounds, watch for the sign indicating Kokanee Park/Gibson Lake Road, which makes a hairpin turn to the left. Follow this gravel road 9½ miles to the parking area and picnic shelter at Gibson Lake, elev. 5,100 feet.

The trail, easily the most heavily used in the park, begins near the parking lot entrance. It climbs steeply and crosses several streams for the first mile. About 2 miles from the parking lot, the trail contours across a flower-filled open slope before reaching Kokanee Lake. This is a photogenic and popular lunch stop, also noted for fine fishing. Follow the trail above the lake around its western shore and on up to 6,700-foot Kokanee Pass. Continue down and past Keen Lake to Kaslo Lake, where a sign directs hikers eastward, up and over a low shoulder. After a short descent, the trail leads into the central park core with its impressive view of Kokanee Glacier and the rocky spine known as the Battleship. Slocan Chief Cabin (vintage 1896) sits on a hump a short distance past the park ranger's hut. The cabin sleeps 20 people on a first-come first-served basis in the summer season. Cabin fees are $5 per person per night. (New management proposals could affect the use of the cabin before 1990. Depending on public comment, the cabin could be left as is or possibly expanded.) Campsites are available just past the cabin. Steep but short trails lead up to the glacier and Smuggler's Ridge.

On the way out, hikers often take the ½-mile side trip from the north end of Kaslo Lake to Enterprise Pass for another good view of the glacier. Hikers with an extra day can continue on the marked route from Enterprise up to Lemon Pass and the Sapphire Lakes area.

An alternate route to Kokanee Glacier comes in from the north via Keen Creek and the Joker Millsite. This is a shorter trail, 6 miles round

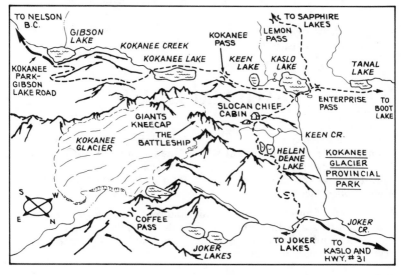

Kokanee Pass en route to Kokanee Glacier and Slocan Cabin. (Rich Landers photo)

trip, but steeper and less scenic. Elevation gain is 1,900 feet.

From Nelson, follow Highway 3A northeast to Balfour, then take Highway 31 north past Ainsworth Hot Springs (popular for after-hike soaks) to Kaslo. Kaslo is approximately 40 miles from Nelson.

At Kaslo, drive east on highway 31A toward New Denver for 4½ miles and turn left on South Fork Kaslo Creek Road. (Drivers who come to the yellow highway closure gates on Highway 31A have gone 500 feet too far.) Drive 15 miles up the Keen Creek drainage to the Joker Millsite trailhead at the end of the narrow and bumpy, but adequately maintained road. (About 8 miles up this road, a new logging road bears off to the right. At this point be sure to bear left and not go up this new road.)

The trail starts behind the bulletin board and takes the first right fork to cross Joker Creek (see Joker Lakes, Hike 98). It is a steep, switchbacking 2½ miles up 1,900 feet to the edge of the park core plateau. Then it is only another ½ mile to Slocan Chief Cabin.

VALHALLA MOUNTAINS
Valhalla Provincial Park

100   GWILLIM LAKES

Round trip 10 miles
Hiking time 10 hours or overnight
High point 7,150 feet
Elevation gain 1,850 feet
Moderately difficult

Hikable late June to mid October
Canadian topo Burton 82 F/13 or
  Slocan 82 F/NW
Information: British Columbia
  Parks, Nelson District

For lovers of towering granite peaks and rock-gouging glaciers, this is a particularly scenic hike high into British Columbia's Valhalla Provincial Park. A hiker has to see this place to believe it. This is grizzly country; hike and camp accordingly.

From the junction of Highways 6 and 3B at Playmore, between Castlegar and Nelson, take an odometer reading (mileages will be from this point) and drive about 10 miles north up the Slocan Valley on Highway 6. Turn left onto a logging road, crossing the Slocan River. Follow the road that appears to be used the most, keeping left at the first two junctions, then keep right for the next three junctions. (Do not be tempted to turn at the Koch Creek junction at 8½ miles.) At 15¾ miles, turn left onto Hoder Creek Road following a Valhalla Provincial Park/Drinnan Lakes sign. (Hikers who come to a gate on the Little Slocan River Road have passed the turn by about 2 miles.) Drive past two turnoffs (one is signed Branch 5). At 22½ miles, bear right, then drive another 5 miles and bear left. At the next spur road keep right. The trailhead parking area is at 29¼ miles. Whew!

In case of a bridge washout or logging closures, here's another access. From the intersection of Highways 6 and 3B between Castlegar and Nelson, make an odometer check (mileages will be from this point). Drive north on Highway 6 up the Slocan Valley about 11 miles to Vallican. Turn west and cross the Slocan River. Drive past Koch Creek, a major stream coming into the Little Slocan River to the left at mile 17, and continue following the road as it bends to the north. At mile 20, cross the Little Slocan River then take the first right and drive past two lakes. At the north end of the second lake (mile 25½), turn sharply left onto Hoder Creek Road. Follow the road up Hoder Creek almost to the end (mile 38) and park near the trailhead, once a steep road into the Drinnan Lake drainage.

From the parking lot, follow the newly constructed trail east, climbing

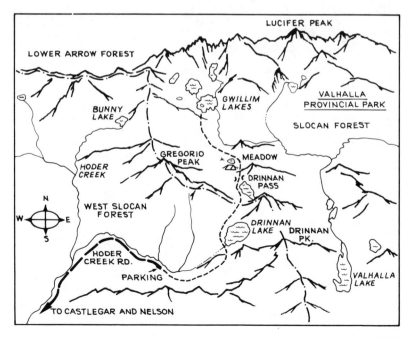

Drinnan Pass, Valhalla Provincial Park. (John Carter photo)

on a well-graded trail built in 1986 to Drinnan Lake. This alpine lake is above timberline and clearcuts and holds trout known to rise to a Royal Coachman or Black Gnat. Around the west or left side of Drinnan Lake the trail wanders, climbing somewhat to Drinnan Pass. A few small alpine tarns and campsites exist around the pass area and excellent vistas of the peaks behind Gwillim Lakes and Gregorio Peak to the west invite the mountaineer. This is some of the best scenery in North America. After passing Drinnan Pass, the trail, which was first cut by the Kootenay Mountaineers in 1980, descends approximately 400 vertical feet to a small lake set amidst a wet, green meadow. After a short, relatively flat stretch, the trail begins a gentle ascent toward Gwillim Lakes. The surrounding valley of Gwillim Creek unfolds as all the peaks one would want to climb become sentinels on the horizon. Summits with the names such as Black Prince, Lucifer, Devils Couch, Mt. Bor and Metasophalis conjure up stories of ancient history. Tread lightly around Gwillim Lakes as the area is very fragile and one's footprints will be seen for years. No open fires are allowed.

APPENDICES

Appendix A: Equipment list

Backpackers often list all the gear they might take on a trip and refer to it every time they assemble their equipment. Following is a sample list. Personalize it as needed. Subtract if possible but be judicious in what is added. Additional ounces eventually add up to pounds you must carry on your back.

Clothing

☐ Wool sweater or pile jacket
☐ Long-sleeved shirt
☐ T-shirts
☐ Socks
☐ Underwear
☐ Shorts
☐ Long pants
☐ Long underwear
☐ Windbreaker
☐ Rain gear (top and bottom)
☐ Gloves or mittens
☐ Visor cap for sun
☐ Wool hat for cold
☐ Bandannas
☐ Boots or hiking shoes
☐ Camp or wading shoes (sneakers)

Shelter

☐ Tent, poles, stakes
☐ Plastic tarp
☐ Sleeping bag and liner
☐ Sleeping pad

Eating

☐ Stove and fuel
☐ Water bottle(s)
☐ Water purification tablets
☐ Pliers (for handling pots)
☐ Pots, pans
☐ Plastic cup and bowl
☐ Spoon (fork optional)
☐ Foil
☐ Pot scrubber
☐ Salt, pepper, sugar, spices
☐ Peanut butter
☐ Hot drinks
☐ Cold drinks
☐ Trail snacks
☐ Breakfasts
☐ Lunches
☐ Dinners

Personals

☐ Toilet paper
☐ Biodegradable soap
☐ Towel
☐ Toothbrush
☐ Floss
☐ Sun protection (glasses, sunscreen)
☐ Flashlight, extra batteries
☐ Candle
☐ Matches

Indispensables

☐ Plastic garbage bag
☐ First aid kit (include moleskin)
☐ Signaling devices (whistle, mirror)
☐ Extra food
☐ Map and compass
☐ Reading material
☐ Fire starter
☐ Nylon cord
☐ Pocket knife
☐ Insect repellent
☐ Mood lifters (hard candy)
☐ Licenses and permits
☐ Repair kit (sewing, tape, etc.)
☐ Pack rain cover

Accessories

☐ Note pad and pen
☐ Field guide to flowers, birds, trees, etc.
☐ Zipper-type plastic bags
☐ Camera and film
☐ Backpack grill
☐ Plastic trowel (for latrines)
☐ Candle lantern
☐ Fishing gear
☐ Thermometer
☐ Collapsible bucket
☐ Binoculars

Appendix B: Administration/Information Sources

General Information

U.S. Forest Service Information Office, Room 112, U.S. Courthouse, W920 Riverside, Spokane, WA 99201, telephone (509) 456-2574.
U.S. Forest Service, Northern Region, P.O. Box 7669, Missoula, MT 59807, telephone (406) 329-3099.
Idaho Panhandle National Forests (headquarters for Coeur d'Alene, Kaniksu and St. Joe national forests) 1201 Ironwood Drive, Coeur d'Alene, ID 83814, telephone (208) 765-7223.
Idaho Department of Lands, Cavanaugh Bay No. 132, Coolin, ID 83821-9704, telephone (208) 443-2516.
Priest Lake State Park, Indian Creek Bay No. 423, Coolin, ID 83821, telephone (208) 443-2200.
Idaho State Parks and Recreation, Statehouse Mail, Boise, ID 83720 (street address not used for mailing is 2177 Warm Springs Avenue), telephone (208) 334-2154.
Washington State Parks and Recreation Commission, 7150 Cleanwater Lane, KY 11, Olympia, WA 98504, telephone (206) 753-2028.

Clearwater National Forest

Supervisor's Office, 12730 U.S. Highway 12, Orofino, ID 83544, telephone (208) 476-4541.
Lochsa Ranger District, Kooskia Ranger Station, Box 398, Kooskia, ID 83539, telephone (208) 926-4275.
North Fork Ranger District, Box 2139, Orofino, ID 83544, telephone (208) 476-3775.
Palouse Ranger District, Route 2, Box 4, Potlatch, ID 83855, telephone (208) 875-1131.
Pierce Ranger District, Kamiah Ranger Station, P.O. Box 308, Kamiah, ID 83536, telephone (208) 935-2513.
Powell Ranger District, Powell Ranger Station, Lolo, MT 59847, telephone (208) 942-3113.

Colville National Forest

Supervisor's Office, 695 South Main, Federal Building, Colville, WA 99114, telephone (509) 684-3711.
Colville Ranger District, 755 South Main, Colville, WA 99114, telephone (509) 684-3711.
Kettle Falls Ranger District, 255 West 11th, Kettle Falls, WA 99141 telephone (509) 738-6111.
Newport Ranger District, 315 North Warren, P.O. Box 770, Newport, WA 99156, telephone (509) 447-3129.
Republic Ranger District, 180 North Jefferson, P.O. Box 468, Republic, WA 99166, telephone (509) 775-3305.
Sullivan Lake Ranger District, Metaline Falls, WA 99153, telephone (509) 446-3205.

Coeur d'Alene National Forest

Fernan Ranger District, E2503 Sherman Ave., Coeur d'Alene, ID 83814, telephone (208) 765-738l.
Wallace Ranger District, P.O. Box 14, Silverton, ID 83867, telephone (208) 752-1221.

Kaniksu National Forest

Bonners Ferry Ranger District, Route 4, Box 4860, Bonners Ferry, ID 83805, telephone (208) 267-5561.
Priest Lake Ranger District, Route 5, Box 207, Priest River, ID 83856, telephone (208) 443-2512.
Sandpoint Ranger District, 1500 Highway 2, Sandpoint, ID 83864, telephone (208) 263-5111.

St. Joe National Forest

Avery Ranger District, H.C. Box 1, Avery, ID 83802, telephone (208) 245-4517.
St. Maries Ranger District, P.O. Box 407, St. Maries, ID 83861, telephone (208) 245-2531.

Kootenai National Forest

Supervisor's Office, 418 Mineral Ave., Box AS, Libby, MT 59923, telephone (406) 293-6211.
Rexford Ranger District, Eureka Ranger Station, P.O. Box 666, Eureka, MT 59917, telephone (406) 296-2536.
Yaak Ranger District, Sylvanite Ranger Station, Route 1, Troy, MT 59935, telephone (406) 295-4717.
Fortine Ranger District, Murphy Lake Ranger Station, P.O. Box 116, Fortine, MT 59918, telephone (406) 882-4451.
Troy Ranger District, Troy Ranger Station, P.O. Box E, Troy, MT 59935, telephone (406) 295-4693.
Libby Ranger District, Libby Ranger Station, 1263 Highway 37 North, Libby, MT 59923, telephone (406) 293-7741.
Fisher River Ranger District, Canoe Gulch Ranger Station, Star Route 2, Box 200, Libby, MT 59923, telephone (406) 293-7773.
Cabinet Ranger District, Cabinet Ranger Station, 2693 Highway 200, Trout Creek, MT 59874, telephone (406) 827-3534.

Lolo National Forest

Supervisor's Office, Building 24, Fort Missoula, MT 59801, telephone (406) 329-3750.
Missoula Ranger District, 5115 Highway 93 South, Missoula, MT 59801, telephone (406) 251-5237.
Ninemile Ranger District, Huson, MT 59846, telephone (406) 626-5201.
Plains/Thompson Falls Ranger District, Plains, MT 59859, telephone (406) 826-3821.
Seeley Lake Ranger District, Drawer G, Seeley Lake, MT 59868, telephone (406) 677-2233.
Superior Ranger District, Superior, MT 59872, telephone (406) 822-4233.

Nez Perce National Forest

Supervisor's Office, Route 2, Box 475, Grangeville, ID 83530, telephone (208) 983-1950.
Selway Ranger Station, Box 91, Kooskia, ID 83539, telephone (208) 926-4258.
Moose Creek Ranger District, Main Post Office, Grangeville, ID 83530, telephone (208) 983-2712.

Umatilla National Forest

Supervisor's Office, 2517 S.W. Hailey, Pendleton, OR 97801, telephone (503) 276-3811.

Pomeroy Ranger District, Route 1, Box 54A, Pomeroy, WA 99347, telephone (509) 843-1891.

Wallowa-Whitman National Forest

Supervisor's Office, P.O. Box 907, Baker, OR 97814, telephone (503) 523-6391.
Baker Ranger Station, Route 1, Box 1, Pocahontas Road, Baker, OR 97814, telephone (503) 523-4476.
Hell's Canyon National Recreation Area, P.O. Box 490, Enterprise, OR 97828, telephone (503) 426-3151.
Eagle Cap Ranger Station, P.O. Box M, Enterprise, OR 97828, telephone (503) 426-3102.
Wallowa Valley Ranger Station, Route 1, Box 83, Joseph, OR 97846, telephone (503) 432-2171.
Wallowa Lake State Park, Route 1, Box 323, Joseph, OR 97846, telephone (503) 238-7488.

Spokane Area

Bureau of Land Management (for Mineral Ridge), N1808 3rd St., Coeur d'Alene, ID 83814, telephone (208) 765-7356.
Dishman Hills Natural Area Association, E10820 Maxwell, Spokane, WA 99206, telephone (509) 926-7949 (Tom Rogers).
Mount Spokane State Park, Route 1 Box 336, Mead, WA 99021, telephone (509) 456-4169.
Riverside State Park, Spokane, WA 99205, telephone (509) 456-3964.
Spokane County Parks and Recreation Department, W1115 Broadway, Spokane, WA 99260, telephone (509) 456-4730.

Columbia Basin

Steamboat Rock State Park, P.O. Box 370, Electric City, WA 99123, telephone (509) 633-1304.
Washington Wildlife Department, Yakima Regional Office, 2802 Fruitvale Blvd., Yakima, WA 98902, telephone (509) 575-2740.
Bureau of Land Management (for Juniper Dunes), E4217 Main Ave., Spokane, WA 99202, telephone (509) 456-2570.

British Columbia

Ministry of Environment and Parks, Parks and Outdoor Recreation Division, West Kootenay District, Rural Route 3, Nelson, B.C. V1L 5P6, Canada, telephone (604) 825-4421.

State and Provincial Wildlife Agencies

Idaho Fish and Game Department, S600 Walnut, P.O. Box 25, Boise, ID 83707, telephone (208) 334-3700.
Montana Fish, Wildlife and Parks Department, E1420 6th Ave., Helena, MT 59620, telephone (406) 444-2535.
Oregon Fish and Wildlife Department, 506 S.W. Mill St., Portland, OR 97201, telephone (503) 229-5406.
Washington Wildlife Department, N600 Capitol Way, Olympia, WA 98504, telephone (206) 753-5710.
Ministry of Environment and Parks, Fish and Wildlife Division, 310 Ward St., Nelson, B.C. V1L 5S4, Canada, telephone (604) 354-6333.

Appendix C: Sources for Topographical Maps

Maps of the Pacific Northwest:

U.S. Geological Survey, Public Inquiry Office, Room 678, U.S. Courthouse, W920 Riverside Ave., Spokane, WA 99201, telephone (509) 456-2524.

Maps anywhere in the United States:

To receive topo maps and information by mail, contact one of the following two U.S. Geological Survey offices in Denver.
   1. *For information only:* USGS, Public Inquiries Office, 169 Federal Building, 1961 Stout Street, Denver, CO 80294, telephone (303) 844-4169.
   2. *For ordering specific maps:* USGS, Branch of Distribution, Box 25286, Denver Federal Center, Denver, CO 80225, telephone (303) 236-7477. (This office now carries maps for both the western and eastern United States.)

Maps of Canada

Ministry of Environment Map Office, Surveys and Resource Mapping Branch, 553 Superior, Victoria, B.C. V8V 1X5, Canada, telephone (604) 387-9307.
Northwest Map Service, W713 Spokane Falls Blvd., Spokane, WA 99201, telephone (509) 455-6981; has topo maps for U.S. and Canada plus aeronautical and nautical maps.

Appendix D: Hiking Groups

Spokane Mountaineers, Inc., P.O. Box 1013, Spokane, WA 99210.
Cascadians, P.O. Box 2201, Yakima, WA 98907.
Boundary Backpackers, Rt. 1 Box 495, Bonners Ferry, ID 83805.
Inter-Mountain Alpine Club, P.O. Box 505, Richland, WA 99352.
Kootenay Mountaineers, Box 3195, Castlegar, B.C. V1N 3A5, Canada.

INDEX

ABOUT THE AUTHORS

RICH LANDERS was graduated in journalism from the University of Montana in 1975. After taking time off to ride his bicycle 5,000 miles across the United States, he worked in New York with *Field & Stream* magazine and in Montana with *Montana Outdoors* magazine. In 1977, he moved to Spokane to become the outdoor editor for *The Spokesman-Review*. In that post he has won numerous writing awards and has been recognized as Conservation Writer of the Year by both the Idaho Conservation League and the Washington Environmental Council. Being a full-time outdoor writer, Rich spends hundreds of days each year in the field with notebook and camera and writes about both trends and issues. He is the Far West Regional editor for *Field & Stream* magazine and his work has been in other publications, including *Outside, Runner's World, Pacific Northwest, Western Outdoors* and *Popular Mechanics*. He has been a trustee for the Spokane Mountaineers for four terms.

IDA ROWE DOLPHIN received both her bachelor's (1965) and master's (1968) degrees from Whitworth College in Spokane. She taught humanities, English and mathematics at Shadle Park High School in Spokane for almost 20 years. She is a past president of the Spokane Mountaineers and is active in the Spokane Mushroom Club and the Native Plant Society. She also has completed a non-fiction book about her experiences as an American civilian prisoner-of-war during the Japanese occupation of the Philippines and her subsequent role within the resistance movement during the latter years of World War II.